Competition Law in Japan

Competition Law in Japan

Second Edition

Hiroshi Yamada
Ryohei Takai
Kaoru Harada
Katsutoshi Kataoka

This book was originally published as a monograph in the International Encyclopaedia of Laws/Competition Law.

Founding Editor: Roger Blanpain
General Editor: Frank Hendrickx
Volume Editors: Francesco Denozza & Alberto Toffoletto

Wolters Kluwer

Published by:
Kluwer Law International B.V.
PO Box 316
2400 AH Alphen aan den Rijn
The Netherlands
E-mail: lrs-sales@wolterskluwer.com
Website: www.wolterskluwer.com/en/solutions/kluwerlawinternational

Sold and distributed by:
Wolters Kluwer Legal & Regulatory U.S.
920 Links Avenue
Landisville, PA 17538
United States of America
E-mail: customer.service@wolterskluwer.com

Printed on acid-free paper

ISBN 978-94-035-2609-6

e-Book: ISBN 978-94-035-2619-5
web-PDF: ISBN 978-94-035-2629-4

The Authors

Hiroshi Yamada graduated from Tokyo University, Faculty of Economics (BA). His major was Positive Economics, *inter alia*, in the field of industrial organization.

Since he entered Japan Fair Trade Commission (JFTC) in 1984, he has been devoted to various tasks, including Case Investigation, M&A Examination and Policy Management. In 2020, he resigned the post of Director General for the Investigation Bureau and left JFTC, and took office as a special advisor in a law firm 'Nagashima, Ohno & Tsunematsu'.

He has taken a position of visiting professor at the Graduate School of Economics of Senshu University since 2024 and also gives lecture on Japanese competition law at some other universities.

Ryohei Takai is Director of the Representation Division of the Consumer Affairs Agency, seconded from JFTC in July 2023. Before the secondment, he was Director of the Litigation Division of the Investigation Bureau at JFTC. He joined JFTC in 1996 and has handled various issues in the agency, including law enforcement, litigation, policy planning, market study and international cooperation.

The Authors

Kaoru Harada joined JFTC in 1999 and handled several case investigations and M&A examinations. She is now seconded to the Legal System Planning Division of the Consumer Affairs Agency.

She graduated from Keio University (Bachelor of Laws) in 1999. In the US, she earned an LLM from Georgetown University Law Center, Washington, DC, in 2004 and passed the Bar Exam in New York in 2005.

She is one of the co-authors of *Antimonopoly Law* (Shuichi Sugahisa (ed.), Takeshi Shinagawa, Daisuke Korenaga and Kaoru Harada, 4th ed., Shojihomu, 2020), which is a practical handbook of Japanese competition law.

Katsutoshi Kataoka is Director of Trade Practice Research Office at JFTC. He joined JFTC in 2003 and has been involved in tasks such as dealing with leniency applications and the 2016 amendment of Antimonopoly Act, including a secondment to the Trans-Pacific Partnership headquarters in the Japanese government.

He graduated from Tokyo University (Bachelor of Laws) in 2003 and earned LLM degrees from the University of Chicago and New York University, passing the bar exam in New York in 2008.

Table of Contents

The Authors 3

List of Abbreviations 13

General Introduction 15

§1. General Background of the Country 15
I. Geography and Population 15
II. Economic System 15

§2. Legal System 16

§3. Historical Background of the Antimonopoly Act 16

Part I. Structure of Japanese Antitrust Law and Its Enforcement 19

Chapter 1. Sources of Antitrust Law 19

§1. National Sources 19

§2. International Sources 20

§3. Secondary Sources 21
I. Cabinet Orders 21
II. Fair Trade Commission's Rules and Designation 22
III. Guidelines 23

§4. Role and Authority of Precedents 25

Chapter 2. Scope of Application 27

§1. Territorial Reach 27

§2. Exemption 27
I. Exemptions in the AMA 27
A. IPRs Exemption 27
B. Acts of Cooperative Associations Exemption 28

C. RPM Exemption 29
II. Exemptions in Each Legislation 30

§3. Special Sectors, State-Owned Enterprises and Public Utilities 33

§4. Sensible Effect and De Minimis 33

Chapter 3. Overview of Substantive Provisions 35

§1. Unreasonable Restraint of Trade 35

§2. Dominant Undertakings 36

§3. Concentrations 36

§4. Other Prohibitions 40
I. Unfair Trade Practices 40
A. Overview 40
B. Specific Practices 41
II. International Agreement 45
III. Monopolistic Situation 46

§5. Tests of Illegality 48
I. Per Se Prohibitions and Naked Restraints 48
II. Balancing Tests 48
III. Merger Tests 48

Chapter 4. Overview of Main Notions 49

§1. Undertaking 49
I. General Remarks 49
II. Trade Association 50

§2. Relevant Market 50
I. General Remarks 50
II. Product Market 51
III. Geographic Market 51

§3. Market Power/Dominant Position 52

§4. Agreement and Concerted Conduct 52
I. General Remarks 52
II. Requirements of Unreasonable Restraint of Trade 52
III. Application to Vertical Agreement 53
IV. International Agreement 54
V. Trade Association 54

§5. Restriction on Competition 55
I. Substantial Restraint of Competition 55
II. Justification 57
III. Impediment to Fair and Free Competition 58

§6. Monopolization and Abuse of Dominance 59

§7. Concentrations 59

§8. Joint Ventures 60

Chapter 5. Consequences of Violations and Enforcement Institutions 61

§1. Administrative Enforcement 61
I. Antitrust Authorities 61
A. Formation and Composition 61
B. Investigating Powers 61
C. Adjudicating Powers (Ascertaining and Sanctioning) 62
1. Cease and Desist Order 62
2. Commitment 63
D. Other Institutional Tasks (Consultancy to Parliament/Government) 67
II. Direct Government's Enforcement Activities 67
III. Other Administrative Agencies Applying Antitrust Rules 67
IV. Administrative Fines 68
A. Surcharge for Unreasonable Restraint of Trade 68
B. Surcharge for Private Monopolization 74
C. Surcharge for Unfair Trade Practices 76
D. Surcharge for Anticompetitive Conduct of Trade Association 80
V. Administrative Injunctions and Other Restrictive Orders 80
VI. Interim Measures 81

§2. Civil Enforcement 81
I. Competent Civil Courts 81
II. Sanctions 82
A. Nullity 82
B. Damages 82
C. Interim Measures 83

§3. Criminal Enforcement 83
I. Criminal Sanctions for Antitrust Violations 83
II. Other Application of Criminal Law to Relevant Conducts 85

Part II. Application of the Prohibition 87

Chapter 1. Restrictive Agreements 87

§1. General Remarks 87

§2. Horizontal Agreements 87
I. Cartels 87
II. Information Exchange Practices 88
III. Cooperation Agreements 89
A. Research and Development 89
B. Standardization 89
C. Joint Production 90
D. Joint Purchasing 90
E. Joint Selling 90

§3. Vertical Agreements 90
I. Distribution 90
A. General Remarks 90
B. Public Utility Service 91
C. Franchising 91
II. Technology Licensing 91

Chapter 2. Dominant Undertakings' Prohibited Practices 93

§1. General Remarks 93

§2. Exploitative Practices 93
I. Excessive/Unfair Pricing 93
II. Discrimination 94
III. Abuse of Superior Bargaining Position 95

§3. Exclusionary Practices 99
I. Predation 99
A. Price-Cost Relationship 100
B. Continuity 101
C. Causing Difficulty to Other Enterprises 101
D. Justifiable Grounds 102
II. Tying 102
III. Rebates 104
IV. Refusal to Deal 105
V. Price Squeeze 106
VI. Interference of Transactions 108

§4. Other Types of Restrictive Conducts 109

Chapter 3. Concentrations 111

§1. General Remarks 111

§2. Horizontal Mergers 111
I. Safe Harbour 112
II. Unilateral Effects 112
A. Analytical Framework for Unilateral Effects 112
1. Homogenous Goods 112
2. Differentiated Goods 113
B. Factors to Be Considered in Deciding Substantial Restraint of Competition Through Unilateral Effects 113
1. Position of the Company Group and the Competitive Situation in the Market 113
2. Import 114
3. Entry 114
4. Competitive Pressure from Related Market 115
5. Competitive Pressure from Customers 115
6. Overall Business Capabilities 116
7. Efficiency 116
8. Financial Conditions of the Company Group 116
III. Coordinated Effects 117
A. Analytical Framework for Coordinated Effects 117
B. Factors to Be Considered in Deciding Substantial Restraint of Competition Through Coordinated Effects 117

§3. Vertical Mergers 117
I. Safe Harbour 117
II. Unilateral Effects 118
III. Coordinated Effects 118

§4. Market/Product Extension Mergers 118

§5. Pure Conglomerate Mergers 119

§6. Joint Ventures 119

Part III. Administrative Procedure 121

Chapter 1. Administrative Investigations Before the Antitrust Authority 121

§1. Initiative 121
I. Complaints 121
II. Ex Officio Investigations 121
III. Leniency Programme 122

A. General Remarks 122
B. Procedure 123
C. Disqualification from the Leniency Programme 131
IV. Market Surveys 132

§2. Powers 132
I. Request for Information 133
A. Grounds and Legal Nature 134
B. Procedures for an Order to Report 134
II. Investigating and Search Powers 134
A. Grounds and Legal Nature 135
B. Procedures and Explanations Given for On-Site Inspection 135
C. Scope of On-Site Inspection 135
D. Procedures Related to Submission and Retention of Materials 136
E. Presence of an Attorney During On-Site Inspection 136
III. Deposition 137
A. Grounds and Legal Nature 137
B. Procedures and Explanations Given for Interview 137
1. Voluntary Interview 137
2. Interrogation 138
C. Prohibited Conducts of Investigator 138
D. Length of Interview 138
E. Procedures for Preparing Records and Affixing Signatures and Seals 139
IV. Cooperation with Other State Institutions 139

§3. Procedure and Right of Defence 139
I. General Remarks 139
II. Procedures for Hearing 140
A. Hearing, Access to File, Briefs 140
1. Hearing 140
2. Submission of Opinion and Access to Evidence 143
B. Statement of Objections 144
C. Final Hearing and Decision 144
III. Attorney Client Privileges 145
A. Background and Overview 145
B. Determination Procedure 148
C. Treatment of Electronic Data 149

Chapter 2. Notifications and Clearance Decisions of Merger Regulations 151

§1. Preliminary Filing Obligations 151
I. Criteria and Thresholds 151

A. Share Acquisition 151
B. Merger 153
C. Joint Incorporation-Type Splits 153
D. Absorption-Type Splits 155
E. Joint Share Transfer 157
F. Acquisition of Business 157
II. Notification Form 158

§2. STRUCTURE OF PROCEEDINGS 159
I. Time Framework 159
A. Consultation Prior to Notification (Voluntary) 160
B. Primary Review 161
C. Secondary Review 161
II. Explanation of Issues and Submission of Written Opinions by the Notifying Company 162
III. Commitment Procedure in the Business Combination Review 162

§3. CLEARANCE AND CONDITIONAL CLEARANCE 163
I. Conditions and Undertakings 163
A. Transfer of Businesses 163
B. Supply of Products under Special Conditions 163
C. Promotion of Imports and Market Entry 164
D. Measures Concerning Behaviour of the Company Group 164
II. Timing 164

Chapter 3. Challenging Administrative Decision 165

§1. GENERAL REMARKS 165

§2. ADMINISTRATIVE APPEALS PROCEDURE 165

Part IV. Criminal Procedure 167

Chapter 1. General Remarks 167

§1. BACKGROUND 167

§2. OVERVIEW OF CRIMINAL INVESTIGATION PROCEDURE IN AMA 168

Chapter 2. Investigating and Search Power 169

Chapter 3. Coordination with Administrative Procedures 181

Chapter 4. Implementation of the Criminal Investigation 182

Chapter 5. Role of Prosecutors 183

Part V. International Aspects 185

Chapter 1. Cooperation under Administrative Agreement 185

§1. General Remarks 185

§2. Cooperation Agreement on Competition Policy 186
I. Notification of Enforcement Activities 187
II. Cooperation on Enforcement Activities Between Competition Authorities 188
III. Coordination on Enforcement Activities Between Competition Authorities 189
IV. Negative Comity 190
V. Positive Comity 191

§3. Competition Chapter of EPA 192

Chapter 2. Other Types of Cooperation and Coordination 193

§1. Cooperation and Coordination Through Multilateral Forum 193

§2. Cooperation and Coordination in East Asia Region 193
I. Top Level Meeting and Conference 193
II. Technical Assistance 194

Selected Bibliography 195

Index 197

List of Abbreviations

AMA	Act on Prohibition of Private Monopolization and Maintenance of Fair Trade
APEC	Asia Pacific Economic Cooperation
ASBP	Abuse of Superior Bargaining Position
CPTPP	the Comprehensive and Progressive Trans-Pacific Partnership
EC	European Commission
EPA	Economic Partnership Agreement
EU	European Union
FTC	Fair Trade Commission (of Japan)
FTTH	Fibre Telecommunications to the Home
GHQ	General Headquarters of the Allied Forces
ICN	International Competition Network
HHI	Herfindahl Hirschman Index
IP(R)	Intellectual Property (Right)
JFTC	Japan Fair Trade Commission
JPY	Japanese Yen
LPG	Liquefied Petroleum Gas
M&A	Merger and Acquisition
METI	Ministry of Economy, Trade and Industry (former MITI)
MITI	Ministry of International Trade and Industry
MOC	Memorandum on Cooperation
NPO	Non-Profit Organization
NTT	Nippon Telegraph & Telephone Company
OECD	Organisation for Economic Co-operation and Development
R&D	Research & Development
RIA	Regulatory Impact Assessment
RPM	Resale Price Maintenance
SII	Structural Impediments Initiative
SSNIP	Small but Significant and Non-transitory Increase in Price
UNCTAD	United Nations Conference on Trade and Development

List of Abbreviations

General Introduction

§1. General Background of the Country

I. Geography and Population

1. Located in the Pacific Ocean, lying to the east of the Asian region, Japan is an archipelago of about 378 thousand square kilometres, including four big islands, Hokkaido, Honshu, Shikoku and Kyushu, and more than six thousand small islands. About 70% of Japan is forested. Since the islands of Japan are located in a volcanic zone on the Pacific Ring of Fire, Japan has more than one hundred active volcanoes and countless onsen, hot springs, while often earthquakes, destructive several times a century, occur.

2. Japan has the world's 12th largest population with over 120 million people as of 2024,[1] but the population has been decreasing since the late 2000s while the population of productive workers (15 years to 64 years) peaked out in 1997. This reduction in population is at an outstanding high speed among developed countries and is concerned to give a negative effect on the economy, contrary to the high economic growth period from the middle of 1950s to 1960s. In order to keep economic growth with a diminishing population, Japan may need to enhance economic efficiency, innovation, etc., and competition law and policy could be one of the drives for them.

II. Economic System

3. Before the gigantic political revolution, *Meiji-Ishin*, in 1868, Japan had been under the feudal system. Under the former system, choice of employment, movement of person, operation of business, etc., were strictly restrained, while some advanced market system such as the rice futures market had already been introduced. After the *Meiji-Ishin*, the government introduced political and economic systems like European countries to catch up with the advanced economies and to resist the imperialist pressure. However, the landlord-tenant system remained until the end of World War II, when the state-controlled economy in Japan was liberalized.

1. United Nations Population Fund, *State of World Population 2024* (2024).

4. In occupied Japan after World War II, the General Headquarters of the Allied Forces (GHQ) ordered Japan to democratize its economy, including dissolution of *Zaibatsu* (a group of companies with a headquarters which financially controls a wide range of subsidiaries), prohibition of monopolies, farmland reform, and establishment of labour rights. As a result of the reformation, our economy was liberalized from the state-controlled economy to some extent, but after GHQ withdrew from Japan in 1952, Japan restarted pursuing a state-controlled economy development. For example, the Ministry of International Trade and Industry (MITI) promoted industrial policy, strategically targeting specific industries such as heavy and chemical industries. Japan enjoyed rapid economic growth from 1954 to 1973, until the first oil crisis took place.

5. Japan's economic growth slowed down after the first oil crisis, but it still enjoyed a relatively high growth rate and a low jobless rate among developed countries. However, after the burst of the bubble economy in 1991, Japanese economy has been stuck. Especially since 1995, Japan has struggled against deflation. The deflation is probably due to the declining birth rate and ageing population. Furthermore, its sovereign debt is at the worst level among developed countries. Japan has to solve these problems, and competition policy and antitrust law can be one of the tools for them to enhance economic efficiency.

§2. Legal System

6. In the seventh century, a constitutional form of government modelled after that of China (Tang), *Ritsuryo*, was introduced. Nevertheless, *Ritsuryo* system had been effective for a couple of centuries. After that until the *Meiji* Revolution, Japanese legal system had been developed by each government in various periods of history, somehow being affected by Chinese one. Japan introduced modern legal system after the *Meiji-Ishin*, from various European countries. For example, the *Meiji* Constitution was based upon German Constitution and Civil Law is a mixture of those of France, Germany, and UK. The legal system in Japan has also been influenced by the American system after World War II.

§3. Historical Background of the Antimonopoly Act

7. As stated before, in occupied Japan after World War II, the GHQ pursued democratization of Japanese economy and one of the tools was Act on Prohibition of Private Monopolization and Maintenance of Fair Trade (Act No. 54 of 1947; hereinafter referred to as 'AMA'). The AMA was aimed to democratize and liberalize the Japanese economy, among others, to dissolve the *Zaibatsu*, which GHQ thought had encouraged the nation and the government to start the war. The AMA was promulgated, and it came into force in 1947 for this purpose. The Japan Fair Trade Commission (hereinafter referred to as 'JFTC') was simultaneously founded as an enforcement agency of the AMA.

8. Under the pressure of GHQ until 1952, the JFTC vigorously enforced the AMA, but after GHQ withdrew from Japan in 1952, the Japanese government intended to incorporate many exemptions to the AMA and other laws in order to weaken its enforcement. Then, the difficult period for the JFTC during which its enforcement level was quite low continued until the oil crisis.

9. Japan suffered from high-level inflation during the oil crisis and soaring of price, which were suspected due to illegal price cartels. Surcharge was introduced as an administrative monetary sanction in 1977 to eliminate those cartels by depriving unreasonable profit originated from the cartels. From 1989 to 1990, US urged Japan to enhance the AMA and JFTC's enforcement in order to reduce US's huge trade deficit to Japan through Structural Impediments Initiative (SII). In 1990, the number of JFTC's staff increased and in 1991, the level of surcharge was raised. After SII, the AMA and its enforcement has been dramatically strengthened. In 2005, the AMA was amended again, increasing the level of surcharge, introducing leniency programme and compulsory investigation for criminal cases. Following the 2005 amendment and the 2009 amendment, the infringements subject to surcharge were extended to non-cartel practices such as unilateral exclusive conduct.

10. In 2013, a bill to amend the AMA was passed in the Diet, which seemed to radically change the structure of the JFTC. The amendment was aiming at abolishing administrative hearing system, which had characterized the JFTC as a unique organization that has administrative as well as judicial function. The amended AMA was enacted in 2015 and all enforcement actions of the JFTC have been subject to the courts' judgment from the first instance except for those which had been examined prior to the amendment.

11. In 2016, the Comprehensive and Progressive Trans-Pacific Partnership (CPTPP) Agreement was approved in Japan and a bill to amend the laws related to the agreement was passed in the Diet. This includes revision of the AMA to adopt the so-called commitment procedure, which enables swift resolution of cases contributing to the early restoration of fair and free competition. The amended AMA which includes the commitment procedure took effect in December 2018.

Subsequently, in 2019, another bill of amendment of the AMA was passed in the Diet. The amendment revised the leniency programme, introducing a system which allows the JFTC to reduce the amount of surcharges if enterprises submit information and documents that contribute to the fact-finding of the case, in addition to the reduction according to the order of application, and abolishing the limit on the number of applicants in the programme, and extended the basis of calculation of surcharges and the calculation term and raised the limit of the amount of criminal fine for juridical person charged with the offence of obstructing investigation. The amended AMA came into effect in December 2020.

Part I. Structure of Japanese Antitrust Law and Its Enforcement

Chapter 1. Sources of Antitrust Law

§1. National Sources

12. Japanese antitrust law regime consists of the AMA and some special laws. For example, the Act Against Delay in Payment of Subcontract Proceeds, etc. to Subcontractors (Act No. 120 of 1956; hereinafter referred to as 'Subcontract Act') was established in 1956 as a special law in order to enhance regulations on ASBPs (Abuse of Superior Bargaining Positions) under the AMA.

13. The Act on Elimination and Prevention of Involvement in Bid Rigging, etc. and Punishment for Acts by Employees that Harm Fairness of Bid Rigging, etc. (Act No. 101 of 2002; hereinafter referred to as 'Involvement Prevention Act') was enacted in 2002 to prevent government employees from being involved in bid riggings for public procurement.

14. Prior to 2009, JFTC was mainly in charge of enforcing the Act Against Unjustifiable Premiums and Misleading Representations (Act No. 134 of 1962; hereinafter referred to as 'Premiums and Representation Act') which was established as a supplementary legislation of the AMA to regulate undue inducement of purchase as a means of unfair trade practices but is now handled by the Consumer Affairs Agency. Nevertheless, JFTC is still involved with its enforcement on the local level because the Consumer Affairs Agency has no local branch and it commissions JFTC's regional offices to investigate the cases related to the Premiums and Representation Act in their jurisdictions.

15. In 2023, 'Freelancers Act (Act on Ensuring Proper Transactions Involving Specified Entrusted Business Operators (Act No. 25 of 2023; hereinafter referred to as 'Freelancers Act')) was established. This Act has two purposes: (a) ensuring proper transactions involving freelance workers mainly by prohibiting enterprises from engaging in ASBP practices toward freelance workers and (b) improving the working environment for freelance workers. The JFTC is responsible for its enforcement to achieve the purpose (a) above. It is to take effect on 1 November 2024.

16. Moreover, in line with a policy of the Government to strengthen monitoring of the business activities of large IT companies, 'Smartphone Software Act' (Act on Promotion of Competition for Specified Smartphone Software (Act No. 58 of 2024) was established in 2024. This Act prohibits the designated large providers of software for smartphones from engaging in certain business practices that may impede fair competition in those industries. It will be enforced by December 2025 at the latest.

17. In addition to these acts, more acts contain articles concerning competition policy. For example, the Unfair Competition Prevention Act (Act No. 47 of 1993) and some legislation regarding IPR (Intellectual Property Rights) such as the Patent Act (Act No. 121 of 1959) are handled by the Ministry of Economy, Trade and Industry (hereinafter referred to as 'METI').

18. Nowadays even industry-specific laws very often include competition policy-oriented articles although some laws still strictly regulate the activities of enterprises and have exemption clauses from the AMA. Under this somewhat complicating regime, however, the AMA has been called as the 'Economic Constitution', at the top in the hierarchy in our competition policy and antitrust regime.

§2. International Sources

19. Article 6 of the AMA prohibits any international agreement or international contract which contains such matters as falling under unreasonable restraint of trade or unfair trade practices. JFTC applied Article 6 to unreasonable restraint of trade cases and unfair trade practices cases, which could have been subject to prohibition of Article 3 and Article 19 respectively if the conducts at question had taken place inside the territory.

20. However, recently, JFTC has come to apply the AMA to cases including conducts outside Japan were subject to Japanese jurisdiction.

21. Moreover, JFTC has tried to enhance cooperation with other authorities. Japan has already concluded the Antimonopoly Cooperation Agreements with the US, Canada, and European Communities. JFTC also concluded several inter-agency cooperation agreements and MOC (Memorandums Of Cooperation). These agreements stipulate notification of enforcement activities when affecting the interest of the other party and assistance to the other party in its enforcement activities.

22. To deepen such cooperative relationships, JFTC concluded with Australia and Canada the so-called second-generation agreements that facilitate the communication of confidential information obtained through enforcement activities, including investigations, and is negotiating with the European Commission (EC) with a view to conclude a similar agreement (as of 2023). Moreover, Japan has concluded the EPA (Economic Partnership Agreements) with various economies, inter alia, those located in the Asian region, which establish more general cooperation such as exchange of information, technical assistance, etc. (*see* Part V below).

§3. Secondary Sources

23. Japanese legal regime has a hierarchy, which includes laws, cabinet orders, rules of ministries, agencies and commissions, internal rules of ministries, etc. from superior rules to inferior ones. Antitrust regime is comprised of four main laws as below:

1. AMA (https://www.jftc.go.jp/en/legislation_gls/AMA.pdf);
2. Subcontract Act (https://www.jftc.go.jp/en/legislation_gls/subcontract.html);
3. Premiums and Representation Act (https://www.japaneselawtranslation.go.jp/en/laws/view/2888);
4. Involvement Prevention Act (https://www.jftc.go.jp/en/legislation_gls/aepibr.html);
5. Freelancers Act (https://www.jftc.go.jp/en/legislation_gls/Act%20on%20Ensuring%20Proper%20Transactions%20Involving%20Specified%20Entrusted%20Business%20Operators%20(Tentative%20translation).html/).
6. Smartphone Software Act (only available in Japanese) (https://laws.e-gov.go.jp/law/506AC0000000058)

24. The regime also includes a wide range of cabinet orders, rules, guidelines, etc. under these laws.

I. Cabinet Orders

25. Among some cabinet orders concerning the Japanese antitrust regime, except for those regarding government structures, the following orders have substantial provisions concerning enforcement of the AMA:

1. AMA Enforcement Order (Cabinet Order for Enforcement of Act on Prohibition of Private Monopolization and Maintenance of Fair Trade (Cabinet Order No. 317 of 1977) stipulates way of calculation of surcharge (*see* Chapter 5, §1, IV below). It also provides threshold of notification of merger transaction (https://www.jftc.go.jp/en/legislation_gls/200902.pdf);
2. Implementing Order of the Act Against Delay in Payment of Subcontract Proceeds, etc. to Subcontractors (Cabinet Order No. 5 of 2001) defines specific services to which the Subcontract Act is applied (https://www.jftc.go.jp/en/legislation_gls/index_files/implementing_order.pdf);
3. Order for Enforcement of the Act on Ensuring Proper Transactions Involving Specified Entrusted Business Operators (Cabinet Order No. 200 of 2024) provides the details necessary for implementation of the Freelancers Act (https://www.jftc.go.jp/en/legislation_gls/Order%20for%20Enforcement%20of%20

the%20Act%20on%20Ensuring%20Proper%20Transactions%20Involving%20Specified%20Entrusted%20Business%20Operators%20(Tentative%20translation).html/).

II. Fair Trade Commission's Rules and Designation

26. Under Article 76(1) of the AMA, JFTC may establish rules with respect to its internal disciplines, proceedings of case handling and procedures for notifications, applications for approval, and other matters. By this general rule-setting power, JFTC has established some rules as follows:

- Business Combination Rules (Rules on Applications for Approval, Reporting, Notification, etc. Pursuant to the Provisions of Articles 9–16 of the Act on Prohibition of Private Monopolization and Maintenance of Fair Trade (JFTC Rule No. 1 of 1953)) (https://www.jftc.go.jp/en/legislation_gls/antimonopoly_rules_files/rules_on_reporting_notification_etc.pdf);
- Investigation Rules (Rules on Japan Fair Trade Commission Investigations (JFTC Rule No. 5 of 2005)) (https://www.jftc.go.jp/en/legislation_gls/20122502.pdf);
- Criminal Investigation Rules (Rules on Compulsory Investigation of Criminal Cases by the Fair Trade Commission (JFTC Rule No. 6 of 2005)) (https://www.jftc.go.jp/en/legislation_gls/antimonopoly_rules_files/compulsoryinvestigation.pdf);
- Hearing Opinions Rules (Rules on Hearings of Opinions by the Fair Trade Commission (JFTC Rule No. 1 of 2015)) (https://www.jftc.go.jp/en/legislation_gls/antimonopoly_rules_files/hearingofopinions.pdf);
- Commitment Procedure Rules (Rules on Japan Fair Trade Commission Commitment Procedures (JFTC Rule No. 1 of 2017)) (https://www.jftc.go.jp/en/legislation_gls/kakuyakukisoku.pdf);
- Leniency Rules (Rules on Reporting the Facts and Submitting the Materials regarding Immunity from or Reduction of Surcharge (JFTC Rule No. 7 of 2020)) (https://www.jftc.go.jp/en/legislation_gls/201225001.pdf);
- Survey Implementation Rules (Rules on Disposition Pursuant to Article 40 of Act on Prohibition of Private Monopolization and Maintenance of Fair Trade (JFTC Rule No. 2 of 2022)) (https://www.jftc.go.jp/dk/guideline/ippanchousa/40joukisoku.html; only available in Japanese).

27. As to unfair trade practices, Article 2(9) of the AMA allows JFTC to designate specific business practices, which are likely to impede fair competition and are prohibited under Article 19 of the AMA (*see* Chapter 3, §4, I below). Based on the provision, JFTC designated and made public practices which may fall under unfair trade practices. The public notice in which JFTC designated unfair trade practices is as follows:

- General Designation (Designation of Unfair Trade Practices (Fair Trade Commission Public Notice No. 15 of 1982)) (https://www.jftc.go.jp/en/legislation_gls/unfairtradepractices_files/unfairtradepractices.pdf).

28. General Designation applies to any conduct in general in all business fields. Other than the General Designation, the JFTC also designates specialized practices in other public notices, which may be employed in some specific business fields. Those public notices are called Specific Designation(s) of Unfair Trade Practices, such as:

– Designation of Specific Unfair Trade Practices in the Newspaper Business (Fair Trade Commission Public Notice No. 9 of 1999) (https://www.jftc.go.jp/en/legislation_gls/index_files/spaper.pdf);
– Designation of Specific Unfair Trade Practices by Shippers Relating to Consignment of Articles (Fair Trade Commission Public Notice No. 1 of 2004; Summary) (https://cms03.jftc.go.jp/en/pressreleases/yearly-2015/March/150311_files/150311.pdf);
– Unfair Trade Practices by Large-scale Retailers Relating to Trade with Suppliers (Fair Trade Commission Public Notice No. 11 of 2005) (https://www.jftc.go.jp/en/legislation_gls/index_files/dsutp.pdf).

29. The JFTC can modify the present designation and newly issue another designation, on its initiative, according to the change of easy-to-fluctuate market structure with the view to prevent anticompetitive conduct more efficiently; however, it has not made major change only twice since it was announced in 1953.

III. Guidelines

30. Other than the rules and designations established by JFTC under the power given by AMA, a much wider range of guidelines were released. Just to mention a few, JFTC has published the following guidelines:

– Predatory Sales Guidelines (Guidelines Concerning Unjust Low Price Sales under the Antimonopoly Act (1984, revised 2009)) (https://www.jftc.go.jp/en/legislation_gls/imonopoly_guidelines_files/unjustlowprice.pdf);
– Distribution Guidelines (Guidelines Concerning Distribution Systems and Business Practices under the Antimonopoly Act (1991, revised 2017)) (https://www.jftc.go.jp/en/legislation_gls/210122.pdf);
– Joint R&D Guidelines (Guidelines Concerning Joint Research and Development under the Antimonopoly Act (1993)) (https://www.jftc.go.jp/en/legislation_gls/imonopoly_guidelines_files/jointresearch.pdf);
– Administrative Guidance Guidelines (Guidelines Concerning Administrative Guidance under the Antimonopoly Act (1994)) (https://www.jftc.go.jp/en/legislation_gls/imonopoly_guidelines_files/administrative.pdf);
– Guidelines Concerning the Activities of Firms and Trade Associations with Regard to Public Bids (1994, revised 2020) (https://www.jftc.go.jp/en/legislation_gls/imonopoly_guidelines_files/20122503.pdf);
– Trade Associations Guidelines (Guidelines Concerning the Activities of Trade Associations under the Antimonopoly Act (1995, revised 2020)) (https://www.jftc.go.jp/en/legislation_gls/imonopoly_guidelines_files/20122502.pdf);

- ASBP Guidelines (Guidelines Concerning Abuse of a Dominant Bargaining Position in Service Transactions under the Antimonopoly Act (1998, revised 2004)) (https://www.jftc.go.jp/en/legislation_gls/imonopoly_guidelines_files/servicetransactions.pdf);
- Electric Power Guidelines (Guidelines for Proper Electric Power Trade (1999)) (https://www.jftc.go.jp/en/legislation_gls/imonopoly_guidelines_files/electric.pdf);
- Gas Guidelines (Guidelines for Proper Gas Trade (2000)) (https://www.jftc.go.jp/en/legislation_gls/imonopoly_guidelines_files/guidelines_gas.pdf);
- Guidelines Concerning Joint Activities for Recycling under the Antimonopoly Act (2001) (https://www.jftc.go.jp/en/legislation_gls/imonopoly_guidelines_files/recycle.pdf);
- Guidelines Concerning the Activities of Associations Conducting of Qualified Professional under the Antimonopoly Act (2001) (https://www.jftc.go.jp/en/legislation_gls/imonopoly_guidelines_files/qualify.pdf);
- Franchise Guidelines (Guidelines Concerning the Franchise System under the Antimonopoly Act (2002)) (https://www.jftc.go.jp/en/legislation_gls/imonopoly_guidelines_files/franchise.pdf);
- Guidelines Concerning Companies which Constitute an Excessive Concentration of Economic Power (2002) (https://www.jftc.go.jp/en/legislation_gls/imonopoly_guidelines_files/Company_Concentration.pdf);
- Merger Guidelines (Guidelines to Application of the Antimonopoly Act Concerning Review of Business Combination (2004, revised 2019)) (https://www.jftc.go.jp/en/legislation_gls/imonopoly_guidelines_files/191217GL.pdf);
- Guidelines Concerning Designation of Specific Unfair Trade Practices by Large-Scale Retailers Relating to Trade with Suppliers (2005, revised 2011) (https://www.jftc.go.jp/en/legislation_gls/imonopoly_guidelines_files/guidelines_large_scale_retailers.pdf);
- Guidelines on Standardization and Patent Pool Arrangements (2005, revised 2007) (https://www.jftc.go.jp/en/legislation_gls/imonopoly_guidelines_files/Patent_Pool.pdf);
- IP Guidelines (Guidelines for the Use of Intellectual Property under the Antimonopoly Act (2007, revised 2016)) (https://www.jftc.go.jp/en/legislation_gls/imonopoly_guidelines_files/IPGL_Frand.pdf);
- Exclusionary Private Monopolization Guidelines (Guidelines for Exclusionary Private Monopolization under the Antimonopoly Act (2009)) (https://www.jftc.go.jp/en/legislation_gls/imonopoly_guidelines_files/20122501.pdf);
- ASBP Guidelines (Guidelines Concerning Abuse of Superior Bargaining Position under the Antimonopoly Act (2010)) (https://www.jftc.go.jp/en/legislation_gls/imonopoly_guidelines_files/101130GL.pdf);
- Investigation Procedure Guidelines (Guidelines on Administrative Investigation Procedures under the Antimonopoly Act (2015)) (https://www.jftc.go.jp/en/legislation_gls/20122504.pdf).
- Business Revitalization Guidelines (Guidelines for Public Support for Revitalization in View of Competition Policy (2016)) (https://www.jftc.go.jp/en/legislation_gls/imonopoly_guidelines_files/160331.pdf);

- Guidelines Concerning Abuse of a Superior Bargaining Position in Transactions between Digital Platform Operators and Consumers that Provide Personal Information, etc. (2019) (https://www.jftc.go.jp/en/legislation_gls/imonopoly_guidelines_files/191217DPconsumerGL.pdf);
- Leniency Guidelines (Guidelines to Reduction System for Cooperation in Investigation (2020)) (https://www.jftc.go.jp/en/legislation_gls/201225002.pdf);
- Determination Procedure Guidelines (Guidelines on Treatment of Objects Recording Confidential Communications Between an Enterprise and an Attorney (2020)) (https://www.jftc.go.jp/en/legislation_gls/20122503.pdf);
- Telecommunication Guidelines (Guidelines for Promotion of Competition in the Telecommunications Business Field (2023; only available in Japanese)) (https://www.jftc.go.jp/dk/guideline/unyoukijun/denki_files/230907denkitsushin.pdf);
- Guidelines Concerning the Activities of Enterprises, etc.Toward the Realization of a Green Society Under the Antimonopoly Act (2024) (https://www.jftc.go.jp/en/legislation_gls/240424EN.pdf).

31. Also, the JFTC makes public its enforcing policy, gives explanation, and provides form for the enterprises to plan business combinations as follows:

- Commitment Procedure Policy (*Policies Concerning Commitment Procedures*, 2018) (https://www.jftc.go.jp/en/legislation_gls/antimonopoly_rules_files/policies_concerning_commitment_procedures.pdf);
- Guidance to fulfil the notification form (*Kisaiyoryo*) (only available in Japanese) (https://www.jftc.go.jp/dk/kiketsu/kigyoketsugo/kaiseiyouryou.html);
- Merger Review Policy (Policies Concerning Procedures of Review of Business Combination (2011)) (https://www.jftc.go.jp/en/legislation_gls/imonopoly_guidelines_files/191217policy.pdf);
- Criminal Accusation and Investigation Policy (Fair Trade Commission's Policy on Criminal Accusation and Compulsory Investigation of Criminal Cases Regarding Antimonopoly Violations (2005)) (https://www.jftc.go.jp/en/legislation_gls/210312.pdf);
- Notification Forms (*Todokedesho*) of Business Combination (only available in Japanese) (https://www.jftc.go.jp/dk/kiketsu/kigyoketsugo/dl/kaiseiyoushiki.html);
- Instruction for Online Submission of Notification of Business Combination (only available in Japanese)(https://www.jftc.go.jp/soudan/madoguchi/teishutsu.html);
- Points to Consider When Submitting An Economic Analysis Report and Data (2022) (https://www.jftc.go.jp/en/legislation_gls/220617EN.pdf).

§4. Role and Authority of Precedents

32. In Japanese legal system, like those in the countries which adopt civil law system, it is not clear whether precedents, not only by the JFTC but also Tokyo District Court, High Court, and Supreme Court, are binding or not. However, regardless of strict academic discussion, practically speaking, it seems difficult for the JFTC to overturn its own precedents and court judgments, especially Supreme

Court's ones, seeming respected. In that sense, precedents are virtually binding and there should be no concern for business to face too arbitrary and unpredictable antitrust enforcement.

Chapter 2. Scope of Application

§1. Territorial Reach

33. The AMA does not have a specific provision that defines or refers to the territorial reach of it. The Supreme Court, however, decided that the agreements that restricted the competition in the Japanese market should be subject to the AMA.[2]

34. Indeed, the JFTC's enforcement record shows its view on the territorial reach. In March 2008, the JFTC took action against some foreign companies, which did not have any presence in Japan in marine hose cartel case. Furthermore, the JFTC, in late 2008, started formal investigation into a proposed transaction between BHP Billiton Limited and BHP Billiton plc and Rio Tinto Limited and Rio Tinto plc, both of which did not have any outlets in Japan. According to these enforcement actions, the JFTC made clear that it would take a legal measure against conduct, which brings anticompetitive effect into Japanese market.

§2. Exemption

I. Exemptions in the AMA

35. The AMA has three exemption clauses, use of IPR, actions of cooperative associations and certain resale price maintenance (RPM). These exemption clauses have been included in the AMA since it was enacted in 1947.

A. IPRs Exemption

36. Article 21 of the AMA provides that its provisions do not apply to acts found to an exercise of rights under the Copyright Act (Act No. 48 of 1970), Patent Act (Act No. 121 of 1959), Utility Model Act (Act No. 123 of 1959), Design Act (Act No. 125 of 1959), or Trademark Act (Act No. 127 of 1959). This provision means that conduct essentially found as the exercise of IPRs is exempted from application of the AMA and that misuse of the IPRs is subject to the act even if the conduct seems to be found as the exercise of IPRs. In the case related to IPRs which the JFTC has handled there was no need to scrutinize whether the conduct at issue met the requirements of the provision. The interpretation of 'acts found to constitute an exercise of IPRs' is explained in the IP Guidelines[3].

37. The IP Guidelines stipulate the principles of applying AMA to IP as follows:

> An act by the right-holder to a technology to block other parties from using its technology or to limit the scope of use may seem, on its face, to be an exercise

2. Cathode Ray-Tube Case (Supreme Court, 12 Dec. 2017).
3. Guidelines for the Use of Intellectual Property under the Antimonopoly Act.

of rights .... [A]ny act that may seem to be an exercise of a right cannot be 'recognizable as the exercise of the rights' provided for in the aforesaid Article 21, provided that it is found to deviate from or run counter to the intent and objectives of the intellectual property systems, which are, namely, to motivate entrepreneurs [sic] to actualize their creative efforts and make use of technology, in view of the intent and manner of the act and its degree of impact on competition. The Antimonopoly Act is applicable to this kind of act .... When determining whether or not any specific act is recognizable as an exercise of the right, attention must be paid to the exhaustion of a right. After a party owning the right to technology legally distributed any product based on the technology in the Japanese market at its own discretion, its right is not infringed by any other party trading in the product in the Japanese market. In other words, the patent or other rights have been exhausted. There is no difference, in the principles of application of the Antimonopoly Act, between the cases where the right-holder imposes restrictions on another party that deals in the product that it has distributed at its own will and where a supplier, in general, imposes restrictions on the dealers that deal in its products.[4]

B. Acts of Cooperative Associations Exemption

38. Article 22 of the AMA provides that the acts of certain cooperative associations are exempted from application of AMA:

(Article 21)

The provisions of this Act do not apply to acts found to constitute an exercise of rights under the Copyright Act, Patent Act, Utility Model Act, Design Act or Trademark Act.

(Article 22)

The provisions of this Act do not apply to such acts by a partnership (including a federation of partnerships) which conforms to the requirements listed in each of the following items and which has been formed pursuant to the provisions of other Acts; provided, however, that this does not apply to cases if unfair trade practices are employed, or if competition in any particular field of trade is substantially restrained, resulting in unjust increases of prices:

(i) The purpose of the partnership is to provide mutual support among small-scale enterprises or consumers;
(ii) The partnership is voluntarily formed, and the partners may voluntarily participate in and withdraw from it;
(iii) Each partner possesses equal voting rights;

4. IP Guidelines, Part 2(1).

(iv) If a distribution of profits among partners is contemplated, the limits of the distributions are prescribed by laws and regulations or in the articles of partnership.

39. Among others, the reason why the application of the AMA for partnership is exempted is interpreted that it is compatible with basic principle of the AMA to strengthen bargaining power and competitiveness of partnerships by allowing some concerted conducts in order to increase market participants.

40. Cooperatives that are protected by this exemption shall be established cooperative laws. The laws include Agricultural Cooperatives Act (Act No. 132 of 1947), Fishery Cooperatives Act (Act No. 242 of 1948), Forestry Cooperatives Act (Act No. 36 of 1978), Small and Medium-Sized Enterprise Cooperatives Act (Act No. 181 of 1949), Consumer Cooperatives Act (Act No. 200 of 1948). Most of these cooperative laws have provisions that cooperatives established in accordance with respective laws shall be deemed as cooperatives of 'small sized enterprises', which is the most important requirement among the above four conditions.

41. There are several cases in which the JFTC took legal measures against cooperatives holding that they had engaged in unfair trade practices; therefore, the exemption provision was limitedly applicable. On the other hand, another proviso, i.e., where competition in any particular field of trade is substantially restrained, resulting in unjust increases of prices, has never been applied in the JFTC's enforcement history.

C. RPM Exemption

42. Since RPM reduces or eliminates price competition among distributors, generally RPM has serious anticompetitive effects and so tends to impede fair competition in principle under the provisions concerning unfair trade practices (see Chapter 3, §4 below). RPM regarding certain products designated by the JFTC and written works, however, is exempted from application of the AMA, unless the RPM tends to unreasonably harm the interests of general consumers' interest, or it is committed by an enterprise who sells the said commodity against the will of the enterprise who produces the said commodity.

43. There are two types of exemptions under this provision. The first one is for certain commodities designated by the JFTC. The commodities shall be daily used by general consumers and free competition exists with respect to them. The purpose of this exemption is to prevent predatory pricing or switch selling on the commodities from impairing their brand image or damaging other distributers. During 1953 to 1959 nine commodities such as cosmetics and medicines were designated by the JFTC. But in 1960s inflation was a big issue and it was criticized that this exemption was a factor of the price increase. After that the JFTC had revoked the designations one by one and the last two designated products were removed in 1997. The JFTC has not designated since then.

44. The second one is for written works. Those which are protected by this provision are newspapers, books, magazines, music-recorded materials including compact cassette and CD. RPM on the works is exempted from application of the AMA without designation by the JFTC. The reason to introduce the written works RPM exemption is unclear and some scholars think that historical practice in these sectors was ratified. Therefore, some argue that there is no economic-based justification for the exemption. On the other hand, some strongly insist that quality and diversity in these sectors would be impaired if the exemption was abolished.

45. The JFTC affirmatively analysed the status and economic impact of the exemption, and considered whether it should be maintained in the 1990s. Although the JFTC, in 2001, reached a conclusion that the exemption should be abolished from the viewpoint of competition policy, it decided not to take action to do so in view of public opinion that the exemption serves promotion and dissemination of culture.

II. Exemptions in Each Legislation

46. In the late 1940s and 1950s, many AMA exemption legislations were introduced in order to develop industries, strengthen competitiveness and stabilize management of companies. Some argue that these exemptions are related to concerted conduct such as cartels. The raison d'être of these exemption legislations has not yet been lost. For instance, nuclear energy insurance cartel is authorized because aviation accident would cause huge damages that individual insurance company cannot assume the risk. Local transportation cartel is approved since such a transportation service is essential for the residence in a rural area.

47. Such exemptions, however, have been acknowledged that they are likely to prevent businesses from making efforts to enhance efficiency and promoting innovation. Thus, review of these exemptions has been conducted by the government since the 1980s.

48. As a result of the review, a number of exemptions have been abolished. As at the end of September 2023, the acts containing AMA exemption provisions are as follows (Table 1).

Table 1 Laws Pertaining Exemption from AMA Application

Name of Law	*Exclusion System Specifics (Foundational Articles)*	*Year of Exemption Enactment*
Insurance Business Act	Insurance cartel	1951
Act on Non-Life Insurance Rating Organization of Japan	Standard rate calculation (automobile liability and earthquake insurance)	1998
Corporate Reorganization Act	Share acquisition for companies undergoing reorganization	1952
Act on securing of Liquor Tax and on Liquor Business Associations	Rationalization cartels	1959
Copyright Act	Arrangement pertaining to secondary usage of commercial records	1970
Act on Coordination and Improvement of the Environmental Health Industry	Cartels preventing excessive competition	1957
Agricultural Cooperatives Act	Certain business of agricultural producers' cooperative association	1999
Export and Import Transaction Act	Export cartels	1952
Act on the Organization of Small and Medium-Sized Enterprise Association	Joint business	1957
Small and Medium-Sized Enterprise Cooperatives Act	Certain business of the National Federation of Small Business Associations	1999
Marine Transportation Act	Cartels on coastwise transport	1949
	Cartels on oceangoing transport	1949
Road Transportation Act	Cartels on joint management among common omnibus operators	1951
Civil Aeronautics Act	Cartels on joint management among domestic air transport operators	1952

Name of Law	*Exclusion System Specifics (Foundational Articles)*	*Year of Exemption Enactment*
	Cartels with foreign air transport operators	1952
Coastal Shipping Cooperatives Act	Cartels on Coastal shipping	1957
	Cartels on shipping space	1957
Act on Special Measures Concerning Rationalization and Revitalization of General Passenger Vehicle Transportation Businesses in Designated Districts	Joint reduction in numbers of taxis	2013
Act Concerning Special Measures of the Act on Prohibition of Private Monopolization and Maintenance of Fair Trade for the Maintenance of Basic Services Associated with the Banking Business and General Passenger Vehicle Transportation Business Operators in Local Areas	Merger of corporations operating basic services in local areas	2020
	Conclusion of joint management agreement between local general passenger vehicle transportation business operators	2020

49. These antitrust exemptions are usually subject to approval by the competent ministers with the consent of or consultation with the JFTC. The exemptions also have conditions to prevent them from inflicting a loss on the public. In other words, each cartel shall not go beyond the extent of the purpose of the exemption and be discriminatory for the parties concerned. The proviso that if unfair trade practices are recognized the exemption that is no longer valid is also installed in these exemption legislations.

50. The number of exemption cartels approved by the competent ministers has been decreasing with abolition of some of the exemption legislations mentioned above, from 1,079 as at the end of FY 1965 to 36 as at the end of September 2023.

§3. SPECIAL SECTORS, STATE-OWNED ENTERPRISES AND PUBLIC UTILITIES

51. As stated above, the AMA is applied to all sectors and enterprises including state-owned enterprises and public utilities as long as they are operating a commercial, industrial, financial, or any other type of business. There is no exemption legislation, which prevents the JFTC from taking actions against state-owned enterprises and public utilities where they engage in AMA violation. In the past, public utility sectors were heavily regulated and competent regulators strictly oversaw almost all activities of public utilities. Therefore, there had been almost no room for the JFTC to apply the AMA in the sectors.

52. Nevertheless, in the 1990s and early 2000s, de-regulation had been implemented. Under the movement opportunity for competition in these sectors has grown. Under that circumstance, the JFTC, in cooperation with the competent ministries, has issued some guidelines such as Electric Power Guidelines,[5] Gas Guidelines,[6] and Telecommunication Guidelines,[7] in order to prevent AMA violation in public utility sectors, and the JFTC also announced that it would closely monitor the sectors and vigorously take actions if it finds any AMA violations.

53. With respect to enforcement in these sectors, the JFTC, in March 2007, issued a decision holding that a telecommunication company had engaged in private monopolization by excluding competitors who tried to enter the fibre optic broadband service market. The company appealed the decision but the Supreme Court upheld the JFTC's decision.[8] There are also a few cases in which the JFTC issued a warning (warning is not a legal action stipulated in the AMA but an administrative guidance to notify the respondent that its conduct may violate the AMA) to an electric power company for suspicion of AMA violation. There is no case in which the JFTC took legal measures against state-owned enterprises.

54. In addition, the JFTC made public the Business Revitalization Guidelines[9]. Those are issued based on consideration of the government support for revitalization in view of the competition policy and indicated key principles to minimize the effect of public support for revitalization on competition on the relevant markets, while also acknowledging that such support is provided to achieve various policy objectives.

§4. SENSIBLE EFFECT AND DE MINIMIS

55. The AMA has neither sensible effect provisions nor so-called *De Minimis* rule. Moreover, the JFTC has not issued any Commission rule, public notice, policy

5. Guidelines for Proper Electric Power Trade.
6. Guidelines for Proper Gas Trade.
7. Guidelines for Enhancing Competition in Telecommunication.
8. NTT-East Case (Supreme Court, 17 Dec. 2020).
9. Guidelines for Public Support for Revitalization in View of Competition Policy.

guidance, etc. on these matters. The AMA's prohibition clauses such as cartels and monopolization, however, have the requirement of 'Substantial restraint of trade'. Thus, concerted conduct between competitors that contains agreement on prices or any other sensitive subjects related to competition might be considered not to be unlawful if it does not 'substantially' restrain competition in the relevant market. However, there are no clear guidelines or case laws in this area.

Chapter 3. Overview of Substantive Provisions

§1. Unreasonable Restraint of Trade

56. Article 2(6) provides the definition of unreasonable restraint of trade, which means conclusion of restrictive agreement in more general term. It is defined as follows:

(Article 2)

(6) The term 'Unreasonable Restraint of Trade' as used in this Act means such business activities, by which any enterprise, by contract, agreement or any other means irrespective of its name, in concert with other enterprises, mutually restrict or conduct their business activities in such a manner as to fix, maintain or increase prices, or to limit production, technology, products, facilities or counterparties, thereby causing, contrary to the public interest, a substantial restraint of competition in any particular field of trade.

57. As seen in the definition above, unreasonable restraint of trade are the business activities which any enterprise, by contract, agreement or any other means irrespective of its name, in concert with other enterprises, mutually restrict or conduct in such a manner as to fix, maintain or increase prices, or to limit production, technology, products, facilities or counterparties thereby causing, contrary to the public interest, a substantial restraint of competition in any particular field of trade. Unreasonable restraint of trade is prohibited under Article 3.

(Article 3)

An enterprise must not effect … unreasonable restraint of trade.

58. Violation of Article 3 is, in principle, subject to a Cease and Desist Order and a Payment Order for Surcharge (hereinafter referred to as 'Payment Order'), both issued by the JFTC. The surcharge is administrative fine (*see* Chapter 5, §1, IV below). The offenders may also be sought damage in civil suit by victims due to Article 25 which exempts the victims from establishing offenders' intention or negligence (*see* Chapter 5, §2, II below).

59. In addition to the administrative and civil measures, the enterprises and their employees may be subject to criminal penalty. Criminal penalty for an individual includes incarceration and fine. The indictment is brought by the Public Prosecutor's Office, but it is made only after an accusation is filed by the JFTC. Both surcharge and criminal penalty can be imposed on the enterprise which engaged in unreasonable restraint of trade (*see* Chapter 5, §3 below).

§2. Dominant Undertakings

60. Article 2(5) provides the definition of private monopolization which is a conduct to monopolize a market. *Private monopolization* is defined as follows:

(Article 2)

(5) The term 'private monopolization' as used in this Act means such business activities, by which any enterprise, individually or by combination, in conspiracy with other enterprises, or by any other manner, excludes or controls the business activities of other enterprises, thereby causing, contrary to the public interest, a substantial restraint of competition in any particular field of trade.

61. Likewise, as in the case of unreasonable restraint of trade, private monopolization is prohibited under Article 3.

(Article 3)

An enterprise must not effect private monopolization.

62. Private monopolization is also subject to both administrative prohibition and criminal penalty. Substantive provisions are the same as those of unreasonable restraint of trade as mentioned above, Articles 3 and 89. The fine and sanction of private monopolization are also the same as those of unreasonable restraint of trade.

§3. Concentrations

63. The AMA provides concentration regulations in Chapter 4, Articles 9–18. There are two beliefs concerning concentration regulations: General Concentration and Market Concentration. As for General Concentration regulations, Article 9 of the AMA provides as follows.

(Article 9)

(1) No company may be established that would cause an excessive concentration of economic power due to share holding (including equity interest; the same applies hereinafter) other companies in Japan.
(2) No company (including a foreign company; the same applies hereinafter) may become a company that causes an excessive concentration of economic power in Japan by acquiring or holding shares in other companies in Japan.
(3) The term 'excessive concentration of economic power' ... means that the overall business scale of a company, its subsidiary companies, and other domestic companies whose business activities it controls through shareholding, is extremely large across a considerable number of business fields;

that a company, its subsidiary companies, and other domestic companies it controls have a great amount of power to influence other enterprises through transactions with their funds; or that a company, its subsidiary companies, and other domestic companies it controls occupy influential positions in a considerable number of interrelated fields of business; and that any of these factors have a large effect on the national economy and impede fair and free competition from moving forward.

64. Especially as for financial institutions, Article 11 prohibits banks and insurance companies from acquiring or holding voting rights in another company in Japan if it results in its holding, exceeding a certain threshold in terms of Excessive Concentration of Economic Power.

(Article 11)

(1) No company engaged in banking or insurance businesses may acquire or hold voting rights in another company in Japan if it results in its holding more than five percent (ten percent for a company engaged in insurance business …) of voting rights of all shareholders.

65. If a company that causes an excessive concentration of economic power is established or if a company acquires or holds the other companies' shares resulting in becoming a company that causes an excessive concentration of economic power, that company will be subject to a Cease and Desist Order.

66. As for market concentration, the AMA prohibits eight types of business combination that substantially restrains competition in any particular field of trade and stipulates individual provisions as follows:

- Article 10: Acquiring or holding shares of any other company;
- Article 13: Interlocking directorates;
- Article 14: Acquiring or holding by a person other than a company;
- Article 15: Effecting merger of companies;
- Article 15-2: Effecting joint incorporation-type split or absorption split;
- Article 15-3: Effecting joint stock transfer;
- Article 16: Engaging in accepting assignment of business;
- Article 17: Circumvention of the prohibition above.

67. Specific provisions are as follows:

(Article 10)

(1) No company may acquire or hold shares of any other companies if its acquisition or holding of shares substantially restrains competition in any particular field of trade, nor may any company use unfair trade practices to acquire or hold shares in another company.

(Article 13)

(1) An officer or an employee (meaning, in this Article, a person other than an officer engaged in the business of a company on a regular basis) of a company may not hold a position as an officer of another company at the same time, if the person's doing so substantially restrains competition in any particular field of trade.

(Article 14)

A person other than a company may not acquire or hold shares in a company if the person's doing so substantially restrains competition in any particular field of trade, nor may a person that is not a company use unfair trade practices to acquire or hold shares in a company.

(Article 15)

(1) No company may effect a merger if any of the following items applies:
 (i) if the merger substantially restrains competition in a particular field of trade.

(Article 15-2)

(1) No company may effect a joint incorporation-type company split (meaning an incorporation-type company split that a company effects jointly with another company; the same shall apply hereinafter) or an absorption-type split if any of the following items applies:
 (i) if the joint incorporation-type company split or absorption-type split substantially restrains competition in a particular field of trade.

(Article 15-3)

(1) No company may engage in a joint share transfer (meaning a share transfer carried out by a company jointly with another company; the same shall apply hereinafter) if it falls under either of the following items:
 (i) if the joint share transfer substantially restrains competition in a particular field of trade.

(Article 16)

(1) No company may engage in any of the following acts if its doing so substantially restrains competition in any particular field of trade, or through unfair trade practices:
 (i) accepting assignment of the whole or a substantial part of the business of another company;
 (ii) accepting assignment of the whole or a substantial part of the fixed assets used for the business of another company;
 (iii) taking on a lease of the whole or a substantial part of the business of another company;
 (iv) undertaking the management of the whole or a substantial part of the business of another company;

(v) entering into a contract which provides for a joint profit and loss account for business with another company.

(Article 17)

No person may engage in any act, irrespective of the name given to that act, that evades the prohibitions and restrictions provided for in the provisions of Articles 9 to 16 inclusive.

68. The business combination that substantially restrains competition in any particular field of trade is subject to a Cease and Desist Order pursuant to Article 17-2:

(Article 17-2)

(1) NoIf an act in violation of the provisions of Article 10, paragraph (1); Article 11, paragraph (1); Article 15, paragraph (1); Article 15-2, paragraph (1); Article 15-3, paragraph (1); Article 16, paragraph (1); or the preceding Article has occurred, the Fair Trade Commission may, pursuant to the procedures provided in Section 2 of Chapter VIII, order the enterprise concerned to dispose of all or some of its shares, transfer a part of its business or take any other measures necessary to eliminate the act in violation of the provisions.

69. Chapter 4 of the AMA, in addition to Articles 9 and 11, also sets forth provisions regarding the notification to the JFTC, with regard to all of the business combination mentioned above. The form and the details of notification, including the threshold to notify, are stipulated in the Business Combination Rules.[10]

70. Each substantive provision regarding M&A in Chapter 4 provides a waiting period. For instance, Article 10(8) provides as follows:

(Article 10)

(8) No company that gave notification in accordance with the provisions of paragraph (2) may acquire the shares under the notification until the expiration of the thirty-day waiting period from the date of acceptance of the said notification; provided, however, that whenever the Fair Trade Commission may, when it finds it to be necessary, it may shorten the relevant period.

71. In case the companies have merged during the waiting period, the JFTC may bring a lawsuit based on Article 18 as follows:

10. Rules on Applications for Approval, Reporting, Notification, etc. Pursuant to the Provisions of Arts 9–16 of the Act on Prohibition of Private Monopolization and Maintenance of Fair Trade.

(Article 18)

(1) If companies have merged in violation of the provisions of Article 15, paragraph (2) and Article 10, paragraph (8) as applied mutatis mutandis pursuant to Article 15, paragraph (3) following the deemed replacement of terms, the Fair Trade Commission may bring an action to have the merger declared invalid.

§4. Other Prohibitions

72. The AMA also prohibits other anticompetitive conducts in addition to restrictive agreement and monopolization: that is, the regulation of unfair trade practices, international agreement or contract, trade association's conducts and monopolistic situation.

I. Unfair Trade Practices

A. Overview

73. Items (i) to (v) of Article 2(9) define some practices as those tend to impede fair competition. In addition to those, JFTC designates fifteen practices which also tend to impede fair competition by a public notice which is known as General Designation,[11] as stated in Chapter 1, §3, II above. These are collectively called as 'unfair trade practice(s)'.

74. The objective of regulation on unfair trade practices is based on the incipient doctrine, which aims to prevent the enterprises from engaging in anticompetitive conduct that restrains the competition in the market, not substantially but to the extent of giving negative effects, in advance of committing serious violation such as unreasonable restraint of trade and private monopolization mentioned above. In this sense, unfair trade practices are the conducts that impede fair competition and may be less significant than those which substantially restrict competition in terms of the degree of anticompetitive effect on a market. Nevertheless, regulation of unfair trade practices plays a role in complementing the gap between the substantial restriction of competition and proper competitive practices.

75. Unfair trade practices are prohibited by Article 19 of the AMA. An enterprise which violates this Article is to receive a Cease and Desist Order pursuant to Article 20 and can be subject to damage suit pursuant to Article 25 (*see* Chapter 5, §1, I, C and §2, II, B below). Besides, certain conducts among those are subject to surcharges (*see* Chapter 5, §1, IV, C below).

11. Designation of Unfair Trade Practices.

(Article 19)

An enterprise must not employ unfair trade practices.

B. Specific Practices

76. Article 2(9) provides the definition of unfair trade practice as follows:

(Article 2)

(9) The term 'unfair trade practices' as used in this Act means an act falling under any of the following items:
 (i) engaging, without justifiable grounds, in any of the following acts, in concert with a competitor:
  (a) refusing to supply to a certain enterprise or restricting the quantity or substance of goods or services supplied to a certain enterprise;
  (b) causing another enterprise to refuse to supply a certain enterprise, or to restrict the quantity or substance of goods or services supplied to a certain enterprise.
 (ii) unjustly and continually supplying goods or services at a price applied differentially between regions or between parties, thereby tending to cause difficulties to the business activities of other enterprises;
 (iii) without justifiable grounds, continuously supplying goods or services at a price far below the cost incurred to supply them, thereby tending to cause difficulties to the business activities of other enterprises;
 (iv) supplying goods to another party who purchases the relevant goods from oneself while imposing, without justifiable grounds, one of the restrictive terms listed below:
  (a) causing the party to maintain the selling price of the goods that one has determined, or otherwise restricting the party's free decision on selling price of the goods;
  (b) having the party cause an enterprise that purchases the goods from the party maintain the selling price of the goods that one has determined, or otherwise causing the party to restrict the relevant enterprise's free decision on the selling price of the goods.
 (v) engaging in any act specified in one of the following by making use of one's superior bargaining position over the counterparty unjustly, in light of normal business practices:
  (a) causing the counterparty in continuous transactions (including a party with whom one newly intends to engage in continuous transactions; the same applies in (b) below) to purchase goods or services other than those to which the relevant transactions pertain;

(b) causing the counterparty in continuous transactions to provide money, services or other economic benefits;
(c) refusing to receive goods in transactions with the counterparty, causing the counterparty to take back such goods after receiving them from the counterparty, delaying payment to the counterparty or reducing the amount of payment, or otherwise establishing or changing trade terms or executing transactions in a way disadvantageous to the counterparty.

(vi) any act falling under any of the following items, which tends to impede fair competition and which is designated by the Fair Trade Commission, other than the acts listed in the preceding items:
(a) unjustly treating other enterprises in a discriminatory manner;
(b) engaging in transactions at an unjust price;
(c) unjustly inducing or coercing the customers of a competitor to deal with one;
(d) dealing with another party on such conditions that will unjustly restrict the business activities of the counterparty;
(e) dealing with the counterparty by making use of one's superior bargaining position unjustly;
(f) unjustly interfering with a transaction between an enterprise in competition with one in Japan or a corporation of which one is a shareholder or an officer and another transaction counterparty; or, if such enterprise is a corporation, unjustly inducing, instigating or coercing a shareholder or officer of such corporation to act against the corporation's interests.

77. On the other hand, General Designation presents the practices which fall on Article 2(9)(vi) as follows:

(Concerted Refusal to Trade)

(1) Without justifiable grounds, any act listed in any of the following items concertedly with another entrepreneur [sic] who is in a competitive relationship with oneself (hereinafter referred to as a 'competitor'):
(i) Refusing to receive supplies of goods or services from a certain entrepreneur [sic] or restricting the quantity or substance of goods or services supplied by a certain entrepreneur [sic];
(ii) Causing another entrepreneur [sic] to refuse to receive supplies of goods or services from a certain entrepreneur [sic], or to restrict the quantity or substance of goods or services supplied by a certain entrepreneur [sic].

(Other Refusal to Trade)

(2) Unjustly refusing to trade or restricting the quantity or substance of goods or services pertaining to trade with a certain entrepreneur [sic], or causing another entrepreneur [sic] to undertake any act that falls under one of these categories.

(Discriminatory Consideration)

(3) In addition to any act falling under the provisions of Article 2, paragraph (9), item (ii) of Act on Prohibition of Private Monopolization and Maintenance of Fair Trade (Act No. 54 of 1947 hereinafter referred to as 'the Act'), unjustly supplying or accepting goods or services for a consideration which discriminates between regions or between parties.

(Discriminatory Treatment on Trade Terms, etc.)

(4) Unjustly affording favourable or unfavourable treatment to a certain entrepreneur [sic] in regard to the terms or execution of a trade.

(Discriminatory Treatment, etc. in a Trade Association)

(5) Unjustly excluding a specific entrepreneur [sic] from a trade association or from a concerted activity, or unjustly discriminating against a specific entrepreneur [sic] in a trade association or a concerted activity, thereby causing difficulties in the business activities of the said entrepreneur [sic].

(Unjust Low Price Sales)

(6) In addition to any act falling under the provisions of Article 2, paragraph (9), item (iii) of the Act, unjustly supplying goods or services for a low consideration, thereby tending to cause difficulties to the business activities of other entrepreneurs [sic].

(Unjust High Price Purchasing)

(7) Unjustly purchasing goods or services for a high consideration, thereby tending to cause difficulties to the business activities of other entrepreneurs [sic].

(Deceptive Customer Inducement)

(8) Unjustly inducing customers of a competitor to trade with oneself by causing them to misunderstand that the substance of goods or services supplied by oneself, or its trade terms, or other matters relevant to such trade are much better or much more favourable than the actual ones or than those pertaining to the competitor.

(Customer Inducement by Unjust Benefits)

(9) Inducing customers of a competitor to trade with oneself by offering unjust benefits in light of normal business practices.

(Tie-in Sales, etc.)

(10) Unjustly causing another party to purchase goods or services from oneself or from an entrepreneur [sic] designated by oneself by tying it to the supply of other goods or services, or otherwise coercing the said party to trade with oneself or with an entrepreneur [sic] designated by oneself.

(Trading on Exclusionary Terms)

(11) Unjustly trading with another party on condition that the said party shall not trade with a competitor, thereby tending to reduce trading opportunities for the said competitor.

(Trading on Restrictive Terms)

(12) In addition to any act falling under the provisions of Article 2, paragraph (9), item (iv) of the Act and the preceding paragraph, trading with another party on conditions which unjustly restrict any trade between the said party and its other transacting party or other business activities of the said party.

(Unjust Interference with Appointment of Officer in One's Transacting Party)

(13) Causing a corporation which is one's transacting party to follow one's instruction in advance, or to get one's approval, regarding the appointment of officers of the said corporation (meaning those as defined by Article 2, paragraph (3) of the Act (The same shall apply hereinafter)), unjustly in light of the normal business practices by making use of one's dominant bargaining position over the party.

(Interference with a Competitor's Transactions)

(14) Unjustly interfering with a transaction between another entrepreneur [sic] who is in a domestic competitive relationship with oneself or with the corporation of which one is a stockholder or an officer, and its transacting party, by preventing the effecting of a contract, or by inducing the breach of a contract, or by any other means whatsoever.

(Interference with Internal Operation of a Competing Company)

(15) Unjustly inducing, abetting, or coercing a stockholder or an officer of a corporation which is in a domestic competitive relationship with oneself or with a corporation of which one is a stockholder or an officer, to take an act disadvantageous to such corporation by the exercise of voting rights, transfer of stock, divulgence of secrets, or any other means whatsoever.

78. Whichever defined in the AMA (Statutorily defined unfair trade practices) or designated by the General Designation (Designated unfair trade practices), these practices can be classified into nine categories. Each practice defined by AMA and designated by General Designation falls under each of one of the categories below.

a. concerted refusal to trade: Article 2(9)(i) of AMA, paragraph (1) of General Designation;
b. discriminatory pricing: Article 2(9)(ii) of AMA, paragraph (3) of General Designation;
c. unjust low-price sales: Article 2(9)(iii) of AMA, paragraph (6) of General Designation;

d. RPM: Article 2(9)(iv) of AMA;
e. abuse of dominant bargaining position: Article 2(9)(v) of AMA, paragraph (13) of General Designation;
f. discriminatory treatment on trade term: paragraphs (2), (4) and (5) of General Designation;
g. unjust high price purchasing: paragraph (7) of General Designation;
h. deceptive customer inducement/customer inducement by unjust benefits/tie-in sales: paragraphs (8)–(10) of General Designation;
i. trading on exclusionary terms/trading on restrictive terms: paragraphs (11) and (12) of General Designation;
j. interference of competitor's business: paragraphs (14) and (15) of General Designation.

79. Practices that fall under unfair trade practices can also be classified into two: one is defined/designated with a requirement of 'without justifiable grounds' and another one defined/designated with that of 'unjustly'. The distinction reflects the likeliness of impeding fair competition and indicates who owes burden of proof. The practices with 'without justifiable grounds' are deemed as illegal in principle; therefore, the defendants should claim their justification when the JFTC probes the practices.

80. On the contrary, the JFTC should prove the unjustness of the practices provided with 'unjustly'. Practices with 'without unjustifiable grounds' respond to (a) concerted refusal to trade defined by AMA; (b) concerted refusal to trade designated by General Designation; (c) unjust low price sales defined by AMA, and (d) RPM above. Among those, some practices will be mentioned in Part II, Chapter 2, §3 and §4 below.

II. International Agreement

81. Article 6 prohibits international agreement or contract.

> (Article 6)
>
> An enterprise must not enter into an international agreement or an international contract which contains such matters which fall under unreasonable restraint of trade or unfair trade practices.

82. International agreement or contract can be subject to a Cease and Desist Order, Payment Order and the damage suit based on Article 25.

III. Monopolistic Situation

83. Article 8(4) regulates 'monopolistic situation', which is defined by Article 2(7), and the detailed requirements are provided by AMA Enforcement Order.[12] The definition of the AMA is as follows:

(Article 2)

(7) The term 'monopolistic situation' as used in this Act means circumstances in which each of the following market structures and negative effect in the market exist in any particular field of business when the aggregate total value of goods of the same description (including goods capable of being supplied without making any material change to the facilities for, or kinds of, such business activities; hereinafter referred to as 'Particular Goods' in this paragraph) and those of any other goods having an extremely similar function and utility thereto, which are supplied in Japan (excluding those exported), or the total value of services of the same description which are supplied in Japan, during the latest one-year period designated by a Cabinet Order, exceeds one-hundred billion yen:
- (i) a single enterprise' share of a field of business (meaning, out of the aggregate volume ... of the Particular Goods and any other goods with an extremely similar function and utility that are supplied in Japan (excluding those exported), or out of the aggregate volume of the services that are supplied in Japan, the ratio of Particular Goods and any other goods with an extremely similar function and utility or services that are supplied by the enterprise; hereinafter the same applies in this item) exceeding one-half or two enterprise' combined share of a field of business exceeding three-fourths during the relevant one-year period;
- (ii) the existence of conditions that make it extremely difficult for any other enterprise to newly enter the relevant particular field of business;
- (iii) the existence of a remarkable increase or of a slight decrease in the price of the Particular Goods or services supplied by the relevant enterprise during a considerable period of time in light of the changes in supply and demand, and changes in the cost of supply, for the Particular Goods or services, and the enterprise falling under any of the following items during the period:
  - (a) That the said enterprise has made a profit at the rate far exceeding the profit rate which is specified by a Cabinet Order as the standard for the business type specified by a Cabinet Order to which the relevant enterprise belongs;
  - (b) That the said enterprise has expended selling and general administrative expenses which are considered to be far exceeding the

12. Cabinet Order for Enforcement of the Act on Prohibition of Private Monopolization and Maintenance of Fair Trade.

standard selling and general administrative expenses for the field of business to which the relevant enterprise belongs.

84. Monopolistic situation is not behavioural violation but structural regulation. In other words, as far as the enterprise meets the above-mentioned requirements, even if it does not participate in any anticompetitive conduct, it can be subject to JFTC's action to restore competition in the market pursuant to Article 8-4 as follows.

However, no enforcement action has been brought since the introduction of the regulation in 1977:

(Article 8-4)

(1) Whenever a monopolistic situation exists, the Fair Trade Commission may order the relevant enterprise, pursuant to the procedures as provided in Section 2 of Chapter VIII, to transfer a part of its business or to take any other measures necessary to restore competition with respect to the relevant goods or services provided, however, that this does not apply if it is found that such measures may, in relation to the relevant enterprise, reduce the scale of business to such an extent that the expenses required for the supply of goods or services that the relevant enterprise supplies will rise sharply, undermine its financial position, or make it difficult to maintain its international competitiveness, or if alternative measures are found to be sufficient for restoring competition with respect to the relevant goods or services can be taken.

(2) In issuing an order pursuant to the preceding paragraph, the Fair Trade Commission must give consideration, based on the matters listed in the following items, to the smooth operation of business activities by the relevant enterprise and enterprises affiliated therewith and the stabilization of life of those employed by the relevant enterprise:
   (i) situations of assets, income and expenditure and other aspects of accounting;
   (ii) situations of officers and employees;
   (iii) location and other locational conditions of factories, workplaces and offices;
   (iv) situations of facilities and equipment for the business;
   (v) substance of patent rights, trademark rights, and other intellectual property rights and other technological features;
   (vi) capacity for and situations of production, sales, etc.;
   (vii) capacity for and situations of funding and acquisition of raw materials, etc.;
   (viii) situations of supply and distribution of goods or services.

§5. Tests of Illegality

I. Per Se Prohibitions and Naked Restraints

85. The JFTC released the Distribution Guidelines[13] in 1991. They illustrate the practices of transaction among manufacturers and distributors and businesses which might fall upon AMA violation with JFTC's enforcing policy. In the guidelines, JFTC declared:

> For example, price-fixing cartels, supply-restraint cartels, purchasing volume cartels, and bid riggings … in principle constitute violations of the Antimonopoly Act.[14]

86. However, no judicial precedent ever ruled cartel or private monopolization from the viewpoint of per se illegal. As discussed below, the provisions of a cartel and that of private monopolization require the 'substantial restriction of competition' in its constitution. When judging these conducts, it should be examined whether 'substantial restrict of competition' is found or not. Even price cartel or bid rigging should be examined, legally, from the standpoint of effects on the competition in the market, and it implies that the JFTC seemingly does not employ the per se illegal doctrine. The JFTC, therefore, practically acknowledges substantial restraints of competition by citing the market share of the parties involved in the conducts in question, and such a way of proving restraints of competition has been approved by the courts.

87. On the other hand, unfair trade practice requires 'impeding fair competition' in its constitution. Some unfair trade practices are declared quasi-'*per se* illegal', just as the above-mentioned unfair trade practice within the Distribution Guidelines. These practices are considered illegal unless the enterprise proves justification for the practices.

II. Balancing Tests

88. For example, as for private monopolization, the JFTC shows some factors to assess the impact of market conduct. Please see later (*see* Chapter 4, §5 below).

III. Merger Tests

89. With regard to the tests by which the JFTC assesses the possible impact of business combination on the market, it makes public in the Merger Guidelines.[15]

13. Guidelines Concerning Distribution Systems and Business Practices under the Antimonopoly Act.
14. Distribution Guidelines, Introduction, para. 3.
15. Guidelines to Application of the Antimonopoly Act Concerning Review of Business Combination.

Chapter 4. Overview of Main Notions

§1. UNDERTAKING

I. General Remarks

90. All prohibition clauses of the AMA begin with 'enterprise (or trade association, i.e. business group which consists of enterprises) must not … '.

91. Concerning enterprise, Article 2(1) provides as follows:

(Article 2)

(1) The term 'enterprise' as used in this Act means a person who operates a commercial, industrial, financial or other business. Any officer, employee, agent or other person who acts for the benefit of any enterprise is deemed to be an enterprise with regard to the application of the provisions of the following paragraph or of Chapter III.

92. As described above, 'Enterprise' means a person who operates a commercial, industrial, financial or any other business. The judicial precedent states, 'Business' means an economic activity by which it receives, continuously or repeatedly, counter-performance in return for the supply of any economic benefit and it does not matter whether 'person' has any legal nature. Consequently, Non-profit Organizations (NPOs), national or local governments, educational institutions, or self-employed individuals/freelance professionals, such as lawyers, accountants, or doctors would fall into the definition of enterprise in the AMA.

93. The person may include state-owned companies and perhaps the state itself if it is considered to meet the requirements of Article 2(1). Therefore, the AMA is applicable to any legal and natural persons as long as they are construed as enterprise. For example, the Supreme Court endorsed, in a private damage suit alleging that the sector of the state for postal service had violated the AMA, the High Court decision holding that the state can be, as the operator of the business issuing and selling postal cards, considered to be an enterprise in the AMA.[16]

94. On the other hand, there could be some conflicts between competition policy and other government policies. To resolve such conflicts, there are some AMA exemption legislation and exemption clauses in the AMA itself (*see* Chapter 2, §2 and §3 above).

16. New Year's Lottery Postal Card Case [Damage Suitcase] (Osaka High Court, 14 Oct. 1994).

II. Trade Association

95. The AMA has provisions specialized to regulate anticompetitive conduct by trade association. Article 2(2) provides the definition of 'trade association' as follows:

> (Article 2)
>
> (2) The term 'trade association' as used in this Act means any combination or federation of combinations of two or more enterprises having as its principal purpose the furtherance of their common interest as enterprises ... .

96. JFTC, in its Trade Associations Guidelines,[17] explains that 'Common interest as enterprises' is interpreted as what contributes, directly or indirectly, economic benefit among its constituent enterprises.[18] The association that does not aim at promoting common interest is not the trade association in the AMA, for instance: pure academic association, philanthropy group, or religious organization, and the like. The JFTC ruled in a specific case that it found any decision made by any branch or subordinate group under the trade association as the trade association's conduct, if its constituent enterprises substantially recognized the decision as what they should comply with. Stated differently, it is not necessary that the decision be done through a formal decision-making process or by the body in accordance with its procedure.

§2. Relevant Market

I. General Remarks

97. The AMA refers to relevant market as a particular field of trade, but the Act does not provide its definition. According to the Merger Guidelines, however, it explains that a particular field of market means the framework to judge whether a suspected conduct causes to restrain competition or whether a reviewed transaction may be to substantially restrain competition. The JFTC determines both the product market and the geographic market, basically, from the demand side's viewpoint of substitutability (substitutability for customers). The JFTC may also deliberate them from the supply side's viewpoint (substitutability for suppliers).

98. When examining substitutability for customers, the JFTC employs so-called SSNIP (Small but Significant and Non-transitory Increase in Price) test. Particularly, the JFTC will suppose that a monopolist in a specific region supplies a specific product. Then, under this assumption, the JFTC considers the degree under which customers can substitute an alternative product or region for the purchase of the product when the monopolist implements an SSNIP with the aim of maximizing its profit. The Merger Guidelines mention that SSNIP is generally considered as a

17. Guidelines Concerning the Activities of Trade Associations under the Antimonopoly Act.
18. Trade Association Guidelines, Part I, 2.

price increase of between 5% and 10% that persists for about a year.[19] If the degree to which an alternative product or region can be substituted for the purchase of the product is small, and the monopolist can succeed in expanding its profits from the price increase, the scope is to be defined as denoting that the effect of the business combination may have some impact on competition.

99. Regarding substitutability for suppliers, the JFTC will consider the degree to which other suppliers can switch, within a relatively short period (mostly within one year), without substantial cost or risk, from the manufacture and sale of another product or region to those of the product, when SSNIP is implemented for the product and region. If the degree is small, and so the monopolist can expand its profit by the price increase, the scope would be such that the effect of the business combination may have some impact on competition.

100. When a market can be defined while another wider (or narrower) market can also be constituted at the same time, the JFTC may define several overlapped markets simultaneously.

II. Product Market

101. When determining the product market, the JFTC is likely to examine the degree of similarity of utility for customers because the degree of product substitutability very often matches the degree of similarity of utility for customers. Thus, JFTC examines the usage, changes in price, quantity, recognition and actions of customers of the product when it determines the product market.

III. Geographic Market

102. When determining the geographic market, as well as the product market, substitutability for customers between the products supplied in each area is considered. The degree of substitutability between the products supplied in each area can very often be determined by the behaviour of customers and suppliers, and existence of issues in the transportation of the product. Thus, the JFTC examines business area of suppliers, the area for customers to purchase, features of goods, type, or cost of transportation when it determines the geographic market.

103. The basic concept above is also applied when the geographic market is determined across the national border. If the customers, both inside and outside Japan for a certain product, purchase products without segregating domestic and foreign suppliers, even if the prices have been raised in Japan, the customers in Japan will be able to substitute the purchase of products from overseas suppliers, which may obstruct the raising of prices in Japan. In such a case, a geographical range can be determined across the national border.

---

19. Merger Guidelines, Part II, 1. (n. 2).

§3. Market Power/Dominant Position

104. The AMA does not directly provide any definition of both market power and dominant position. Especially, Article 2(5) on private monopolization does not include the exact concept of dominant position as the explicit requirements. It can be said that the concept of substantial restriction of competition is extremely vital to judge if a conduct violates monopolization regulation instead (see §5 below).

§4. Agreement and Concerted Conduct

I. General Remarks

105. The AMA prohibits concerted practices among enterprises which substantially restrain competition as unreasonable restraint of trade, and they comprise horizontal cartel, such as price-fixing and quantity limiting, bid rigging and market/customer allocation. It bans these hardcore cartels such as price-fixing and bid riggings as well as non-hardcore cartels such as patent standardization, joint R&D and collective purchasing or production, though there is no distinction between them in the statute. Group boycott (concerted refusal to deal) is a conduct that falls under unfair trade practice but could also be prohibited as unreasonable restraint of trade when it meets substantial restraint of trade.

II. Requirements of Unreasonable Restraint of Trade

106. It is generally recognized that the regulation on unreasonable restraint of trade has two main requirements, on conduct and effects on competition. The requirement on effects that the conduct tends to substantially restrain competition will be mentioned in §5 below.

107. The requirement on conduct is that the conduct should be executed in a manner to mutually restrict business activities in concert with other enterprises. Traditionally, some have argued that 'mutually' and 'in concert with other enterprises' are independent requirements; however, the recent judgment declared that it was obvious that the agreement in question had restricted the business activities of the members and they had mutually and concertedly restrained each activity, because they had acknowledged and accepted actions of other members through the agreement, thereby their conduct had satisfied the requirement of 'mutually' and 'concertedly'.[20]

108. It is broadly believed that the mere fact there appears consistency of the action among the enterprises in question is not sufficient to meet the requirement, but the existence of 'communication of intent' among them is needed.

---

20. Tama Area Bid-rigging Case (Supreme Court, 20 Feb. 2012).

109. On this point, the JFTC made a decision in its administrative judgment as follows:

> It is still not sufficient that the mere fact the [respective] conducts [of enterprises] eventually result in external consistency meets the requirement of 'in concert with.' Moreover, it is needed that [the fact] any communication of intent existed among enterprises is found.[21]

110. The Tokyo High Court also judges in the same line of this decision as follows:

> It should be believed that it is necessary to be found that communication of intent existed between them. 'Communication of intent' means that enterprises' intent, on which some enterprises respectively perceive or anticipate that they raised prices or put the same matter into practice, existed. ... It is not sufficient that one merely perceives or admits the other raised prices. However, that enterprises obviously agree to restrict their business with each other is not necessarily required. It is sufficient that each enterprise perceives the other's price raising and admits it tacitly if it is found appropriately so.[22]

In sum, whether explicitly or implicitly, existence of *communication of intent* among enterprises is required to acknowledge violation of unreasonable restraint of trade.

III. Application to Vertical Agreement

111. The requirement of mutuality and concerted practice is not limited to horizontal agreement but applicable to vertical agreement. However, the JFTC has come to hesitate to apply unreasonable restraint of trade to vertical agreement such as RPM and has employed regulation of private monopolization or unfair trade practices to challenge it for a long time. It may be partly because the JFTC has been bound to an old ruling that an agreement 'mutually [to] restrict ... their business activities in the statute'.[23]

112. There has been a strong disagreement to this judgment in academia and the judgment was not of the Supreme Court but merely of the Tokyo High Court. Indeed, the JFTC has challenged some cases in which the enterprises on different transaction levels were involved in a horizontal agreement in the last decade. Also, the judgment of the same court held as follows in a different case forty years later:

> The representative (of appellant [X]) claims that [X] does not correspond to the 'enterprise' defined in the AMA because the 'enterprise' needs to be those

21. Plywood Cartel Case (JFTC Administrative Hearing Decision, 30 Aug. 1949).
22. Toshiba Chemical Case (Tokyo High Court, 25 Sep. 1995).
23. Newspapers Distributional Channel Agreement Case (Tokyo High Court, 9 Mar. 1953).

which are in competitive relationship but [X] was not nominated in the bidding by the procurement body hence it was not competing with other violators which were nominated, quoting the judgement of The Tokyo High Court of 1953 .... However, the court doubts that the definition of 'enterprises' should be limited to those which are in competitive relationship under the current Act which has been revised since ... the court held in 1953, and it is not adequate at least to interpret the meaning of the 'enterprise' in a limited way such as the appellant claims.[24]

113. That was not a case targeting vertical agreement, but the coverage of unreasonable restraint of trade may be gradually expanded to vertical agreement as the scope of the participants of agreement is broadened.

IV. International Agreement

114. As stated in Chapter 1, §4, II above, enterprises are prohibited from entering an international agreement that contains matters which fall under unreasonable restraint of trade.

V. Trade Association

115. Trade association's anticompetitive conducts are prohibited by Article 8 of the AMA. Those are subject to a Cease and Desist Order and the damage suit based on Article 25. Also, it can be subject to surcharges only when the conduct violates Article 8(i), which falls under unreasonable restraint of trade, and/or Article 8(ii), which corresponds to international agreement/contract, which falls under unreasonable restraint of trade.

116. When price-fixing is conducted by a trade association composed of some enterprises that meet the requirements provided by Article 2(2), it is also prohibited pursuant to Article 8(i).

117. Moreover, when a trade association restricts present or future members of participants into particular business activities or unjustly restricts the operations or activities of its constituents, these conducts are forbidden by items (iii) or (iv) of Article 8.

118. If a trade association agrees to the same international agreement or contract, it also violates Article 8(ii) of the AMA.

24. Blindfold Seal Bid-rigging Case [Criminal case] (Tokyo High Court, 14 Dec. 1993).

(Article 8)

A trade association must not engage in any act which falls under any of the following items:

(i) substantially restraining competition in any particular field of trade;
(ii) entering into an international agreement or an international contract as provided in Article 6;
(iii) limiting the present or future number of enterprises in any particular field of business;
(iv) unjustly restricting the functions or activities of the constituent enterprises (meaning an enterprise who is a member of the trade association; the same applies hereinafter);
(v) inducing an enterprise to employ such an act as falls under unfair trade practices.

§5. Restriction on Competition

I. Substantial Restraint of Competition

119. As stated in §4 above, the concept of substantial restriction of competition is important to enforce the AMA, because major substantive provisions such as unreasonable restraint of trade, private monopolization, and merger regulation (regulations on business combination) sets this requirement in its constitution as antitrust violations can cause harmful results. As to what substantial restriction of competition is, the court ruled as follows:

> 'Substantial restriction of competition … to be considered is whether a situation appears or at least is about to appear where competition itself has decreased and whereby a certain enterprise or a group of enterprises can, according to its own will, manipulate price, quality, quantity, or other various conditions, thereby controlling the market to some extent'.[25]

120. There have been some judgments rendered after this ruling of the Tokyo High Court since then, and the Supreme Court finally set forth the interpretation of substantial restraint of trade in two cases.

121. The first case was on a private monopolization case, and the Court ruled that it was obvious that the conduct in question had resulted in substantial restraint of competition that is to establish, maintain, or strengthen the market controlling power.[26] Subsequently, the Supreme Court ruled in a bid rigging case as follows:

25. Toho-Subaru Case [Business Combination] (Tokyo High Court, 19 Sep. 1951).
26. NTT-East Case (*supra* n. 9).

> Substantial restraint of competition is to impair the function of competition which the market has, and is interpreted as to cause a situation in which a certain enterprise or a certain group of enterprises can freely to some extent control successful tenderers and their price, in a bid rigging.[27]

122. Comparing those decisions above, it is obvious that the Supreme Court made the old and traditional interpretation of the Tokyo High Court's decision mentioned above reflected on its rulings, and the recent two decisions of the Supreme Court implied the same thing that the substantial restraint of competition is to establish, maintain and strengthen the market controlling power that enables a certain enterprise to control the market freely, to some extent, in price, quantity and other terms and conditions of transactions, and they are applicable not only to bid rigging but also to non-hardcore ones, private monopolization and mergers.

123. Indeed, the JFTC has cited the Tokyo High Court's ruling in some guidelines even before the Supreme Court rendered the judgment. The Exclusionary Private Monopolization Guidelines[28] quote the above-mentioned the Tokyo High Court's judgment, from a more analytical point of view, as for what factors of '*establishing, maintaining, or strengthening the state in which a certain entrepreneur or a certain group of entrepreneurs can control the market at will by being, to some extent, free to influence price, quality, quantity, and other various conditions after competition itself has lessened*'.[29]

124. The guidelines show several basic frameworks to assess it as follows:

- Market environment of alleged enterprises and their competitors, including:
  i. market share and its rank;
  ii. competitive environment;
  iii. competitors' condition.
- Potential competitive pressure, including:
  i. statutory entry barrier;
  ii. actual entry barrier;
  iii. substitutability between the entrants' and the enterprise's products.[30]
- Customer's countervailing bargaining power
- Efficiency
- Other exceptional circumstances to assure consumer interests.

125. Substantial restriction of competition can be in theory classified into two types in its processes to affect the competition in the market; those are 'competition avoidance' and 'competition foreclosure.' The former refers to a price cartel or bid

27. Tama Area Bid-rigging Case (*supra* n. 21).
28. Guidelines for Exclusionary Private Monopolization under the Antimonopoly Act.
29. Exclusionary Private Monopolization Guidelines, Part III, 2. (1).
30. *Ibid.*, Part III, 2, (2).

rigging. The latter means conduct excluding incumbent competing rivals from the market or blocking potential rivals from newly penetrating a market to maintain a market power.

126. Paragraphs (5) and (6) of Article 2 provide the term of 'contrary to the public interest'. According to traditional interpretation, public interest means a situation where competition is guaranteed. Therefore, when the competition is substantially restricted, such a situation itself should immediately be concluded to violate the AMA. In this regard, whether the competition is restricted 'substantially' or not may be the point of an argument.

II. Justification

127. There are a few cases where a conduct which is likely to restrain the competition is justified and thus it is believed as innocent, since it does not meet the requirement of substantial restriction of competition. In such a case, possible justifications would be acceptable considering both the aim and its measures.

128. The first case is that a conduct can be justified because it is supposed to achieve more favourable condition for national economy than any other means would do, even if it causes restriction of competition. For instance, agreeing among the enterprises not to handle inappropriate goods and services for the consumers out of a market could be justifiable because such an agreement will serve to protect consumers' interests.

129. The second case is that a conduct aims at securing creative activities or incentive for R&D. A simple example is the execution of IPR, which is exempted due to Article 21.

130. The third case is that a conduct is carried out to avoid a certain difficulty caused by physical, technical, or economic reason. For instance, refusing to deal on such grounds as lack of capacity of supply.

131. In addition, the conduct with any merit such as improving efficiency or promote competitiveness, rescuing a failing company, or serving to achieve other policy goals.

132. As for the last point, a certain conduct which enterprises are forced to engage in by governmental regulation or administrative guidance, also known as *gyosei-shido*, may give negative effects on competition; therefore, the JFTC made public Administrative Guidance Guidelines[31] which revealed its views concerning administrative guidance. Also, such regulations and guidance should be assessed

31. Guidelines Concerning Administrative Guidance under the Antimonopoly Act.

and reviewed in the light of effectiveness and adequateness. In line with the policy above, most of the governmental regulations are subject to Regulatory Impact Assessment (RIA).

III. Impediment to Fair and Free Competition

133. Unfair trade practice is, as stated above, prohibited as anticompetitive conduct which tends to impede fair competition. As for the conduct which tends to impede fair competition, the JFTC interprets that it does not necessarily restrict substantial competition in the market, but it is sufficient if the conduct implies any tendency to impede fair and free competition. The JFTC ruled in its decision as follows:

> When the JFTC judges whether or not the conduct in question meets the requirements of unfairness ..., it adapts criteria to see if the conduct concerned has competitive restrictive effect or not. It should be interpreted that the conduct concerned does not necessarily have to be proved to the extent that it restricts substantial competition in the relevant market, but that it is sufficient only to say that it proves to a certain extent that it impedes fair and free competition. Interpretation like this should be valid, given the AMA prohibits unfair trade practices as a preventive measure against private monopolization and the like.[32]

134. The JFTC interprets 'free competition' as the situation where neither free competition among enterprises is infringed nor an enterprise is prevented from entering the market. If a conduct is likely to impede free competition or diminish competition, the JFTC will suspect that a certain enterprise employs unfair trade practices.

135. Second, regarding the fairness, the JFTC considers that free competition should be achieved by appropriate manners of business, especially, on price, quality and service. For instance, misleading representations or pyramid schemes are inadequate in the way of business and therefore incompatible with fair and free competition.

136. Third, concerning the market as a competitive and level playing field, any enterprise should be assured to freely decide whether to accept or refuse transaction, terms and conditions of transactions, trading partners based on its initiative and without inhibition.

137. Some of the practices that the AMA illustrates as unfair trade practices are, however, very often seen in the usual business scene; therefore, JFTC specifically examines them considering whether they may be justified when it enforces the law. As stated in Chapter 4, §4, III above, the JFTC is used to apply the AMA to the

32. Taisho-Seiyaku Case (JFTC Administrative Hearing Decision, 28 Mar. 1953).

RPM which is a conduct categorized as a cartel in other jurisdictions. Nevertheless, the JFTC declares that some practices, including RPM, in particular, tend to seriously impede fair competition and regards them as illegal in principle, and thus make them subject to surcharge.

§6. MONOPOLIZATION AND ABUSE OF DOMINANCE

138. Private monopolization can be divided into two types: controlling type monopolization and exclusionary type monopolization. The difference between the two types may be obscure, but enforcement could be different.

139. 'Controlling' means depriving, directly or indirectly, other enterprises of the freedom of decision on their business by setting limitation on them. For instance, controlling may be caused by:

- acquiring competitor's equities, or getting interlocked by dispatching executives;
- deciding subordinate company's price or sales market; or
- instructing subordinate company's price to bid in bidding.

140. By its nature, the behaviour of controlling requires the existence of other entity to be targeted, such as existing or potential competitors or enterprises competing subordinate company.

141. On the other hand, 'exclusionary' means various conducts that would cause difficulty for other enterprises to continue their business activities or for newcomers to commence their business activities, according to the Exclusionary Private Monopolization Guidelines. It should be justified that an enterprise obtains high market share or makes potential competitors hesitate to enter the market by offering its products at a lower price with a higher quality. That is the function of competition in its nature that the AMA aims to promote.

142. With regard to the relationship with unfair trade practice, certain types of them are considered in the framework of the AMA as preliminary of private monopolization, as mentioned in §5, III above.

§7. CONCENTRATIONS

143. As stated in Chapter 3, §3 above, the AMA regulates two types of concentration: 'general concentration' and 'market concentration'.

144. General concentration prohibits enterprises from acquiring or holding shares of other enterprises in Japan, which would result in the excessive concentration of economic power.

145. Historically, the regulation of general concentration reflects on the situation prior to World War II where certain Japanese companies had excessive economic power in Japanese domestic commerce. These powerful companies backed the Imperial Japanese Army, which resulted in Japan's entry into the war.

146. On the contrary, market concentration is directly related to traditional antitrust regulation. Market concentration regulation prohibits business combination that substantially restrains competition in any particular field of trade. Merger regulation aims at preventing market structures from causing substantial restriction of competition. Therefore, the phrase of 'if... substantially restrains' is interpreted as the situation that the business combination in question is likely to cause substantial restriction of competition. Also, that of 'substantial restriction of competition' is considered the same as that of cartel and monopolization stated above.

§8. Joint Ventures

147. In the context of behavioural conduct, the AMA does not have any specific provision or definition concerning alliances between enterprises, including joint ventures. If they are involved in a cartel or trade association's anticompetitive behaviour, such conduct should be examined in the same manner as other anticompetitive conducts.

148. On the other hand, in the context of review of the business combination, the Merger Guidelines define what constitutes a joint venture (*see* Part II, Chapter 3, §6 below).

Chapter 5. Consequences of Violations and Enforcement Institutions

§1. Administrative Enforcement

I. Antitrust Authorities

A. Formation and Composition

149. The JFTC, an enforcer of the AMA and related laws, is an independent administrative commission. The commission consisted of a Chairman and four Commissioners constitutes a panel to make all the decisions on the activities of the JFTC (hereinafter referred to as 'Commission' in this sense.). The Chairman and Commissioners are chosen from among experts in law and economics and appointed by the Prime Minister with consent of the Diet. The term of office of the Chairman and Commissioners is five years. When each of them reaches the age of 70 during their term, they retire from office.

150. Under the Commission, General Secretariat takes charge of the actual practice such as case investigation, merger review and implementation of competition policies including advocacy activities. The headquarters of the JFTC is located in Tokyo, and eight local offices are also in charge of the enforcement of the AMA and other matters.

B. Investigating Powers

151. According to Article 47, the JFTC may take the following measures in order to conduct the necessary investigation with regard to a case:

- to order persons concerned with a case or witnesses to appear to be interrogated, or collect their opinions or reports;
- to order expert witnesses to appear to give expert opinions;
- to order persons holding books and documents and other object to submit such objects, or keep such submitted objects at the JFTC;
- to Enter any business office of the persons concerned with a case or other necessary sites, and inspect conditions of business operation and property, books and documents, and other materials.

152. When the JFTC investigates a case which, the JFTC considers, should be subject to criminal penalty, designated staff members of the JFTC may exercise criminal investigation powers such as search and seizure with the warrant issued by the court (*see* §3 below).

153. Besides those powers above, the JFTC may use administrative investigating power in order to gather necessary information under Article 40. That power has been exercised for the purpose of collecting information in the course of market study.

C. Adjudicating Powers (Ascertaining and Sanctioning)

1. Cease and Desist Order

154. After the investigation, the JFTC may issue an administrative order for prompt elimination of illegal acts. This order is called a 'Cease and Desist Order'. A Cease and Desist Order must be rendered in writing, and shall indicate the measures necessary to eliminate the violation or to ensure the elimination of the violation, and the facts found by the JFTC and the application of laws and regulations thereto.

> (Article 7)
>
> (1) Whenever an act in violation of the provisions of Article 3 or the preceding Article occurs, the Fair Trade Commission may, pursuant to the procedures provided in Section 2 of Chapter VIII, order the relevant enterprise to cease and desist the relevant act, to transfer a part of the relevant enterprise's business, or to take any other measures necessary to eliminate the act in violation of the provisions.
>
> (2) Whenever the Fair Trade Commission finds it to be particularly necessary, even if an act in violation of the provisions of Article 3 or the preceding Article has already ceased to exist, the Fair Trade Commission may, pursuant to the procedures provided in Section 2 of Chapter VIII, order the following person to take measures to make public that the act has been discontinued and to take any other measures necessary to ensure the elimination of the relevant act; provided, however, that this does not apply if seven years have passed since the date of discontinuation of the relevant act:
>
> (i) enterprise that committed the relevant act;
>
> (ii) if the enterprise that committed the relevant act is a juridical person, any juridical person surviving, or established as a result of the merger the enterprise ceased to exist;
>
> (iii) if the enterprise that committed the relevant act is a juridical person, any juridical person who has acquired all or part of the business involving the relevant act from the enterprise by virtue of a company split;
>
> (iv) any enterprise that has acquired all or part of the business involving the relevant act from the enterprise that committed the relevant act.

(Article 20)

(1) If an act in violation of the provisions of the preceding Article has occurred, the Fair Trade Commission may, pursuant to the procedures provided in Section 2 of Chapter VIII, order the enterprise to cease and desist from engaging in the relevant act, delete the relevant clauses from the contract, or take any other measure necessary to eliminate the relevant act.
(2) The provisions of Article 7, paragraph (2) applies mutatis mutandis to an act in violation of the provisions of the preceding Article.

(Article 61)

(1) A Cease and Desist Order must be rendered in writing, and the written Cease and Desist Order is to indicate the measures necessary to eliminate the violation or to ensure that the violation is eliminated, and the facts found by the Fair Trade Commission and the application of laws and regulations thereto, and the chairman and commissioners who attended the meeting pursuant to the provisions of Article 65, paragraph (1) must affix their names and seals thereto.
(2) A Cease and Desist Order is to take effect by serving a copy of the written Cease and Desist Order to the addressee thereof.

2. Commitment

155. As mentioned in the General Introduction, §3, the CPTPP Agreement was approved in Japan and the Bill to amend the laws related to the agreement was passed by the Diet in 2016. That includes revision of the AMA to adopt the so-called commitment procedure. The amendment came into force in December 2018. In the commitment procedure, the JFTC and suspected violators communicate with each other throughout all the procedures after the launch of the investigation by the JFTC. The commitment procedure is expected to facilitate early resolution of competitive concerns and effective enforcement of the AMA. In addition to the amendment of the AMA, the JFTC released Commitment Procedure Rules[33] and Commitment Procedures Policy[34] to clarify the procedures. The Commitment Procedures Policy provides that the commitment procedure does not apply to cartel conduct.

(Article 48-2)

If the Fair Trade Commission believes there to be a fact in violation of the provisions of Article 3, Article 6, Article 8, Article 9, paragraphs (1) or (2), Article 10, paragraph (1), Article 11, paragraph (1), Article 13, Article 14, Article 15, paragraph (1), Article 15-2, paragraph (1), Article 15-3, paragraph (1), Article 16, paragraph (1), Article 17 or Article 19 and recognizes that it is necessary

33. Rules on Fair Trade Commission Commitment Procedures.
34. Policies Concerning Commitment Procedures.

for promotion of fair and free competition, it may notify the party conducting the act that was the reason for that suspicion of the following matters in writing …:

(i) the overview of the relevant act;
(ii) the clauses of laws and regulations for which there is suspicion of violation;
(iii) the fact that it is possible to make an application for approval under the provisions of Article 48-3, paragraph (1).

(Article 48-3)

(1) When a party that has received a notice pursuant to the provisions of the previous article intends to formulate and conduct measures that are necessary in order to exclude the act that was the reason for the suspicion, it may create a plan (hereinafter referred to as the 'Exclusion [sic] Measures Plan' in this Article and Article 48-5) related to the measures that it intends to conduct (hereinafter referred to as the 'Exclusion [sic] Measures' in this Article to Article 48-5) submit that plan to the Fair Trade Commission within sixty days after the relevant notice and apply for its approval, pursuant to the provisions of the Rules of the Fair Trade Commission.
(3) When there has been an application for approval pursuant to the provisions of paragraph (1), the Fair Trade Commission is to approve the plan if the Fair Trade Commission finds that Exclusion [sic] Measures Plan conforms to both of the following items:
   (i) the Exclusion [sic] Measures are sufficient for excluding [sic] the act that was the reason for the suspicion;
   (ii) the excluding [sic] Measures are expected to be reliably conducted.

(Article 48-4)

The provisions of Article 7, paragraphs (1) and (2) … (and) Article 7-2, paragraph (1) … shall not apply for the act that was the reason for suspicion related to that approval and the act related to the excluding [sic] Measures, if the Fair Trade Commission gave the approval of paragraph (3) of the preceding Article.

(Article 48-6)

Whenever the Fair Trade Commission finds it to be particularly necessary for promotion of fair and free competition, even if the act that was the reason for the suspicion of violation of the provisions of Article 3, Article 6, Article 8, or Article 19 has already ceased to exist, it may notify the party stated in item (i) in the form of a document of the matters in item (ii) in writing.

(i) the following party
   (a) the party who committed the act that was the reason for the suspicion.

(b) if the party who committed the act that was the reason for the suspicion is a juridical person, any juridical person surviving, or established as a result of the merger the juridical person ceased to exist.

(c) if the party who committed the act that was the reason for the suspicion is juridical person, any juridical person who has acquired all or part of the business involving the relevant act from the juridical person by virtue of a company spilt.

(d) any party who acquired all or part of the business involving the relevant act from the party who committed the act that was the reason for the suspicion.

(ii) the following matters

(a) overview of the act that was the reason for the suspicion.

(b) clause of the laws and regulations for which there was suspicion of violation.

(c) the fact that it is possible to make an application for approval under the provisions of paragraph 1, Article 48-7

156. The commitment procedures begin when, during the period from the start of an investigation to the issuance of a notification of Hearing (*see* Part III, Chapter 1, §3, II), the JFTC finds that it is appropriate to apply the procedures and issues a written notification on the commitment procedures (hereinafter referred to as 'Notice of Commitment Procedures') to the suspected violator. Bid rigging, cartels and suspected violators who were subject to a legal measure under the same provision with the suspected violation within ten years are excluded from the procedures. In the Notice of Commitment Procedures, the JFTC describes an outline of the suspected violation based on the facts that have been acknowledged as of the time of issuing the Notice of Commitment Procedures in order that the suspected violator can consider the Elimination Measures referred to in Article 48-3(1). The JFTC may also issue the Notice of Commitment Procedures even if the suspected violation already ceased pursuant to Article 48-6(1). In this case, the suspected violator considers the measures to ensure the elimination (hereinafter referred to as 'Measures to Ensure Elimination').

157. Suspected violators may at any time, even before issuance of Notice of Commitment Procedures, consult with the JFTC, including confirming whether or not the commitment procedures are applicable to the case or indicating its desire for application of commitment procedures.

158. When the suspected violator received the Notice of Commitment Procedures, it will decide whether to apply for commitment approval. If the notified enterprise (meaning the suspected violators that received the Notice of Commitment Procedures; the same applies hereinafter) applies for commitment approval, it should submit application by Form No. 1 when the Notice of Commitment Procedures is issued pursuant to Article 48-3(1), or Form No. 3 when it is issued pursuant to Article 48-6(1), both of which are annexed to the Commitment Procedure Rules, together with a plan of Commitment Measures or Measures to Ensure Elimination (hereinafter referred to as 'Commitment Plan' inclusive), within sixty days from the date of the Commitment Procedure Notice. The application should include the attachments required by the Commitment Procedures Rules, such as documents showing that the Commitment Measures are sufficient for eliminating the suspected violation (requirements of sufficiency). On the contrary, if it decides not to apply for commitment approval, the investigation procedure will resume.

159. The Commitment Measures should also be reliable (requirement of reliability). The details of these requirements are explained in the Commitment Procedures Policy.

(1) Requirements of Sufficiency

The JFTC will assess whether or not the Commitment Measures satisfy the requirement of sufficiency based on the specific facts and their effects on competition. In assessing, the JFTC refers to the content of measures employed in similar cases in the past.

(2) Reliability of Measures Implemented

Even in the case the requirement of sufficiency is satisfied, the suspected violation would not be surely eliminated unless the Commitment Measures are implemented by the notified enterprise by the deadline. Therefore, the JFTC also assesses the Commitment Measures, considering their reliability. For instance, the Commitment Measures will not be approved in principle if the notified enterprise is unlikely to reach consent with the third parties to amend the contract by the time designated in the measures when the Commitment Measures involve amendments to the contract for elimination of the suspected violation.

160. In this regard, the Commitment Procedures Policy also shows seven typical examples as follows:

i. Cessation of the suspected violation, or confirmation of its cessation, etc.
ii. Notification to trading partners and others, or publicizing information to customers and others.
iii. Development of a compliance programme.
iv. Amendments of contracts.
v. Transfer of businesses etc.
vi. Recovery of monetary value provided by trading partners and others.
vii. Reporting on the state of implementation.

161. The JFTC will approve the Commitment Plan pursuant to Article 48-3(3) or Article 48-7(3) of the AMA when it determines the Commitment Measures satisfy both requirements. The JFTC declares that it will not take any action against the suspected violation subject to the Commitment Measures after it approves the Commitment Plan. On the other hand, if the JFTC determines that the Commitment Measures do not conform to the requirements, it will render a decision to dismiss the application pursuant to Article 48-3(6) or Article 48-7(5). In such a case, the investigation will be resumed back to the issuance of the Notice of Commitment Procedures.

162. After the approval of a Commitment Plan, in order to make clear what kinds of specific acts could have an adverse effect on free and fair competition and to ensure transparency and predictability regarding the enforcement of the law related to Commitment Procedures, the JFTC will make public an outline of the approved Commitment Plan and of the suspected violation related to such approval, and other necessary matters.

163. The JFTC should render a decision to rescind the approval of the Commitment Plan, and the investigation also will be resumed when the JFTC finds that the approved Commitment Measures are not implemented or that the enterprise obtained the approval of the Commitment Plan based on false or wrongful facts.

D. *Other Institutional Tasks (Consultancy to Parliament/Government)*

164. Pursuant to Article 44, the JFTC shall report annually to the Diet, through the Prime Minister, on the enforcement of this act. The annual report is made public on the JFTC's website (http://www.jftc.go.jp/en/about_jftc/annual_reports/index.html).

(Article 44)

(1) The Fair Trade Commission must report annually to the Diet, through the Prime Minister, on the enforcement of this Act.

165. The JFTC may submit to the Diet, through the Prime Minister, its opinions on matters necessary to attain the purpose of the AMA, but this right has never been exercised in the past.

II. Direct Government's Enforcement Activities

166. Though is administratively attached to the Cabinet Office, there are no governmental bodies other than the JFTC which can be engaged in enforcement activities of the AMA.

III. Other Administrative Agencies Applying Antitrust Rules

167. As stated in the previous section, there are no other administrative agencies enforcing the AMA in Japan. However, JFTC's activities of advocacy has made the views of the competition policy accepted in business laws under the jurisdiction of other ministries or agencies.

168. Furthermore, the courts have played a role in applying the AMA, in the cases in which the addresses of the JFTC's Cease and Desist Orders and Payment Orders were rendered. The courts also have made decisions on application of the AMA in private suits.

IV. Administrative Fines

169. Surcharge is a kind of administrative fines in the Japanese legislation. The AMA provides that the JFTC must render a Payment Order to the parties who committed a violation to pay to the national treasury a surcharge in such cases as unreasonable restraint of trade, private monopolization and a certain types of unfair trade practices, in addition to elimination of illegal acts. The amount of surcharge is calculated in accordance with a certain formula stipulated in Articles 7-2 to 9, 8-3 and 20-2 to 7 of the AMA.

170. The surcharge rate varies in the types of violation. Pursuant to Article 62, the Payment Order is issued in a written form and states the amount of the surcharge to be paid, the basis of its calculation, the violation to which it pertains, and the time limit for payment. Detailed method of calculation of amount of sales and purchases, surcharge calculation rate applied to each business type, etc., are provided from Articles 4 to 14 of AMA Enforcement Order.

A. *Surcharge for Unreasonable Restraint of Trade*

171. The basic surcharge calculation rate for unreasonable restraint of trade is 10% of the amount of the sales and purchases of the relevant goods or services that the enterprise supplied and purchased in the particular field of trade connected with the violation. The sales amount of the relevant goods or services includes those of wholly owned subsidiary companies of the violator, who did not implement the act in violation by themselves but received instructions or information from the violator and supplied and purchased the subject goods in accordance with the instructions or information (such subsidiaries are defined as 'Non-Violating Supplying Co-Subsidiary, etc.' and 'Non-Violating Purchasing Co-Subsidiary, etc.' in the AMA).

172. The time period for calculation of the sales amount of the relevant goods or services is the same as the time period of the violation. However, calculation period would be ten years in case where the violation begun before the date which is back to ten years from the date on which the JFTC started investigation. In other words, the maximum calculation period for surcharge is ten years, even if the period of violation is more than ten years. The special calculation rate which is applied to a violator who is small- and medium-sized enterprise is 4%.

173. If there are economic benefits gained by joining the cartel conduct such as money which the enterprise and its wholly owned co-subsidiary gained irrespective of its name, such as charges, remuneration and kick back, with regard to not supplying the goods or services connected with the relevant violation to others or not receiving the good or services from others, the benefits are added to the sales amount.

(Article 7-2)

(1) If an enterprise effects unreasonable restraint of trade or enters into an international agreement or an international contract containing particulars, falling under unreasonable restraint of trade, that is related to the price of goods or services or substantially restrain supply or purchase volume, market share or transaction counterparties with respect to goods or services and thereby affects their price, the Fair Trade Commission must order the enterprise, pursuant to the procedures as provided in Section 2 of Chapter VIII, to pay to the national treasury a surcharge of an amount equivalent to the total sum of ten percent of the amount listed in items (i) to (iii) inclusive below and the amount listed in item (iv) below; provided, however, that if the amount thus calculated is less than one million yen, the Commission may not order the payment of such a surcharge:

(i) the amount of sales of the relevant goods or services that the enterprise and its Specified Non-Violating Supplying Co-Subsidiary, etc. supplied in the particular field of trade connected with the relevant violation (limited to the violation related to supplying goods or services; hereinafter the same applies in this item) (excluding the goods or services that the Specified Non-Violating Supplying Co-Subsidiary, etc. supplied to the enterprise and the goods or services that the enterprise or the Specified Non-Violating Supplying Co-Subsidiary, etc. supplied to the Supplying Co-Subsidiary of the enterprise, etc.), and the relevant goods or services that the enterprise and the Specified Non-Violating Supplying Co-Subsidiary, etc. supplied to the Supplying Co-Subsidiary, etc. in the particular field of trade (excluding the goods or services that the Supplying Co-Subsidiary, etc. (limited to the Violating Supplying Co-Subsidiary, etc. or Specified Non-Violating Supplying Co-Subsidiary, etc. of the enterprise) received from the enterprise or the Specified Non-Violating Supplying Co-Subsidiary, etc. in order to supply the goods or services to others) for the Period of Implementation connected with the violation, calculated using the method provided by Cabinet Order;

(ii) the amount of purchases of the relevant goods or services that the enterprise and its Specified Non-Violating Purchasing Co-Subsidiary, etc. received in the particular field of trade connected with the relevant violation (limited to the violation related to receiving goods or services; hereinafter the same applies in this item) (excluding the goods or services that the Specific Non-Violating Purchasing Co-Subsidiary, etc. received from the enterprise and the goods or services that the enterprise or the Specified Non-Violating Purchasing

Co-Subsidiary, etc. received from the Purchasing Co-Subsidiary, etc. of the enterprise), and the relevant goods or services that the enterprise and the Specified Non-Violating Purchasing Co- Subsidiary, etc. received from the Purchasing Co-subsidiary, etc. in the particular field of trade connected with the violation (excluding the goods or services that the Purchasing Co-Subsidiary, etc. (limited to the Violating Purchasing Co-Subsidiary, etc. or the Specified Non-Violating Purchasing Co-Subsidiary, etc.) received from others in order to supply the goods or services to the enterprise or the Specified Non-Violating Purchasing Co- Subsidiary, etc.) for the Period of Implementation connected with the violation, calculated using the method provided by Cabinet Order;

(iii) the amount, calculated using the method provided by Cabinet Order, equivalent to the price for the business that is closely connected to the goods or services connected with the relevant violation such as manufacturing, sales, or management of all or part of the goods or services which, provided by Cabinet Order, which the enterprise and its wholly owned co-subsidiary, etc. (limited to the wholly owned subsidiary, etc. that has never committed a violation; the same applies in the following item) conducted;

(iv) the amount, calculated using the method provided by Cabinet Order, equivalent to economic benefits such as money which the enterprise and its wholly owned co-subsidiary, etc. gained irrespective of its name such as charges and remuneration, with regard to not supplying the goods or services connected with the relevant violation to others (excluding the Supplying Co-Subsidiary, etc. of the enterprise, other enterprises that committed a violation and their Supplying Co-Subsidiary, etc.) or not receiving the goods or services from others (excluding the Purchasing Co- Subsidiary, etc. of the enterprise, other enterprises that committed a violation and their Purchasing Co-Subsidiary, etc.).

(2) In cases under the preceding paragraph, if an enterprise falls under either of the following items (excluding the cases where one or more co-subsidiaries, etc. of the enterprise do not fall under either of the preceding items), the term 'ten percent' appearing in the paragraph shall be replaced with 'four percent':

(i) any company whose amount of stated capital or total contribution amount is not more than three hundred million yen and any company or individual whose number of regular employees is not more than three hundred, which operates as its principal business, a manufacturing, construction, transportation or other business (excluding the business types listed in items (ii) to (iv) inclusive and the business types provided by Cabinet Order pursuant to item (v));

(ii) any company whose amount of stated capital or total contribution amount is not more than one hundred million yen and any company or individual whose number of regular employees is not more than one hundred, which operates a wholesale business (excluding business types provided by Cabinet Order pursuant to item (v)) as its principal business;

(iii) any company whose amount of stated capital or total amount of contribution is not more than fifty million yen and any company or individual whose number of regular employees is not more than one hundred, which operates as its principal business, business belonging to service business (excluding the business types provided by Cabinet Order pursuant to item (v));

(iv) any company whose amount of stated capital or total amount of contribution is not more than fifty million yen and any company or individual whose number of regular employees is not more than fifty, which operates as its principal business, business belonging to retail business (excluding the business types provided by Cabinet Order pursuant to the following item);

(v) any company whose amount of stated capital or total amount of contribution is not more than the amount provided by Cabinet Order for each of its business types and any company or individual whose number of regular employees is not more than the number provided by Cabinet Order for each of its business types, which operates as its principal business, business belonging to any of the business types provided by Cabinet Order;

(vi) of cooperative partnerships and other partnerships established pursuant to special Acts with the principal purpose of company in business (including federation of partnerships), any partnership which has a scale comparable to the scale provided in each of the preceding items for the individual business type in the preceding items as provided by Cabinet Order.

(3) In cases where Fair Trade Commission orders an enterprise to pay a surcharge pursuant to the provisions of paragraph (1), if the enterprise has not respond to the request from the Commission or the staff who engage in the administrative affairs pertaining to investigations into the case connected with the violation (such as the investigators designated pursuant to Article 47, paragraph (2)) to submit reports or materials regarding facts connected with the violation that should form the basis for the calculation of the surcharge for the violation, the Commission may order the enterprise to pay the surcharge, by estimating the amount listed in each of the items in paragraph (1) for the Period of Implementation where the facts that should form the basis for the calculation of the surcharge cannot be ascertained because the reports and materials regarding the facts have not been submitted, using a reasonable method provided in the Rules of the Fair Trade Commission, in light of materials obtained from the enterprise, its Specified Non-Violating Supplying Co-Subsidiaries, etc., its Specified Non-Violating Purchasing Co-Subsidiaries, etc. or other enterprises that supply or receive goods or services connected with the violation, or other materials.

174. The surcharge rate is increased 50% for repeated offender for ten years, and violator who played leading roles such as planning the violation, requiring other enterprise (violator) to engage in, or not to discontinue, a violation, or requiring other violator obstruct JFTC's investigation. Thus, if a violator falls in both conditions, i.e., repeated offender and ringleader, the basic calculation rate will be 20% of the amount of sales and purchases of the relevant goods or services.

(Article 7-3)

(1) If an enterprise is ordered to pay a surcharge pursuant to the provisions of paragraph (1) of the preceding Article, the term 'the total sum' in the same paragraph (including the cases where these are applied mutatis mutandis pursuant to paragraph (2) of the same Article following the deemed replacement of terms) is deemed to be replaced with 'the total sum, multiplied by 1.5', if the enterprise falls under any of the following items; provided, however, that this does not apply if the enterprise is subject to the application of the provisions of paragraph (3):

(i) a person that was subject to an order pursuant to the provisions of paragraph (1) of the preceding Article or paragraph (1) or (2) of Article 7-9 (limited to when the order has become final and binding), a notice pursuant to the provision of paragraph (7) of the following Article or paragraph (3) of Article 7-7, or a decision pursuant to paragraph (2) of Article 63 (hereinafter referred to in this paragraph as 'Payment Order, etc.') within the ten years prior to the Investigation Start Date connected with the relevant violation (limited to a person committing a violation on or after the day of the Payment Order, etc.) ;

(ii) a person whose wholly owned subsidiary was subject to a Payment Order, etc. (limited to the case when the wholly owned subsidiary was that of the person on the date of the Payment Order, etc.) within the ten years prior to the Investigation Start Date connected with the relevant violation (limited to a person committing a violation on or after the day of the Payment Order, etc.), excluding persons who fall under the previous item;

(iii) a juridical person who is an enterprise who merged with another juridical person who is an enterprise subject to a Payment Order, etc. within the ten years prior to the Investigation Start Date connected with the relevant violation, or succeeded through a transfer or company split to all or part of the business connected to the violation related to the Payment Order, etc. from another juridical person who is an enterprise subject to a Payment Order, etc. within the ten years prior to the Investigation Start Date connected with the relevant violation (limited to a person committing the violation on or after the date of the merger, transfer or split), excluding persons that fall under the previous item (i) or (ii).

(2) If an enterprise is ordered to pay a surcharge pursuant to the provisions of paragraph (1) of the preceding Article, the term 'the total sum' in the same

paragraph (including the cases where these are applied pursuant to paragraph (2) of the same Article following the deemed replacement of terms) shall be replaced with 'the total sum, multiplied by 1.5', if the enterprise falls under any of the following items; provided, however, that this does not apply if the enterprise is subject to the application of provisions of the following paragraph:

(i) a person that has, at the request of another enterprise, designated a price, supply volume, purchase volume, market share or transaction counterparty in relation to the goods or services involved in the violation, continuously to other enterprises, either individually or in concert with others;

(ii) a person that has, at the request of another enterprise, designated a price, supply volume, purchase volume, market share or transaction counterparty in relation to the goods or services involved in the violation, continuously to other enterprises, either individually or in concert with others;

(iii) a person that has committed any of the following acts to materially facilitate the relevant violation, either individually or in concert with others, in addition to the person listed in the preceding two items:

(a) requiring, requesting or instigating another enterprise to perform, or not to discontinue, the relevant violation;

(b) designating price, supply volume, purchase volume, market share or a transaction counterparty to another enterprise in connection with the goods or services involved in the violation, or about business activities constituting the violation (excluding exclusively designating about one's own transactions);

(c) requiring, requesting or instigating another enterprise to hide or disguise, at the time of the Fair Trade Commission investigation, the materials related to the violation or the facts that should be the basis of its calculation of the surcharge of the violation or to submit the false reports or materials related to the facts at the time of the investigation;

(d) requiring, requesting or instigating another enterprise not to report the facts or provide materials pursuant to the procedures provided in the following Article, paragraph (1), items (i), paragraph (2), items (i) to (iv) or paragraph (3), item (i) or (ii), or not to apply for conference pursuant to the procedures provided in Article 7-5, paragraph (1).

(3) If an enterprise is ordered to pay a surcharge pursuant to the provisions of paragraph (1) of the preceding Article, the term 'the total sum' in the same paragraph (including the cases where these are applied pursuant to paragraph (2) of the same Article following the deemed replacement of terms) shall be replaced with 'the total sum, multiplied by 2,', if the enterprise falls under any items of the paragraph (1) and any items of the preceding paragraph.

B. Surcharge for Private Monopolization

175. The surcharge calculation rate varies in the types of violation. 10% is applied to the control type of private monopolization and 6% is applied to the exclusionary type violation. Likewise, in unreasonable restraint of trade, the amount of surcharge is calculated based on the sales amount of the relevant goods or services that the enterprise supplied in the particular field of trade connected with the violation. The calculation period and other relevant conditions are also the same as those of surcharge for unreasonable restraint of trade.

(Article 7-9)

(1) If an enterprise effects private monopolization (limited to that arising from the control of the business activities of other enterprise) that is related to the price of goods or services supplied by the relevant other enterprise (hereinafter referred to as 'Controlled Enterprise' in this paragraph) or substantially restrains the supply volume, market share or transaction counterparties with respect to goods or services supplied by the Controlled Enterprise and thereby affects their price of goods or services, the Fair Trade Commission must order the enterprise, pursuant to the procedures as provided in Section 2 of Chapter VIII, to pay to the national treasury a surcharge of an amount equivalent to the total sum of ten percent of the amount listed in items (i) and (ii) below and the amount listed in item (iii) below; provided, however, that if the amount thus calculated is less than one million yen, the Commission may not order the payment of such a surcharge:

(i) the sales amount of the relevant goods or services that the enterprise and its Specified Non-Violating Supplying Co-Subsidiary, etc. supplied to the Controlled Enterprise (including the goods or services necessary for the Controlled Enterprise to supply the goods or services in the particular field of trade connected with the relevant violation; the same applies in the following item and item (iii)), the goods or services that the enterprise and the Specified Non-Violating Supplying Co-Subsidiary, etc. supplied in the particular field of trade (excluding the goods or services that the Specified Non-violating supply Co-subsidiary, etc. supplied to the enterprise and the goods or services that the enterprise or the Specified Non-Violating Supplying Co-Subsidiary, etc. supplied to the Controlled Enterprise and Supplying Co-Subsidiary, etc. of the enterprise) and the goods or services that the enterprise and the Specified Non-Violating Supplying Co-Subsidiary, etc. supplied to the Supplying Co-Subsidiary, etc. in the particular field of trade (excluding the goods or services that the Supplying Co-Subsidiary, etc. (limited to the Violating Supplying Co-Subsidiary, etc. or the Specified Non-Violating Supplying Co-Subsidiary, etc.) received from the enterprise or the Specified Non-Violating Supplying Co-Subsidiary, etc. in order to supply the goods or services to others) in the Period of Implementation for the violation connected with the violation, calculated using the method provided by Cabinet Order;

(ii) the amount, calculated using the method provided by Cabinet Order, equivalent to the price for the business that is closely connected to the goods or services connected with the relevant violation such as manufacturing, sales, or management of all or part of the goods or services, provided by Cabinet Order, which the enterprise and its wholly owned co-subsidiary, etc. (limited to the enterprise and its wholly owned subsidiary, etc. not in violation; the same applies in the following item) conducted;

(iii) the amount, calculated using the method provided by Cabinet Order, equivalent economic benefits such as money which the enterprise and its wholly owned co-subsidiary, etc. gained irrespective of its name such as charges and remuneration, with regard to not supplying the goods or services connected with the relevant violation to others (excluding the Supplying Co-Subsidiaries, etc. of the enterprise and other enterprises that committed a violation and their Supplying Co-Subsidiary, etc.).

(2) If an enterprise effects private monopolization (limited to that engaged in by excluding the business activities of other enterprises, and excluding those which fall under the provisions of preceding paragraph), the Fair Trade Commission must order the enterprise, pursuant to the procedures as provided in Section 2 of Chapter VIII, to pay to the national treasury a surcharge in an amount equivalent to six percent of the sales amount of the goods or services that the enterprise and its Specified Non-Violating Supplying Co-Subsidiary, etc. supplied in the particular field of trade connected with the relevant violation (excluding the goods or services supplied to the other enterprises that supply the goods or services in the particular field of trade), the goods or services that the enterprise and the Specified Non-Violating Supplying Co-Subsidiary, etc. supplied to the other enterprises (excluding the Supplying Co-Subsidiary, etc. of the enterprise) supplying the goods or services in the particular field of trade (including the goods or services necessary for the other enterprises to supply the goods or services) and the goods or services that the enterprise and the Specified Non-Violating Supplying Co-Subsidiary, etc. supplied to the Supplying Co-Subsidiary, etc. in the particular field of trade (excluding the goods or services that the Supplying Co-Subsidiary, etc. (limited to the Violating Supplying Co-Subsidiary, etc. or the Specified Non-violating Supplying Co-subsidiary, etc.) received from the enterprise or the Specified Non-Violating Supplying Co-Subsidiary, etc. in order to supply the goods or services to others) in the Violation Period connected with the violation, calculated using the method provided by Cabinet Order; provided, however, that if the amount thus calculated is less than one million yen, the Commission may not order the payment of such a surcharge.

C. Surcharge for Unfair Trade Practices

176. Some practices that fall under unfair trade practices, under certain circumstances, are subject to surcharge. They are abuse of superior bargaining position, concerted refusal to trade, discriminatory pricing, unjustly low-price sales and RPM. Except for abuse of superior bargaining position, surcharge is imposed only on repeated violators who engaged in the same conduct in the past ten years. Calculation rate for abuse of superior bargaining position is 1% of the violator's sales to the counterparty to the act in violation. With regard to discriminatory pricing, unjustly low-price sales and RPM, calculation rate is 3% of the sales amount for the goods or services provided in the same item that the enterprise supplied. As for concerted refusal to trade, calculation rate is 3% of the sales amount for goods or services that the relevant enterprise supplied to the competitor of an enterprise to which it refused to supply the goods or services or to which it supplied the goods or services in limited quantities or with limited content.

(Article 20-2)

If an enterprise under either of the following items has committed an act in violation of the provisions of Article 19 (limited to acts that fall under Article 2, paragraph (9), item (i)), the Fair Trade Commission must order the enterprise, pursuant to the procedures provided in Section 2 of Chapter VIII, to pay to the national treasury a surcharge in an amount equivalent to three percent of the sales amount for goods or services identical to those set forth in (a) of the same item that the relevant enterprise supplied, through the act in violation during the Violation Period, to the competitor of an enterprise to which it refused to supply the goods or services or to which it supplied the goods or services in limited quantities or with limited content (for an act in violation under the provisions of (b) of the same item, the sales amount for goods or services identical to those set forth in (b) of the same item that the relevant enterprise supplied to the other enterprise prescribed in (b) of the same item (hereinafter referred to as 'the Refusing Enterprise' in this Article) (including goods or services that were necessary in order for the Refusing Enterprise to supply the relevant type of goods or services), for goods or services identical to those that the enterprise supplied to the competitor of an enterprise to which the Refusing Enterprise refused to supply the goods or services or to which it supplied the goods or services in limited quantities or with a limited content, and for goods or services identical to those that the refusing company supplied to the relevant enterprise), which is calculated using the method prescribed by the Cabinet Order; provided, however, that the Commission may not order the payment of such a surcharge if, with regard to the relevant violation, the enterprise has received an order pursuant to the provisions of Article 7-2, paragraph (1) (including the cases where these are applied mutatis mutandis pursuant to Article 8-3 following the deemed replacement of terms; the same applies in the following Article to Article 20-5 inclusive) or an order pursuant to the provisions of Article 7-9, paragraph (1) or (2) (limited to when the relevant order is final and binding; the same applies in Articles 20-4 and 20-5), a notification pursuant to the provisions of Article 7-4, paragraph (7) or Article 7-7, paragraph (3), or a decision pursuant to the provisions of Article 63, paragraph (2), or if the amount of surcharge pursuant to this Article is less than one million yen:

(i) a person who received an order pursuant to the provisions of the preceding Article (limited to an order related to Article 2, paragraph (9), item (i); the same applies in the following item) or an order pursuant to the provisions of this Article (limited to when the relevant order is final and binding; the same applies in the following item), within ten years before the Investigation Start Date in relation to the case connected with the relevant violation;

(ii) an enterprise whose wholly owned subsidiary was subject to an order pursuant to the provisions of the preceding Article (limited to the case when the wholly owned subsidiary was that of the relevant enterprise on the date of the order) or of this Article (limited to the case when the wholly owned subsidiary was that of the enterprise on the date of the order) within the ten years before the Investigation Start Date for the case connected with the relevant violation.

(Article 20-3)

If an enterprise under either of the following items has committed an act in violation of the provisions of Article 19 (limited to an act that falls under Article 2, paragraph (9), item (ii)), the Fair Trade Commission must order the enterprise, pursuant to the procedures provided in Section 2 of Chapter VIII, to pay to the national treasury a surcharge in an amount equivalent to three percent of the sales amount for the goods or services provided in the same item that the enterprise supplied ,through the act in violation during the Violation Period, which is calculated using the method provided by Cabinet Order; provided, however, that the Commission may not order the payment of such a surcharge if, with regard to the act in violation, the enterprise has received an order pursuant to the provisions of Article 7-2, paragraph (1), Article 7-9, paragraph (1) or (2) or provisions of the following Article (limited to when the relevant order is final and binding), a notification pursuant to the provisions of Article 7-4, paragraph (7) or Article 7-7 paragraph (3), or a decision pursuant to the provisions of Article 63, paragraph (2), or if the amount of the surcharge pursuant to this Article is less than one million yen:

(i) an enterprise that was subject to an order pursuant to the provisions of Article 20 (limited to an order related to Article 2, paragraph (9), item (ii); the same applies in the following item) or an order pursuant to the provisions of this Article (limited to when the relevant order is final and binding; the same applies in the following item), within ten years before the Investigation Start Date for the case connected with the relevant violation;

(ii) an enterprise whose wholly owned subsidiary was subject to an order pursuant to the provisions of Article 20 (limited to the case when the wholly owned subsidiary was that of the enterprise on the date of the order) or of this Article (limited to the case when the wholly owned subsidiary was that of the enterprise on the date of the order) within the ten years before the Investigation Start Date for the case connected with the violation.

(Article 20-4)

If an enterprise under either of the following items has committed an act in violation of the provisions of Article 19 (limited to an act that falls under Article 2, paragraph (9), item (iii)), the Fair Trade Commission must order the enterprise, pursuant to the procedures provided in Section 2 of Chapter VIII, to pay to the national treasury a surcharge in an amount equivalent to three percent of the sales amount for the goods or services provided in the same item that the enterprise supplied ,through the act in the violation during the Violation Period, which is calculated using the method provided by Cabinet Order; provided, however, that the Commission may not order the payment of such a surcharge if, with regard to the act in violation, the enterprise has received an order pursuant to the provisions of Article 7-2, paragraph (1) or Article 7-9, paragraph (1) or paragraph (2), or the provisions of Article 7-4, paragraph (7) or Article 7-7, paragraph (3), or if the amount of the surcharge pursuant to this Article is less than one million yen:

(i) an enterprise that was subject to an order pursuant to the provisions of Article 20 (limited to an order related to Article 2, paragraph (9), item (iii); the same applies in the following item) or an order pursuant to the provisions of this Article (limited to when the relevant order has become final and binding; the same applies in the following item), within ten years before the Investigation Start Date of the case connected with the relevant violation;
(ii) an enterprise whose wholly owned subsidiary was subject to an order pursuant to the provisions of Article 20 (limited to the case when the wholly owned subsidiary was that of the enterprise on the date of the order) or of this Article (limited to the case when the wholly owned subsidiary was that of the enterprise on the date of the order) within the ten years before the Investigation Start Date for the case connected with the violation.

(Article 20-5)

If an enterprise under either of the following items has committed an act in violation of the provisions of Article 19 (limited to an act that falls under Article 2, paragraph (9), item (iv)), the Fair Trade Commission must order the enterprise, pursuant to the procedures provided in Section 2 of Chapter VIII, to pay to the national treasury a surcharge in an amount equivalent to three percent of the sales amount for the goods or services provided in the same item that the enterprise supplied ,through the act in the violation during the Violation Period, which is calculated using the method provided by Cabinet Order; provided, however, that the Commission may not order the payment of such a surcharge if, with regard to the act in violation, the enterprise has received an order pursuant to the provisions of Article 7-2, paragraph (1) or Article 7-9, paragraph (1) or paragraph (2), or the provisions of Article 7-4, paragraph (7) or Article 7-7, paragraph (3), or if the amount of the surcharge pursuant to this Article is less than one million yen:

(i) an enterprise that was subject to an order pursuant to the provisions of Article 20 (limited to an order related to Article 2, paragraph (9), item (iv); the same applies in the following item) or an order pursuant to the provisions of this Article (limited to when the order has become final and binding; the same applies in the following item), within ten years before the Investigation Start Date for the case connected with the relevant violation;

(ii) an enterprise whose wholly owned subsidiary was subject to an order pursuant to the provisions of Article 20 (limited to the case when the wholly owned subsidiary was that of the enterprise on the date of the order) or of this Article (limited to the case when the wholly owned subsidiary was that of the enterprise on the date of the order) within the ten years before the Investigation Start Date for the case connected with the violation.

(Article 20-6)

If an enterprise has committed an act in violation of the provisions of Article 19 (limited to an act under Article 2, paragraph (9), item (v) that the enterprise engaged in on a continuous basis), the Fair Trade Commission must order the enterprise, pursuant to the procedures provided in Chapter VIII, Section 2, to pay to the national treasury a surcharge in an amount equivalent to one percent of the enterprise's sales to the counterparty to the act in violation, which is calculated using the method provided by Cabinet Order, for the violation period (if the enterprise engaged in the act in violation against a counterparty to which it supplied goods or services, a surcharge during the Violation Period in an amount equivalent to one percent of the amount of purchases by the counterparty, which is calculated using the method provided by Cabinet Order, and if there were multiple counterparties to the act in violation, the surcharge in an amount equivalent to one percent of the total sales amount to the counterparties or one percent of the total amount of purchases by the counterparties, which is calculated using the method provided by Cabinet Order); provided, however, that the Commission may not order the payment of such a surcharge if the amount of the surcharge is less than one million yen.

D. Surcharge for Anticompetitive Conduct of Trade Association

177. If a trade association engages in the act substantially restraining competition in any particular field of trade, the JFTC will issue Payment Order to the constituent enterprises of the trade association. The calculation rate and other relevant conditions of surcharge for the constituent enterprises are as the same as those for unreasonable restraint of trade. If a trade association had engaged in the unreasonable restraint of trade and the constituent enterprise had sold the goods following the decision of the trade association, the surcharge that enterprise must pay would be 10% of the sales amount of the goods during the period of the violation.

(Article 8-3)

The provisions of Article 2-2 (excluding paragraph (14)), Article 7-2, Article 7-4 (excluding paragraph (4), items (ii) and (iii)), Article 7-5, Article 7-6 and Article 7-8, paragraphs (1), (2) and (6) apply mutatis mutandis to cases in which an act is committed in violation of the provisions of Article 8, item (i) (limited to when an act is committed that constitutes an unreasonable restraint of trade) or item (ii) thereof (limited when an international agreement or an international contract is concluded that contains matters constituting unreasonable restraint of trade) …

V. Administrative Injunctions and Other Restrictive Orders

178. Upon petition by the JFTC, the court may make injunction order to the person engaging in an act suspected of violating the AMA if the court finds there to be an urgent necessity of doing so pursuant to Article 70-4(1). Article 85(ii) provides that such a petition of urgent injunction is subject to the exclusive jurisdiction of the Tokyo District Court.

(Article 70-4)

(1) Upon petition by the Fair Trade Commission, if the court finds there to be an urgent necessity of doing so, the court may order the person engaging in an act suspected of violating the provisions of Article 3; Article 6; Article 8; Article 9, paragraph (1) or (2); Article 10, paragraph (1); Article 11 paragraph (1); Article 13; Article 14; Article 15, paragraph (1); Article 15-2, paragraph (1); Article 15-3, paragraph (1); Article 16, paragraph (1); Article 17; or Article 19 to temporarily stop engaging in the act, stop exercising voting rights, or stop executing business as an officer of a company, or may rescind or modify such order.

(Article 85)

Any following action and case is subject to the exclusive jurisdiction of the Tokyo District Court:

(ii) any case provided for in Article 70-4, paragraph (1) … .

VI. Interim Measures

179. The AMA does not provide interim measures as enforcement tool for the JFTC.

§2. CIVIL ENFORCEMENT

I. Competent Civil Courts

180. Regarding a claim for injunction under Article 24 of the AMA, they may bring a suit at the district court which has a jurisdiction on that case pursuant to Article 84-2. Regarding a claim for damages under Article 25 of the AMA, the Tokyo District Court had a jurisdiction pursuant to Article 85-2. Those who have the ground of claims under the Civil Code (Act No. 89 of 1896) can bring a suit under the Code of Civil Procedure (Act No. 109 of 1996) regarding the jurisdiction.

(Article 84-2)

(1) When a court listed in one of the following items has jurisdiction over an action to suspend or prevent an infringement under the provisions of Article 24 pursuant to the provisions of Articles 4 and 5 of the Code of Civil Procedure, the action may also be filed with the court set forth in the relevant item:
  (i) a district court located within the jurisdiction of the Tokyo High Court (excluding Tokyo District Court), Osaka District Court, Nagoya District Court, Hiroshima District Court, Fukuoka District Court, Sendai District Court, Sapporo District Court or Takamatsu District Court: Tokyo District Court;
  (ii) a district court located within the jurisdiction of the Osaka High Court (excluding Osaka District Court): Tokyo District Court or Osaka District Court;
  (iii) a district court located within the jurisdiction of the Nagoya High Court (excluding Nagoya District Court): Tokyo District Court or Nagoya District Court;
  (iv) a district court located within the jurisdiction of the Hiroshima High Court (excluding Hiroshima District Court): Tokyo District Court or Hiroshima District Court;
  (v) a district court located within the jurisdiction of the Fukuoka High Court (excluding Fukuoka District Court): Tokyo District Court or Fukuoka District Court;

(vi) a district court located within the jurisdiction of the Sendai High Court (excluding Sendai District Court): Tokyo District Court or Sendai District Court;
(vii) a district court located within the jurisdiction of the Sapporo High Court (excluding Sapporo District Court): Tokyo District Court or Sapporo District Court;
(viii) a district court located within the jurisdiction of the Takamatsu High Court (excluding the Takamatsu District Court): Tokyo District Court or Takamatsu District Court.

(Article 85-2)

The jurisdiction of the first instance over any actions concerning compensation for damages pursuant to the provisions of Article 25 is to lie with the Tokyo District Court.

II. Sanctions

A. Nullity

181. Neither AMA nor relevant laws have any provision which stipulates that the act to violate the AMA could be nullified. However, anyone who believes that a specific act is offensive to public order and morals including those which the AMA protects can bring a suit to any district court. The act could be nullified pursuant to Article 90 of the Civil Code.

(Article 90) [Civil Code]

A juridical act that is against public policy is void.

B. Damages

182. AMA provides, by Article 25, that consumers or enterprises that have incurred damage due to the violation of the acts prohibited by the AMA may claim for damages at any district courts. If the damages are caused by the AMA violations, the violators are liable for damages regardless of their intentions or negligence.

183. They may also claim for damages in tort under Article 709 of the Civil Code.

(Article 25)

(1) An enterprise that has committed an act in violation of the provisions of Articles 3, 6 or 19 (for enterprise that have committed acts in violation of

the provisions of Article 6, limited to enterprises that have effected unreasonable restraint of trade or employed unfair trade practices in the international agreement or contract concerned) and any trade association that has committed an act in violation of the provisions of Article 8 is liable for damages suffered by another party.

(2) No enterprise or trade association may be exempted from the liability provided in the preceding paragraph by proving the non-existence of intention or negligence on its part.

(Article 709) [Civil Code]

A person that has intentionally or negligently infringed the rights or legally protected interests of another person is liable to compensate for damage resulting in consequence.

C. Interim Measures

184. A person may bring a claim for injunction on the ground of unfair trade practice by an enterprise or a trade association.

(Article 24)

A person whose interests are infringed upon or likely to be infringed upon by an act in violation of the provisions of Article 8, item (v) or Article 19 and who is thereby suffering or likely to suffer extreme damage is entitled to seek the suspension or prevention of such infringements from an enterprise or a trade association that infringes upon or is likely to infringe upon such interests.

§3. CRIMINAL ENFORCEMENT

I. Criminal Sanctions for Antitrust Violations

185. Chapter XI of the AMA (Articles 89-100) stipulates criminal penalties. Imprisonment with work or fine are imposed against violation of unreasonable restraint of trade, private monopolization pursuant to Article 89(1). Article 95(1) provides that an individual who carried out a conduct that falls under unreasonable restraint of trade is subject to criminal penalties and fine, and that an enterprise involved that the individual belongs to is also subject to criminal fine. The details on criminal procedure will be mentioned in Part IV below.

(Article 89)

(1) A person who falls under any of the following items are punished by imprisonment with work for not more than five years or by a fine of not more than five million yen:

(i) a person who, in violation of the provisions of Article 3, has effected private monopolization or unreasonable restraint of trade;
(ii) a person who, in violation of the provisions of Article 8, item (i), has effected substantial restraint of competition in any particular field of trade.

(2) An attempt to commit a crime falling under the preceding paragraph will be punished.

(Article 95)

(1) If a representative of a juridical person, or an agent, an employee or any other worker of a juridical person or of an individual has, with regard to the business or property of the juridical person or individual, violated the provisions referred to in any of the following items, in addition to the offender being punished, the juridical person or individual is sentenced to the fine prescribed in each of those items:
(i) Article 89: Fine of not more than five hundred million yen.

186. Other than this, those who committed a crime shall be punished; for example, a person will be punished by imprisonment with work or fines when it does not comply with decisive order, refused administrative investigation, etc. The penalties for these violations are provided from Articles 89 to 91 (*see* Table 2). The jurisdiction of the first instance over any action involving those crime lies in the district courts pursuant to Article 84-3.

(Article 84-3)

The jurisdiction of the first instance over any action involving a crime provided for in Articles 89 to 91 inclusive are to lie in the district courts.

187. Even if the offenders and their enterprise are criminally fined, the JFTC imposes surcharge on the enterprise under administrative procedure. However, the amount corresponding to half the amount of the criminal fine is deducted from a surcharge in such a case pursuant to Article 7-7(1).

(Article 7-7)

(1) In the case under Article 7-2, paragraph (1), if a final and binding decision on the same case sentences the relevant enterprise to a fine, instead of the amount calculated pursuant to the provisions of the same Article, Article 7-3, paragraph (2) or (3) of Article 7-4, or paragraph (3) of Article 7-5, the Fair Trade Commission is to deduct from the relevant amount the amount equivalent to one-half of the amount of the relevant fine; provided, however, that this does not apply if the surcharge amount calculated pursuant to the provisions of Article 7-2, Article 7-3, paragraph (2) or (3) of Article 7-4, or paragraph (3) of Article 7-5 does not exceed the amount equivalent to one-half of the amount of the relevant fine, or if the surcharge amount after the relevant deduction is less than one million yen.

188. Major criminal sanctions under the AMA are provided in Table 2.

Table 2 Major Criminal Sanctions

Types of illegal acts	*Individual*	*Enterprise*
Cartel Private monopolization	Imprisonment with work: up to 5 years Fine: up to JPY 5 million	Fine: up to JPY 500 million
Violation of final Cease and Desist Order	Imprisonment with work: up to 2 years Fine: up to JPY 3 million	Fine: up to JPY 300 million
Failure to notify M&A cases to the JFTC	Fine: up to JPY 2 million	Fine: up to JPY 2 million
Obstruction of inspection Refusal to report	Imprisonment with work: up to 1 year Fine: up to JPY 3 million	Fine: up to JPY 3 million

II. Other Application of Criminal Law to Relevant Conducts

189. Regarding bid riggings in public tendering, Article 96-6 ('Obstruction of Auction and Bids') of the Penal Code (Act No. 45 of 1907) may be applied.

190. In addition, Article 8 of the Involvement Prevention Act[35] stipulates that the staff in charge of tendering of public organizations will be punished when they are involved in bid rigging, by, for instance, informing an enterprise the target price or other secret information concerning the biding.

(Article 96-6) [Penal Code]

(1) A person who, by the use of fraudulent means or force, commits an act which impairs the fairness of a public auction or bid held for concluding a contract, is punished by imprisonment for not more than 3 years or a fine of not more than 2,500,000 yen, or both.
(2) The same applies to a person who colludes for the purpose of preventing a fair determination of price or acquiring a wrongful gain.

35. Act on Elimination and Prevention of Involvement in Bid Rigging, etc. and Punishment for Acts by Employees that Harm Fairness of Bid Rigging, etc.

(Article 8) [Involvement Prevention Act]

If an employee, in respect of concluding an agreement for the sale and purchase, lease, contract, etc., by bidding etc. by the government, etc. for which such employee works, has conducted any acts that harm the fairness of the bidding, etc. by inciting any enterprise or person to conduct bid rigging, informing any enterprise or person the target price or any other secret concerning the bidding, etc. or by any other method, in breach of his/her duties, the employee shall be sentenced to imprisonment with labor not exceeding five years or punished with a fine not exceeding 2,500,000 yen.

Part II. Application of the Prohibition

Chapter 1. Restrictive Agreements

§1. General Remarks

191. Unreasonable restraint of trade is, as described in Part I, Chapter 3, §1 above, prohibited by Article 3 of the AMA. Article 19 also prohibits enterprises from engaging in unfair trade practices stipulated in Article 2(9) and other practices designated by the JFTC, some of which include restrictive agreements, both horizontal and vertical.

§2. Horizontal Agreements

I. Cartels

192. Unreasonable restraint of trade is a conduct equivalent to cartel. Among the conducts that fall under unreasonable restraint of trade, those which pertain to prices of goods or services, or those which substantially restrain the volume of supply or purchase, market share or transaction counterparties thereby affecting the prices are subject to surcharge pursuant to Article 7-2.

193. As noted above, the difference between hardcore cartels and non-hardcore ones is not clear in a sense that both require a substantial restraint of competition. Nevertheless, most of the conducts categorized as hardcore cartel is those which may affect the price of goods and services, and such cartels are subject to surcharge excluding RPM, then it may be possible that hardcore cartels except for RPM are subject to surcharge.

194. For the JFTC to acknowledge the violation of Article 3, it should identify a particular field of trade where a substantial restraint of trade occurs. Preciseness necessary for this identification depends on cases. For example, the particular field of trade may consist of the whole market of a good, for example, when its manufacturers, distributors and retailers are involved in a violation. Even transactions with potential competitors may be included. On the other hand, it may be limited to transactions with particular customers if the violation is solely targeted to such transaction.

195. Horizontal agreement prohibited by Article 3 includes bid riggings (so-called '*Dango*'). It is also subject to surcharge. Generally, in bid rigging cases, amount of surcharge is calculated by summing specific goods or services targeted by the conduct in question. On this point, the Tokyo High Court ruled as follows. This decision was upheld by the Supreme Court and has been established:

> The 'goods or services in question (subject to surcharge)' refers to the goods or services that are the target of the violation. It should be interpreted that it refers to the works which specifically anti-competitive effect appeared due to being brought up for coordination among the participants of the agreement, in such a bid rigging case. Considering that the surcharge has a sanctioning element to prevent the enterprises from engaging in unreasonable restraint of trade, the works which shall be subject to surcharge need to be those which anti-competitive effect appeared due to coordination procedure in which the enterprise in question (appellant) was directly or indirectly involved.[36]

196. For identifying the targeted goods or services, the JFTC focuses on communication among the participants in the agreement, particularly on how to decide successful tenderer and its price.

197. By the 2009 amendment, which came into effect in 2010, group boycott has been subject to surcharge, too. Group boycott is a practice designated as unfair trade practice; however, there has not yet been a case in which surcharge was imposed.

198. Requirements for non-hardcore cartels are basically the same as elaborated below, although a comparison between anticompetitive effects and procompetitive one is more carefully considered, and surcharge is not imposed.

II. Information Exchange Practices

199. There are various types of information exchange. Information exchange could be illegal when it is related to prices of goods or services, quantities of supply, etc., restraining competition. The more it is linked to future expectation and specific transaction rather than past and general statistics, etc., the more likely it is to fall under unreasonable restraint of trade, or trade association's illegal conduct under Article 8.

200. The basic idea for information exchange seems to appear in the 'Information Activities' of trade association:

> If an information activity of this kind results in the formation of a tacit understanding or common intent among constituent firms to restrain competition, or if it is used as a means or a method of restraining competition, the case shall

36. Machida Area Bid-rigging Case (Tokyo High Court, 20 Feb. 2004).

> in principle be found to constitute a violation of the Act. That is, if a trade association's information activities lead to restrictive conduct by the association, such as … Fixing prices, etc., … Restricting resale prices, … Restricting quantities, … Restricting customers, … Allocating markets, … Allocating contracts, predetermining the bidder expected to win a contract, etc., … Restricting the construction or expansion of facilities, etc., and … Restricting entry, etc., or if they accompany such restrictive conduct, such cases shall … be found to constitute a violation … .[37]

III. Cooperation Agreements

201. Other than information exchange, cooperation agreements could be prohibited as unreasonable restraint of trade.

A. Research and Development

202. In the Joint R&D Guidelines,[38] the JFTC announces that cooperation agreements for research and development may be prohibited as unfair trade practices, unreasonable restraint of trade, private monopolization, or subject to M&A regulations, under certain circumstances. With respect to unreasonable restraint of trade, the Joint R&D Guidelines point out that the concerted activities for R&D may be correspondent with non-hardcore cartel.

203. The Joint R&D Guidelines also indicate whether they fall under violation depends on the number of participants, market share, object, necessity, coverage, and duration, etc. For example, the closer the cooperation agreement is to the product market, the more likely the agreement is prohibited since it is close to a hardcore cartel in the product market.

204. Moreover, the Joint R&D Guidelines also say that cooperation agreements concerning research and development are usually not regarded as non-hardcore cartels when the combined market share of participants is 20% or less.

B. Standardization

205. Standardization could also be prohibited as unreasonable restraint of trade, but it is not likely unless it restraints competition tools directly. Rather standardization could be illegal as a group boycott if it excludes outside competitors and its anticompetitive effect exceeds procompetitive one.

---

37. Trade Association Guidelines, Part II, 9.
38. Guidelines Concerning Joint Research and Development under the Antimonopoly Act.

C. *Joint Production*

206. Joint production can cause procompetitive effect through increasing efficiency in production, for example, achieving economies of scale by integrating production facilities. On the other hand, joint production could also restrain competition by, for example, price or supply restriction, or market allocation. Although there is no enforcement case or guidelines except some consultations to the JFTC by businesses, the JFTC would see its effect as rather anticompetitive than procompetitive.

D. *Joint Purchasing*

207. Joint purchasing could cause dead weight loss through decreasing supplies. The JFTC has challenged in some cases which included joint purchasing conduct. On the other hand, there are many cases concerning joint purchasing which were brought to the JFTC for preliminary consultation and raised no problem because, for example, the market share of the parties was small.

E. *Joint Selling*

208. Joint selling is more likely prohibited under unreasonable restraint of trade than other types of cooperation agreements because it may give effects to lessen the number of competitors in nature, and therefore it is close to hardcore cartels. In fact, joint selling can be used to disguise hardcore cartel and the JFTC has taken action against such disguised hardcore cartel cases. However, joint selling could bring about procompetitive effect by, for example, expanding distribution channels, allowing participants to have other distribution channels, different from just intending in maintaining prices or restricting participants' distribution channels. In those cases, the JFTC would carefully consider various elements including procompetitive effect.

§3. Vertical Agreements

I. Distribution

A. *General Remarks*

209. There are several types of vertical agreements for distribution to be illegal under the AMA. In this regard, the Distribution Guidelines cover customer allocation, boycotts, RPM and so on, which may fall under unreasonable restraint of trade or various types of unfair trade practices. In the Distribution Guidelines, boycotts including a vertical agreement could be prohibited as unreasonable restraint of trade. Nevertheless, they do not refer to RPM as unreasonable restraint of trade, but as a certain type of unilateral conduct. As explained in Part I, Chapter 4, §4, III above, since the Tokyo High Court judgment in 1953, the JFTC has not handled RPM cases under unreasonable restraint of trade.

210. For example, when a manufacturer discontinues supply to wholesalers for the purpose of preventing them from selling to price-cutters, it would fall under paragraph (2) (other refusal to trade) or (12) (trading on restrictive terms of the General Designation). When a distributor interferes with parallel imports by prohibiting retailers to handle unauthorized articles, the conduct could be banned by paragraph (12) or (14) (interference with a competitor's transactions of the General Designation).

211. Such cases imply that the conduct which might be immediately prohibited as anticompetitive agreement in other jurisdictions are regulated under unfair trade practices, examining their anticompetitive effects on case-by-case basis in Japan.

B. Public Utility Service

212. Public utility service industries have been deregulated since 1980s. The three guidelines mentioned in Part I, Chapter 2, §3 above, Electric Power Guidelines, Gas Guidelines and Telecommunication Guidelines, were published under such circumstances. These guidelines explain unjust low-price sales to exclude competitors, interference with trades between customers and competitors, and other industry-specific anticompetitive conduct. There have been some warnings and enforcement cases by the JFTC in these industries.

C. Franchising

213. Franchise system could cause illegal conduct against the AMA due to superior bargaining position of franchisers. The Franchise Guidelines[39] had been first published in 1983 and was considerably revised later in 2002. The guidelines recommend franchisers to explain certain points in detail, which are essential for franchisees to operate business before they conclude a contract with franchisers. The guidelines also explain what conduct could be prohibited as ASBP, tie-in and RPM which may come under unfair trade practice. After the 2009 amendment to the AMA, surcharge is imposed in ASBP cases.

II. Technology Licensing

214. Legal frameworks to protect IPRs in relation to technology may encourage business to conduct R&D and may serve as a driving force for creating new technologies and products based on such technologies. In this sense, IPRs can have

39. Guidelines Concerning the Franchise System under the Antimonopoly Act.

procompetitive effects. In addition, technology transactions assist in promoting competition by enabling increased efficiency in the use of technology through combinations of different technologies, the formation of new markets for technologies and their associated products, as well as increase of competing parties. In a free-market economy, the system for protection of the IPRs motivates market players to actualize their creative efforts and contribute to the development of the national economy. It is important to ensure that their basic purposes are respected and that technologies are traded without impedance.

215. Under the system of IPRs, however, competition in technologies and products may be diminished if a right-holder does neither allow other businesses to use its technology nor grant other players licence to use the technology on the condition that their R&D, production, sales or any other business activities are restricted. Then, their conduct could be prohibited by the AMA.

216. For comprehensive recognition of the principles by which the JFTC applies the AMA to restrictions pertaining to the use of technology, it published the Guidelines for Patent and Know-How Licensing Agreements under the Antimonopoly Act in 1999, which were abolished and reborn in 2007 as the IP Guidelines.[40] Article 21 of the AMA and the IP Guidelines cover, as stated in Part I, Chapter 2, §2 above, restrictions pertaining to the use of technology protected by the IPRs related legislation, such as Patent Act, the Utility Model Act, the Act on the Circuit Layout of a Semiconductor Integrated Circuits (Act No. 43 of 1985), the Plant Variety Protection and Seed Act (Act No. 83 of 1998), the Copyright Act and the Design Act, and any technology protected as know-how.

217. Part II of the IP Guidelines explains the basic principles according to which the AMA applies to restrictions pertaining to the use of technology, and then Part III clarifies, targeting (i) any conduct of inhibiting any other party from using the technology, (ii) any conduct of licensing other parties to use the technology within a limited scope and (iii) any conduct of imposing restrictions on activities conducted by other parties licensed to use the technology, how the conduct could be prohibited as unreasonable restraint of trade, private monopolization or unfair trade practices with past enforcement cases.

40. Guidelines for the Use of Intellectual Property under the Antimonopoly Act.

Chapter 2. Dominant Undertakings' Prohibited Practices

§1. General Remarks

218. Conduct like monopolization in the US and abuse of dominance in the EU are regulated as private monopolization and/or unfair trade practices in Japan.

219. Private monopolization is divided into two types, i.e., controlling type and exclusionary type, as stated in Part I, Chapter 4, §6 above. There are only a few cases of the former type of private monopolization and the violation is seen under only exceptional circumstances.

220. One of the control type private monopolization cases in which the JFTC challenged was related to anticompetitive conduct in the agricultural industry in 2015.[41] In this case, the JFTC found that the federation of agricultural cooperatives, which implemented tenders as a representative of ordering parties, controlled the business activities of participants in bidding of public tender through designating successful tenderers and managing to have the designated successful tenderers to win the biddings regarding the works related to country elevator (a facility for drying, husking and storage of grains) ordered by the agricultural cooperatives.

221. The latter is more common, and most of the cases that the JFTC has challenged fall under this type. Telecommunication company's case mentioned in Part I, Chapter 2, §3. above as well as §2 and §3 below is an example of exclusionary type.

§2. Exploitative Practices

I. Excessive/Unfair Pricing

222. Though the AMA has some provisions, which prohibit unfair pricing, there have been no case in which the JFTC challenged the pursuit of excessive profit by setting a high price. The JFTC has mainly focused on the unduly low pricing conduct including selling goods at a discriminately low price to certain consumers whose object was excluding competitors.

223. The exception, however, might be the telecommunication company case which was the case in which a dominant company in the telecommunication market set a high price for the companies who utilized the fibre optic broadband service that provided the advanced service for small volume customers.[42] In this case, the JFTC acknowledged that the dominant company's price raised the cost of the service providers, which was competing with the dominant company in the market of small volume business and its pricing would result in exclusion of the competitors out of

41. Fukui Prefectural Federation of Agricultural Cooperative Association Case (JFTC Cease and Desist Order, 16 Jan. 2015).
42. NTT-East Case (*supra* n. 9).

the market that fell under private monopolization. The company appealed to the Court and the Tokyo High Court upheld the JFTC's decision (*see* §3, V below).

224. As another type of charging detriment upon enterprises, the AMA prohibits abusive conduct of superior bargaining position which falls under unfair trade practice.

225. Not being the case where a legal action was taken, the JFTC cautioned an electrical power company in 2012. In that case, the company unilaterally announced increase in electricity rates, due to the nuclear power plant accident and subsequent cost-up, for small volume customers such as supermarkets and small-sized factories despite that the conditions of transactions could not be altered until the term of contract expired. Also, the company sent a document to its customers that it regards the alternation of conditions of transactions as accepted unless the customers raised objection.

226. The JFTC acknowledged that the electric supplier was in the position superior to its customers, who had no choice but to accept the increase in rate for fear of suspension of electricity supply. In this case, the company had pledged that it would reconsider the new electricity rates and negotiate with them in a good faith before closing the investigation. The JFTC examined this and concluded not to take any formal action on the ground that it would solve the anticompetitive concerns.

227. Though these are not the cases of exploitation in a strict sense, it is considered that the conduct above may have been alleged as violation of Article 102 of TFEU (Treaty on the Functioning of the European Union).

II. Discrimination

228. Enterprises can freely decide the conditions of transactions and are permitted to offer more favourable conditions to obtain more customers than the competitors. However, discriminative dealing may impose any disadvantage on specific customers, which results in excluding them out of the market. Therefore, the AMA prohibits the conduct of discriminating amount of remuneration of goods without good reason, thereby tending to cause difficulties to the business activities of other enterprises (Article 2(9)(ii)) and regulates other discriminative treatment (General Designation, paragraphs 3 and 4).

229. As stated before, the conducts such as discrimination and predation are considered as a means of monopolization. Moreover, the AMA has a regulatory framework of unfair trade practice, which is a kind of pre-emptive regulation for monopolization. Therefore, those conducts mentioned above are prohibited even if they do not cause substantial restraint of competition which the monopolization clause requires.

230. The JFTC issued a Cease and Desist Order to a cooperative operated by manufacturers of plastic tile, which unduly discriminated selling price of tile between members and non-members and provided a certain rebate for members as violation of the AMA in 1980.[43]

231. On the contrary, in a private suit in which the pricing of an LPG (Liquefied Petroleum Gas) supplier was alleged to violate the AMA, the Tokyo High Court, in 2005, held that price discrimination is not illegal in nature but is only prohibited in case where it is unduly practised, because the price differs by region and other elements, and the regulation of price discrimination purports to ensure competition in efficiency among enterprises by means of price competition.[44] The court concluded that it is adequate to find out whether even the competitors no less efficient than the party concerned cannot offer the price in rivalry with the party and that it should be considered whether the price is below the cost to decide its unfairness.

III. Abuse of Superior Bargaining Position

232. Generally, it depends on the will of enterprises on what condition to enter transaction; however, if an enterprise in the superior bargaining position over the other party makes use of its position unjustly in the light of normal business practices, the conduct may impede the transaction based on free and voluntary will of the parties concerned as well as may cause disadvantage on one side and advantage on another side, thereby may impede fair competition.

233. ASBP does not require that violator has dominant or is in a monopoly position in a relevant market. It is sufficient for the violator to have relatively superior bargaining position against its trading partner. The regulation also does not necessarily require economic analysis about competitive effects in the relevant market. Whether the conduct at issue is abusive is judged after seeing if it is unjust in light of normal business practice on a case-by-case analysis.

234. Typical conduct of ASBP found in the cases in which the JFTC issued a Cease and Desist Order is to coerce purchase of any other products or services than those that are identified in the contract of supply, provision of labour force without compensation in the event of open sale, payment of monetary contribution as a measure for settling the accounts.

235. ASBP is subject to Cease and Desist Order and Payment Order. Payment Order has been applicable to the conduct since the 2009 amendment. The JFTC, in line with this amendment, issued the ASBP Guidelines[45] to enhance the predictability for businesses.

---

43. Toyo Linoleum Case (JFTC Recommendation Decision, 7 Feb. 1980).
44. Nippon Gas Case (Tokyo High Court, 31 May 2005).
45. Guidelines Concerning Abuse of Superior Bargaining Position under the Antimonopoly Act.

236. This regulation comprises two requirements:

i. to be in the superior bargaining position; and
ii. to make use of its position unjustly in light of the normal business practices.

237. With regard to requirement i above, the ASBP Guidelines explain as follows:

> In order for one party to a transaction (Party A) to have superior bargaining position over the other party (Party B), it is construed that Party A does not need to have a market-dominant position nor an absolutely dominant bargaining position equivalent thereto, but only needs to have a relatively superior bargaining position as compared to the other transacting party. When Party A has superior bargaining position over Party B, who is a counterparty, it means such a case where if Party A makes a request, etc., that is substantially disadvantageous for Party B, Party B would be unable to avoid accepting such a request, etc., on the grounds that Party B has difficulty in continuing the transaction with Party A and thereby Party B's business management would be substantially impeded. … In determining the presence or absence of superior bargaining position, the degree of dependence by Party B on the transactions with Party A, position of Party A in the market, the possibility of Party B changing its counterparty, and other concrete facts indicating the need for Party B to carry out transactions with Party A are comprehensively considered.[46]

238. On the other hand, concerning requirement (ii), the ASBP Guidelines mention the requirement of 'unjustly in light of the normal business practices' in section III, as follows:

> The requirement, 'unjustly in light of normal business practices,' indicates that the presence or absence of ASBP is determined case-by-case from the viewpoint of maintaining/promoting fair competition where entrepreneur [sic] compete to provide better quality or lower prices. The term 'normal business practices' means business practices that are endorsed from the viewpoint of the maintenance/promotion of the said fair competition. Therefore, an act is not immediately justified merely because it complies with the currently existing business practices.[47]

239. The AMA indicates three types of conduct that may fall under the ASBP, and the ASBP Guidelines show some examples which may correspond to each type of conduct along with it as follows:[48]

---

46. ASBP Guidelines II. 1.-2.
47. *Ibid.*, III.
48. *Ibid.*, IV.

a. causing a transacting party in continuous transactions (including a party with whom one intends to newly engage in continuous transactions; the same applies in (b) below) to purchase goods or services other than those to which the relevant transactions pertain:
   i. an enterprise causes a transacting party to purchase goods or services by making a request that could be taken to mean that the purchase would have an influence on future transactions, such as suggesting the termination of transactions with the transacting party or a reduction of the transaction volume in the event of a failure to make the purchase;
   ii. an enterprise causes a transacting party, to purchase goods or services by having a person, such as a staff member in charge of purchasing, who could have an influence on the transactional relationship with the counterparty request the purchase;
   iii. an enterprise causes a transacting party to purchase goods or services by organizationally or systematically requesting the purchase;
   iv. an enterprise causes a transacting party to purchase goods or services in the case where the transacting party has expressed its intention not to make a purchase or where the transacting party is clearly found to have no intention of making a purchase even in the absence of such expression, by repeatedly requesting that the purchase be made or by one-sidedly sending goods to the transacting party;
   v. an enterprise requests a transacting party with whom the enterprise places an order for the processing of components to recommend a purchaser of the goods produced by a manufacturer, a transacting party of the enterprise, and causes the transacting party to purchase the said goods should the transacting party fail to recommend a purchaser;
   vi. in computerizing receipts/placement of orders, an enterprise, despite the fact that a transacting party has already signed a contract with another enterprise on Internet services that can respond to the said computerization, and therefore has been receiving such services, requests the transacting party to designate and use an Internet service provider that provides more expensive Internet services, and causes the transacting party to use the said provider, suggesting that the enterprise would not continue transactions with the transacting party.

b. Causing a transacting party in continuous transactions to provide money, services or other economic benefits:
   i. an enterprise requests and causes a transacting party to pay a monetary contribution, etc. for holding an event, refurbishing the selling space, or placing an advertisement that does not directly contribute to the sales promotion of the transacting party's goods or services;
   ii. an enterprise requests and causes a transacting party to pay a monetary contribution as a measure for improving the settling accounts of the enterprise;
   iii. an enterprise causes a transacting party to pay, at the time of opening its new store or refurbished store, an amount equivalent to a certain percentage of the transacting party's amount of supply to the said store as a monetary contribution over a fixed period, without clarifying the amount of the

payment, the basis for the calculation of the amount, and the purpose of the payment in advance, in order to secure the said store's gross profits;

iv. in a case where it had been decided in advance that an enterprise receives a rebate on attaining a certain sales volume during a fixed period, the enterprise requests and causes a transacting party to pay, the said rebate in spite of the fact that it has not attained the sales volume;

v. when placing an advertisement for a discount sale upon opening its new store or refurbished store, an enterprise requests, and causes a transacting party to pay, an amount of monetary contribution that exceeds the expenses actually required for placing the said advertisement;

vi. an enterprise unilaterally requests a supplier to pay fee for using a facility ('centre fee') for its distribution operation, such as a delivery centre, without sufficiently discussing the amount of the fee and the basis for the calculation of the amount with the supplier, and causes the supplier to pay an amount that exceeds a reasonable amount of fee for the level of use of the said facility;

vii. an enterprise suspends the acceptance of the supply of goods in respect to transaction, which has been continued in order to gain money under the pretext of a 'newly-introduced monetary contribution,' and thereafter causes the transacting party to resume supply of the same goods. Through these measures, the enterprise requests the transacting party to provide money and causes the transacting party to pay the money.

c. refusing to receive goods in transactions with the transacting party, causing the trading party to take back such goods after receiving them from the transacting party, delaying payment to the transacting party or reducing the amount of payment, or otherwise establishing or changing trade terms or executing transactions in a way disadvantageous to the transacting party:

i. an enterprise requests and causes a transacting party to dispatch employees, etc., of the transacting party to engage in operations that only benefit the enterprise without paying the expenses for the dispatch;

ii. an enterprise causes a supplier to dispatch employees, at the time of a discount sale upon opening its new store or refurbished store, in order to have them engage in sales operations, and has those employees engage in the sales operations of not only the goods supplied by the said supplier, but also the goods of other suppliers, thereby causing the supplier that has dispatched the employees to bear a burden that exceeds the scope as deemed reasonable considering direct benefit, etc.;

iii. while offering to bear the expenses for the dispatch of employees, etc. by transacting parties, an enterprise merely decides a uniform amount of daily allowance as dispatch expenses, and although expenses such as transportation expenses and accommodation expectations occur depending on an individual transacting party's circumstances, the enterprise causes the transacting parties to dispatch employees, etc. without paying such expenses;

iv. in a case where an enterprise bears the expenses for the dispatch of employees, etc. by transacting parties, and such expenses to be borne include daily allowances, transportation expenses, and accommodation expenses, an enterprise uniformly decides that the daily allowance should be set at an amount lower than an appropriate amount corresponding to the salary of the said employee, etc. or the contents of the operations pertaining to the dispatch;

v. an enterprise causes a transacting party to pay the wage for a part-time worker whom it has employed for its inventory operations;

vi. in a case where a contract only stipulates that a transacting party transports goods to a warehouse of an enterprise, the enterprise causes the transacting party to engage free of charge in loading and unloading work, etc., in the warehouse of the enterprise, which has not been set forth in the contract in advance.

§3. Exclusionary Practices

240. The AMA illustrates some practices in it, which relate to exclusionary conduct, such as concerted refusal to supply (Article 2(9)(i)), price discrimination (Article 2(9)(ii)) and predatory pricing (Article 2(9)(iii)). Also, the General Designation sets out refusal to trade (paragraphs (1) and (2)), discriminatory treatment (paragraphs (3)–(5)), predatory pricing (paragraph (6)), unjustly high price purchasing (paragraph (7)), inducement of customers by unjust benefit (paragraph (9)), tie-in sales (paragraph (10)), dealing with exclusionary terms (paragraph (11)), etc. All these practices except for the first one which falls under private monopolization are categorized in unfair trade practices. In sum, the AMA prohibits various types of exclusionary conducts specifically. The followings are brief notes on some of them.

I. Predation

241. Predation including predatory pricing would be one of the most popular means of exclusion. The Exclusionary Private Monopolization Guidelines refer to predation as one of the typical exclusionary conducts. Nevertheless, the clause concerning private monopolization above neither has a clear definition of predation nor case law what the predation means.

242. Price competition through each enterprise's efforts essentially constitutes the core of the competition on the merits (meaning the competition by which enterprises attract customers by supplying high-quality and low-cost products), which the competition policy aims to maintain and promote. In this sense, low prices in themselves would by no means be considered improper, as a matter of course. Indeed, there is no problem in providing goods at a low price that has been achieved through an enterprise's efficient operations.

243. However, if an enterprise tries to acquire customers by offering a low price that totally disregards profitability, such behaviour may run counter to the purposes of the competition law and policy and, if so, needs to be regulated. This is because an act of winning away the customers of a competitor by setting such a low price that the supply of the goods cannot be continued unless the losses thereby incurred were compensated for by profits from the supply of other goods, or by other sources of funds. Indeed, the enterprise might raise its price to recoup for its profit loss after its rivals exit the market. Such situation does not reflect enterprises' efforts or the proper competition process, and it could tend to cause difficulties to the business activities of competitors that are just as efficient as or more efficient than the enterprise which engaged in the price cutting and could harm the fair competition order.

244. The Act defines the predation as a type of unfair trade practice as follows: 'Without justifiable grounds, supplying goods or services continuously for a price which is excessively below the cost required for the supply, thereby tending to cause difficulties to the business activities of other enterprises'.

245. This regulation consists of three requirements:

i. to supply goods or service continuously at a price excessively below the cost for the supply;
ii. to cause difficulties to other enterprises' business activities;
iii. to have no justifiable grounds.

A. *Price-Cost Relationship*

246. With regard to the requirement i above, it can be divided into two elements: price-cost relationship and continuity.

247. The Predatory Sales Guidelines[49] state as follows:

> [An] appropriate price/cost relationship would be one that can be used to determine whether or not a certain price setting obviously lacks economic rationality for the price cutter. In this respect, a price setting that would expand losses as more goods are supplied can be deemed to lack economic rationality unless there are special circumstances. Thus, it is appropriate to determine whether or not a certain price setting lacks economic rationality by comparing the costs that arise by supplying the goods that were made subject to price cutting (hereinafter referred to as the 'price-cut goods') and the price of said goods … . The costs required for the supply are divided into costs that would not be generated unless the price-cut goods were supplied (hereinafter referred to as 'variable-featured costs') and the other costs. If an entrepreneur [sic] sets a low price that is insufficient for even recovering the variable-featured costs, losses would expand as more price-cut goods are supplied. [50]

To summarize, the price below the variable-featured costs is presumed to be 'a price which is excessively below the costs required for the supply'.

49. Guidelines Concerning Unjust Low Price Sales under the Antimonopoly Act.
50. Predatory Sales Guidelines, 3(1)A(C).

B. Continuity

248. The Predatory Sales Guidelines explain as follows:

> [I]n order for price cutting to be regarded as unjust low-price sales, it needs to negatively affect the decision regarding the continuation of business, etc. of entrepreneur [sic] that are just as efficient as the price cutter .... The term 'continuously' either means that an entrepreneur [sic] engages in price cutting repeatedly over a considerable period of time, or that an entrepreneur [sic] is objectively predicted to be engaged in price cutting for such duration judging from said entrepreneur's [sic] sales policy, etc., and does not necessarily require price cutting to be carried out every day in a continuous manner. For example, even when price cutting is carried out only on specific dates, such as every weekend, there are cases where the entrepreneur [sic] can be regarded as supplying the price-cut goods continuously, depending on the purchasing behavior of consumers.[51]

249. In other words, to fulfil the requirement of continuity the fact is needed that the enterprise is engaging in predatory selling over a considerable period of time, or is likely to engage in the conduct for the duration.

C. Causing Difficulty to Other Enterprises

250. The requirement (ii) is called 'effect requirement'. The Predatory Sales Guidelines state as follows:

> The phrase 'tending to cause difficulties to the business activities of other entrepreneur' [sic] does not necessarily require that price cutting makes business activities difficult in actuality [sic], but it includes cases where a concrete possibility of the price cutting inviting such result is found based on various circumstances .... The presence or absence of such possibility is determined on a case-by-case basis, by comprehensively taking into consideration the actual status of other entrepreneurs [sic] as well as the size and type of business of the price cutter, the quantity of the price-cut goods, the duration of the price cutting, the status of advertising and publicity associated with the price-cut goods, the characteristics of the price-cut goods, and the price cutter's intention or purpose of price cutting.[52]

251. However, this requirement is burdensome for the JFTC to challenge the predation. Indeed, it may be the reason why there have been only a few cases in which it took legal measures though hundreds of complains a year have been

51. *Ibid.*, 3 (1) B.
52. *Ibid.*, 3, (2), B.

reported to the JFTC is that the fact can be hardly found that the conduct affects the other enterprises' business. The JFTC consequently closes the case by just issuing caution in most cases.

D. *Justifiable Grounds*

252. As stated above, the JFTC has just a few cases in which the JFTC took legal measures against predatory pricing, therefore there is no precedent judgment. Nevertheless, the Predatory Sales Guidelines state as follows:

> 'For example, in cases where the market price of the price-cut goods declines due to a supply-and-demand imbalance or the replacement cost of the raw materials for the price-cut goods becomes lower than the acquisition cost of said raw materials, it is considered a case which has "justifiable grounds" for setting a low price according to the market conditions of the goods or the raw materials, or in the case where the price of the raw materials soars unexpectedly in a transaction for procuring the raw materials after the price of the goods is decided, and as a result, the price of the price-cut goods becomes excessively below the costs required for the supply, "justifiable grounds" are considered to exist'.[53]
>
> 'If there is a need to make clearance sales of products such as perishable goods whose quality is likely to deteriorate rapidly or seasonal goods whose peak sales periods are over, "justifiable grounds" are considered to exist for setting a price lower than the variable-featured costs. The same applies when setting a reasonably low price for any damaged item'.[54]

II. Tying

253. Also, the AMA has no clear definition about tying as the conduct of possible violation. However, the Exclusionary Private Monopolization Guidelines explain tying as one of typical exclusionary conduct and elaborate elements to consider in determining illegality. The guidelines state as follows:

> [W]here an entrepreneur [sic] supplies one product (tying product) only on the condition that the trade partners also purchase another product (tied product) may cause difficulty in the business activities of competitors who are unable to easily find alternative trade partners in the market of the tied product, and therefore may undermine competition in the market of the tied product. Thus, supplying (or purchasing) only on the condition that the trade partners also purchase (or supply) another product ... may fall under Exclusionary Conduct.[55]

53. *Ibid.*, 3, (3).
54. *Ibid.*, 3, (3), Note 10.
55. Exclusionary Private Monopolization Guidelines, Part II, 4, (1).

254. This regulation has two requirements. First, the tying product and tied product should be different products. The guidelines explain as above:

> Assessment over whether or not the product required to purchase on condition for the supply of a product is deemed to be 'another product' is made from the viewpoint of whether or not each of the combined product has a distinctive character and is traded independently. Specifically, comprehensive consideration is given to the respective products in terms of factors such as whether the users are different from each other, whether the contents and functions are different from each other (including whether the contents and functions of the combined products differ substantially from those of each product before combination), and whether the users can separately purchase each of them (including whether each of the combined products is normally sold or used as a single unit).[56]

255. Second, where the tying makes competitors unable to easily find alternative trading partners in the market of the tied product and causes difficulty in their business activities, the tying is construed as exclusionary conduct. The guidelines declare this policy as follows:

> The JFTC will comprehensively consider the following factors to assess whether or not such conduct would cause difficulty in the business activities of competitors who are unable to easily find alternative trade partners in the market of the tied product.[57]

256. The factors to be taken into consideration at assessment of illegality, illustrated in the guidelines are as follows:

i. conditions of the entire market of the tying and the tied products;
ii. position of the enterprise in the market of the tying product;
iii. positions of the enterprise and its competitors in the market of the tied product;
iv. period of the conduct, number of the trade partners, and quantity of transaction;
v. conditions of the conduct.

257. Tying is subject to the regulation of unfair trade practice in addition to private monopolization. Analytical framework is like that of private monopolization. The difference is, as well as other unfair trade practices, that substantial restraint of competition is required for private monopolization but tying under the unfair trade practice regulation requires only the likelihood to impede fair competition as the result of the conduct. So, even if an enterprise who engages in tying is not in a dominant position in the market of the tying product, it possibly be condemned by the regulation on unfair trade practices. Also, it is not necessary for the tying conduct

56. *Ibid.*
57. *Ibid.*, Part II, 4, (2).

to enhance the market position in the tied product. Tying unpopular product to rare and blockbuster product might be subject to tying clause under unfair trade practice regulation. The measure against tying as unfair trade practice is only Cease and Desist Order and Payment Order is not rendered.

III. Rebates

258. Rebates are regarded as one of the typical exclusionary conducts under the private monopolization regulation, although the provision of the AMA does not clearly describe the conduct as the two practices mentioned above. The Exclusionary Private Monopolization Guidelines set out as follows:

> [W]hen an entrepreneur [sic] gives rebates to trade partners on the condition that the amount or volume of purchase from the entrepreneur [sic] or the proportion of amount (volume) of purchase from the entrepreneur [sic] to the total amount (volume) of its purchase reaches a particular threshold or more during a specified period, such conduct may have effects in restraining the trade partners' dealings of competitors' products. Thus, where Rebates-giving to the trade partners on the condition for certain amount of purchase from the alleged entrepreneur [sic], etc. has effects in restraining the trade partners' dealings of the competitors' products, such conduct may have the same effect as Exclusive Dealing.[58]

259. In determining whether rebates have the same effect as exclusive dealing, the guidelines explain that the JFTC takes into consideration such factors as the following:

i. level of rebates;
ii. threshold of giving rebates;
iii. progressiveness of rebates;
iv. retroactivity of rebates.

260. Where the threshold of rebates-giving is set for each trading partner respectively, the trading partners would be more likely to purchase more products from the enterprise than when the same criteria are set for all the trading partners. Because the enterprise can set the criteria in accordance with the specific circumstances of each trading partner so that the rebates function more effectively to have the trading partners deal with the enterprise's products with greater preference than with the competitors' products. Thus, such rebates-giving is regarded as highly effective in restraining the dealings of the competitors' products.

261. If rebates are given, however, for the volume of purchase, especially in case where the threshold is set at the level of entire quantity of purchase, the rebates

58. *Ibid.*, Part III, 3(3).

function more effectively in making the trading partners buy products from the enterprise with greater preference than with those from the competitors. Then, the trading partners would be more likely to discontinue purchasing from competitors. Such a way of providing rebates is regarded as highly effective in restraining the dealings of competitors' products.

262. Exclusionary dealing is one of the unfair trade practices and some types of rebates such as loyalty rebate is often regarded as a tool to achieve exclusionary monopolization. The analytical framework of rebates under unfair trade practice regulation is, therefore, the same as that of private monopolization. But as well as other unfair trade practices rebates as unfair trade practice do not need to meet substantial restraint of competition standard.

263. The Distribution Guidelines explain coverage rebate, similar to loyalty rebate.[59] Distribution Guidelines state that providing rebates is illegal as unfair trade practices in cases where an influential manufacturer provides coverage rebates, and if the provision has the function of restricting distributors' handling of competing products and may result in making it difficult for new entrants or competitors to easily secure alternative distribution channels. Rebate, in theory, may also be subject to unjust low-price sales provision of unfair trade practice. The Predatory Sales Guidelines, however, do not refer to rebate as to how the JFTC deals with rebate in the context of analysis of unjust low-price sales. There has been no case where rebate was considered to be unjust low-price sales.

IV. Refusal to Deal

264. Refusal to deal is also one of the unfair trade practices, which may constitute private monopolization.

265. However, an enterprise has the discretion to select to whom and on what conditions it supplies a product. This principle is generally accepted in the competition community in Japan. It is thus an exceptional case where refusal to deal is challenged as a possible violation of private monopolization that neither does the AMA provide detailed description nor is there case law in which the conduct was alone considered to be a violation of private monopolization. Also, there are not any guidelines which mention refusal to deal as stand-alone exclusionary conduct.

266. Under the unfair trade practice regulation, refusal to deal is designated in the General Designation. The Distribution Guidelines explain unfair trade practice regulation in detail and illustrate a typical case in which the refusal to deal provision may fall under unfair trade practices. According to the guidelines, it is prohibited when an influential firm in a market engages in such conduct as a means of

59. Distribution Guidelines, Part I., Ch. 3., 2 (2) a.

achieving such unjust purposes in the light of the AMA as excluding its competitors from a market, and if such conduct may make it difficult for the refused firm to carry on normal business activities.

> *In cases where an enterprise engages in, for example, the conduct mentioned in ... i. below... as a means to secure the effectiveness of its illegal practice under the Antimonopoly Act, such conduct is illegal as unfair trade practices (Paragraph 2 (Other Refusal to Trade) of the General Designation). Moreover, in cases where an influential enterprise in a market ... engages in, for example, the conduct mentioned in ... ii. or iii. below as a means to achieve unjust purposes under the Antimonopoly Act (such as exclusion of its competitor from a market), and if such conduct tends to make it difficult for the refused competitor to carry on normal business activities, such conduct is illegal as unfair trade practices (Paragraph 2 of the General Designation):*
>
> *i. an influential manufacturer in a market, by causing distributors not to deal with its competitor, reduces the competitor's business opportunities and prevents the competitor from easily finding alternative trading partners, and, with a view to ensure the effectiveness of such conduct, refuses to deal with distributors not complying with this request (this conduct also falls under Paragraph 11 (Trading on Exclusive Terms) of the General Designation) ...;*
> *ii. an influential material manufacturer in a market, in an attempt to prevent a finished product manufacturer from manufacturing by itself some of materials supplied by the material manufacturer to it, stops its supply to the finished product manufacturer of main materials which have been being supplied by the material manufacturer to the finished product manufacturers;*
> *iii.* an influential material manufacturer in a market, in an attempt to exclude competitors of its customer (more specifically, an enterprise which has a close relation with the material manufacturer and which manufactures a finished product by making use of materials supplied by the manufacturer) from a market for the said finished product, stops its supply to those competitors of materials which have been being supplied by the material manufacturer to them. [60]

V. Price Squeeze

267. None of the AMA provision and General Designation clearly articulated price squeeze. In addition, since there is no general designation directly relevant to price squeeze, the conduct would be only subject to the private monopolization regulation. There is a high-profile case law with respect to price squeeze. The JFTC,

60. *Ibid.*, Part II., Ch. 3., 2.

in 2007, issued a Cease and Desist Order to a vertically integrated telecommunication company. The company was alleged to have been engaged in private monopolization in the optical fibre telecommunications services market by excluding the business activities of other telecommunications carriers. The exclusion was achieved by price squeeze. The telecommunication company appealed the JFTC's order, but the Supreme Court affirmed the order in the end. The outline of the case is as follows: [61]

268. The telecommunication company was engaged in the regional telecommunications business in the eastern part of Japan. It had an extremely large market share in almost all areas of the region, in terms of the volume of holdings of subscriber optical fibre facilities indispensable for providing optical fibre telecommunications services, and in terms of the number of optical fibre telecommunications to the home (FTTH services). Therefore, it was extremely important for those who had no subscriber optical fibre equipment to connect with the subscriber optical fibre equipment owned by the telecommunication company in the subscriber optical fibre equipment connection market (upstream market) to provide services in the FTTH service market (downstream market). Under the circumstances, the telecommunication company provided FTTH services at a price of the customer fee, which was lower than the connection fee paid to the telecommunication company by other telecommunications carriers. Therefore, in order to win customers, other telecommunications carriers had to set a customer fee that could counter against the customer fee of the telecommunication company while paying the telecommunication company the connection fee, i.e., the other telecommunications carriers would be forced to suffer a large deficit, because it would generate negative margins. It has become extremely difficult for other telecommunications carriers to enter the FTTH service business. Such conduct by the telecommunication company was deemed to exclude the business activities of other telecommunications carriers who intended to connect the subscriber optical fibre equipment owned by the telecommunication company and provide FTTH services.

269. Through the debate, in this case, the JFTC did not argue that price squeeze claims are cognizable under the private monopolization regulation. The Exclusionary Private Monopolization Guidelines, however, clearly provide as to how the JFTC deals with price squeeze. First, the guidelines state that price squeeze may be considered as exclusionary conduct under private monopolization regulations as follows:

> [I]f an entrepreneur [sic] carries out, beyond reasonable degree, refusal to supply, imposing restriction on the quantity or contents, or applies discriminatory treatment to the condition or implementation of supply in the upstream market … concerning a product necessary for the trading customers to carry out business activities in the downstream market, such conduct may cause difficulty in the business activities in the downstream market of the trading customers who are unable to easily find an alternative supplier in the upstream market, and

61. NTT-East Case (*supra* n. 9).

> may undermine competition in the downstream market. Thus, carrying out Refusals, beyond reasonable degree, concerning a product necessary for the trading customers to carry out business activities in the downstream market ... may fall under Exclusionary Conduct.[62]

270. The Guidelines also elaborate the factors of assessment of price squeeze. They explain that the following circumstances are likely to be considered that the conduct causes difficulty in the business activities of the enterprises who would be competitors in the downstream market. That means the possibility that the price squeeze conduct is condemned as private monopolization would be high. The guidelines state as follows:

> [I]f the prices of products in the upstream market that an entrepreneur [sic] supplies to some trading customers are set at a higher level than those for other trading customers, going beyond reasonable degree, on the basis of differences in the details of supply and other conditions, those trading customers will have to increase the price of their products in the downstream market because the purchasing costs will be higher for them. In this case, particularly when the purchasing costs for those trading customers is higher than the selling price of the products sold by other trading customers in the downstream market or the selling price of the product sold by the alleged entrepreneur [sic] in the downstream market, if the entrepreneur [sic] itself sell it there, it is considered that those trading customers cannot compete with other trading customers (or the alleged entrepreneur [sic]) through economically reasonable business activities. Accordingly, such a case would be more likely to be deemed to cause difficulty in the business activities of the trading customers who are unable to easily find an alternative supplier in the upstream market.[63]

VI. Interference of Transactions

271. Unjust interference with a competitor is a practice designated by the General Designation (paragraph (14)). The JFTC sometimes employs this regulation to challenge the practices of distributors of imported goods which intend to exclude their competitors that sell goods imported via the third parties or the third countries (parallel import). Actually, the JFTC sometimes took legal measure against the enterprises which dealt with imported goods with brand names such as shoes, which interfered business activities of its competitors who sold goods of parallel import by prohibiting or restricting its counterparties from transacting with competitors.

272. Interfering competitor's business by intentionally damaging its reputation may also lead to exclusionary practice. The JFTC issued a Cease and Desist Order in 2020 and a Payment Order in 2021 against Mainami Aviation Services Co.,

62. Exclusionary Private Monopoly Guidelines, Part II., 5(1).
63. *Ibid.*, Part II., 5(2).

Ltd.[64] It was a case of exclusionary conduct concerning the sale of the aviation fuel by 'into-plane fuelling' service at Yao Airport located in Osaka prefecture. This is the first case where the JFTC issued a Payment Order against violation of exclusionary private monopolization since the introduction of surcharge as sanction for violation of the conduct in 2009.

Mainami Aviation Services has been having its users not be refuelled from SGC Saga Aviation Co., Ltd., which was a competitor of Mainami Aviation Services. The conducts which the JFTC acknowledged are as follows:

i. Mainami Aviation Services, alleging that Mainami Aviation Services would not bear responsibility for aircraft-related accidents caused by mixing the aviation fuel of Mainami Aviation Services with that of SGC Saga Aviation, has notified its customers that it would not continue to fuel their aircraft if the users are refuelled from SGC Saga Aviation;
ii. Mainami Aviation Services, as a condition to accept requests related to fuelling from its customers who are fuelled by the service of SGC Saga Aviation, has requested its users to sign a document describing that they shall not seek Mainami Aviation Services' liability for aircraft-related accidents caused by mixing the aviation fuel of Mainami Aviation Services with that of SGC Saga Aviation or to remove the fuel from the customers' aircraft.

273. The JFTC acknowledged that the conducts above excluded business activities of SGC Saga Aviation and led to substantial restraint of competition in the field of into-plane fuelling service at Yao Airport. So, the JFTC issued a Cease and Desist Order to have Mainami Aviation Service to stop the conducts and to let its customers and employees know the actions that the company takes abiding by the Cease and Desist Order. The JFTC also imposed JPY 6.12 million surcharge on Mainami Aviation Services.

274. Mainami Aviation Services filed a lawsuit with the Tokyo District Court against these orders, arguing that there were no effects of exclusion and that there were justifiable reasons from the viewpoint of safety. However, the Court dismissed the case in February 2022. Then, the company appealed against the District Court judgment to the Tokyo High Court. The Court, in January 2023, upheld the District Court judgment, finding that the justifiable reasons were not backed by any evidence. The enterprise's appeal to the Supreme Court was rejected in September 2023.

§4. OTHER TYPES OF RESTRICTIVE CONDUCTS

275. Private monopolization regulation contains control type conduct. Nevertheless, it is not so clear what conduct constitutes 'control' in the definition of private monopolization. Though it is generally recognized that not only direct control

64. Mainami Aviation Service Case (JFTC Cease and Desist Order, 7 Jul. 2020; Surcharge Payment Order, 19 Feb. 2021).

but also indirect control is covered, there is no clear guidance about the boundary of indirect control. In an old case in the 1950s it was considered that the enterprise who had a large market share and was the price leader controlled the relevant market concerning the condition and business practices in the market[65]. In that case, the enterprise was neither in a dominant position in the market nor had capital ties or interlocking directorate relationship with its competitors and counterparties. But this case was a rare case and there has been no similar case since then. So, indirect control would probably be raised under only exceptional circumstances.

---

65. Noda Soy-sauce Case (JFTC Administrative Hearing Decision, 27 Dec. 1955).

Chapter 3. Concentrations

§1. General Remarks

276. As stated before (*see* Part I, Chapter 3, §3 above), the AMA regulates eight types of business combination as follows:

i. acquisition or possession of the shares of a company;
ii. interlocking directorates;
iii. shareholding by a person other than a company;
iv. merger of companies;
v. joint incorporation-type split or absorption split;
vi. joint share transfer;
vii. acquisition of business;
viii. circumvention of the prohibition above.

277. Chapter IV of the AMA prohibits a business combination, where it is to substantially restrain competition in any particular trade of field, or where it is created by way of unfair trade practice. Prohibited business combinations are subject to Cease and Desist Order pursuant to Article 17-2.

278. The JFTC published the Merger Guidelines to clarify its policy to review business combinations. The guidelines set out the analytical framework and the criteria for assessing whether a certain business combination may be to substantially restrain competition in accordance with the categories of business combinations, i.e., horizontal, vertical and conglomerate ones.

§2. Horizontal Mergers

279. The Merger Guidelines define the 'horizontal business combinations (horizontal mergers)' as 'business combinations between companies with a competitive relationship in the same particular field of trade'.[66]

280. The guidelines indicate that horizontal mergers reduce the number of competing units in a market and directly influence the competition in the market, and consequently they are more likely to cause an effect of substantially restraining competition than vertical and conglomerate ones.

281. In the review of a horizontal merger, the JFTC first determines whether that merger falls under one of the Safe Harbour criteria. If not, the JFTC examines both the unilateral effects and the coordinated effects of the merger.

---

66. Merger Guidelines, Part III, 2.

I. Safe Harbour

282. The Merger Guidelines disclose that the JFTC normally considers that a horizontal merger will not cause substantial restraint of competition in the market when a horizontal merger falls under either of the following range defined from i. to iii. below ('Safe Harbour') indicated by Herfindahl Hirschman Index (HHI) value after the merger and increment of HHI value:

i. HHI value after the merger is not more than 1,500;
ii. HHI value after the merger is more than 1,500 but not more than 2,500 while the increment of HHI value is not more than 250;
iii. HHI value after the merger is more than 2,500 while the increment of HHI value is not more than 150.[67]

283. The HHI value is calculated by summing squared market share of each company in a market. The market share of each company is the percentage of its sales volume to total sales volume in a market. When it is not appropriate to calculate the share based on the volume (e.g., when the price differs among products and sales results are usually calculated on monetary bases), the market share can be calculated by sales in monetary terms.

284. According to the guidelines, the possibility of a merger to substantially restrain competition is ordinarily considered little in the light of past cases in case the HHI value is not more than 2,500 and the market share of the company group after the merger is not more than 35%.

II. Unilateral Effects

A. Analytical Framework for Unilateral Effects

285. Depending on whether goods are homogenous or differentiated in a relevant market, the framework to examine the unilateral effects of a horizontal merger varies as follows.

1. Homogenous Goods

286. When goods are characterized as homogenous, customers of the goods can easily switch suppliers to the competitors if the merging parties raise the price. However, in some cases, the competitors cannot increase their sales without raising their prices, or the customers cannot switch suppliers to the competitors. In such cases, the merging parties are likely to have certain power to control the conditions

67. Merger Guidelines, Part IV, 1(3).

of transactions including price. As a result, the horizontal merger may have the effects of substantially restraining competition.

2. Differentiated Goods

287. Customers may buy goods of another brand that is next in their order to preference to the first brand when the price of the goods with the first brand is increased in case the goods are characterized as differentiated by brand, etc.; in other words, the goods have higher substitutability between these brands. The JFTC considers that the company group is likely to have certain power to control the conditions of transactions in a market where the companies are merging which compete each other by the goods with substitutable brands while other competitors do not sell such goods. As a result, the effects of the horizontal merger to substantially restrain competition may appear.

B. Factors to Be Considered in Deciding Substantial Restraint of Competition Through Unilateral Effects

288. To decide a horizontal merger may have unilateral effects of substantially restraining competition in a market, the JFTC comprehensively takes the following factors into consideration.

1. Position of the Company Group and the Competitive Situation in the Market

289. The market condition such as market share and competitive situation is crucial to evaluate the effect of the merger on competition in the market. The factors below are explained in detail in the Merger Guidelines:

i. Market Share and Ranking
The guidelines mention that the larger the market share the merging parties have or the larger they increase the market share after the merger, the larger the impact the merger will have on competition. Similarly, when the merger raises the ranking of the merging parties in terms of market share to a high position or raises it to a great degree, the merger will have much more impact on competition.
ii. Competition among the Parties, etc. in the Past
There are cases in which the merging parties have competed vigorously against each other or one of them has boosted the competition in the market. Such actions of the merging parties can lead to a price reduction or an improvement in the quality or variety of goods. In such cases, the merger may have a substantial impact on competition as it eliminated the possibility of the price reduction or quality improvement described above, even though the merging parties' share or their rank in the market is not high.
iii. Market Share Differences from Competitors

The guidelines mention that the larger the difference in market share between the merging parties and the competitors the larger the impact the merger will have on competition. In considering the difference in market share between the merging parties and their competitors, the JFTC also examines the surplus capacity of supply of the competitors and the degree of substitutability between goods sold by the merging company and those by the competitors.

iv. Competitors' Surplus Capacity of Supply and Degree of Differentiation
When the surplus capacity of supply of the competitors is not much, JFTC considers that the merger's impact on competition may be significant, even though the market share differences between the merging parties and the competitors are not large.[68]

2. Import

290. 'Import' refers to supply from outside the defined geographic market. The JFTC considers that the competitive pressure of imports may prevent the merging parties from exercising their power to control the conditions of transactions in the market if the imports are expected to increase within approximately two years when the merging parties raise the price of their goods. It examines all the conditions below when it determines whether import pressure is sufficient:

i. Degree of Institutional Barriers
When there are no institutional barriers, such as tariffs, import pressure will be probably stronger.

ii. Degree of Import-Related Transportation Cost, Problems in Distribution
When import-related transportation costs are low and there is no distribution problem for importing, import pressure will be probably promising.

iii. Degree of Substitutability Between the Imported Product and the Merging Parties' Product
When the substitutability of the merging parties' product with imported product is high, it is likely to serve strong incentive for customers to purchase and use the imported product.

iv. Potential for Supply from Overseas
When a foreign supplier has surplus capacity enough to increase supply without raising price, it will probably deter the merging parties from raising domestic prices.[69]

3. Entry

291. The JFTC also considers that the competitive pressure of entrance may diminish the negative impact of the merger on competition if a newcomer is

68. Merger Guidelines, Part IV. 2(1).
69. *Ibid.*, Part IV. 2(2).

expected to enter the market within approximately two years. It examines all the conditions below when evaluating entry pressure:

i. Degree of Institutional Barriers to Entry
   Entry pressure is likely to function to deter the merging parties from raising their price when there is no institutional barrier such as regulations to entry.
ii. Degree of Barriers to Entry in Practice
   The examples of barriers to entry in practice given in the Merger Guidelines are scale of capital for entry, technical issues and conditions for the purchase of raw materials, and sales conditions. Newcomers will be probably encouraged to enter, and the market environment will be conducive to entry when there is no problem with such barrier.
iii. Degree of Substitutability Between Entrants' Products and the Merging Parties' Product
   The customers are likely to switch their purchase to the entrant's product when the product that the entrant is planning to supply and the merging parties' product are highly substitutable.
iv. Potential for Market Entry
   It is necessary to assess the potential for market entry when the merging party increases the price of their product. Entry pressure is considered as higher when there is already a potential entrant with a significant scale to the market.[70]

4. Competitive Pressure from Related Market

292. The 'related market' implies the neighbour market means that the competing product (i.e., a product with similar utilities to customers) market or the geographic market neighbouring the defined market. When the probability of competing products replacing demand for such goods is high in the near future, it will be evaluated as a factor stimulating competition in the market. The same is applied when there is a vigorous competition in neighbouring markets.

5. Competitive Pressure from Customers

293. When customers have a countervailing bargaining power against the merging parties, it can be difficult for the merging parties to raise the price. To determine whether the customers have competitive pressure, factors such as competition among customers and possibility for customers to switch to other suppliers are considered.

70. *Ibid.*, Part IV. 2(3).

6. Overall Business Capabilities

294. After the merger, the merging parties' overall capacities, such as procurement ability or technical and marketing capabilities, can be increased. When the competitors will have difficulties to compete with the merging parties because of such overall business capabilities as a result of the merger, such a situation may be taken into consideration.

7. Efficiency

295. According to the Merger Guidelines, the efficiency of the merger is examined in the light of these aspects below:

- (i) Specificity to the Merger
  Improvements in efficiency, such as economics scale or integration of production facilities, should be specific to the merger. On the contrary, such improvement in efficiency is not considered specific to the merger when it can be achieved by any other means with less restrictive effect on competition,
- (ii) Materialization
  Improvements in efficiency should be materialized. In order to determine that, the JFTC may consider the merging parties' internal documents leading to the decision of the merger, explanatory material for the shareholders and so on.
- (iii) Contribution to the Interests of Customers
  The outcome of improvements in efficiency through the merger must be returned to customers through price reduction, improvement of quality, supply of new products, etc.[71]

8. Financial Conditions of the Company Group

296. To evaluate the business ability of the merging parties, the financial conditions, such as the business results of the merging parties, are also taken into consideration.

297. When one of the merging parties is considered as so-called the failing firm, the possibility of the horizontal merger to substantially restrain competition in the defined market by unilateral conduct is usually thought to be small. Similarly, it is considered that the acquisition of the 'failing division' does not usually cause problems on competition.

298. To be considered as the 'failing firm', it should be obvious that one of the merging parties would be highly likely to go bankrupt and exit the market in the near future without the merger. Moreover, it should be difficult to find any other

71. *Ibid.*, Part IV. 2(7).

companies that can rescue the party with a merger that should have less impact on competition. The same criteria are applied to the consideration of 'failing division'.

III. Coordinated Effects

A. Analytical Framework for Coordinated Effects

299. As a result of the reduction in the number of competitors by a merger, there may be a case that the competitors will be able to predict each other's behaviour easily and their coordinated conduct, such as following price raise could bring profits to them. Given market structure, such as the concentration of the defined market, the characteristic of the goods or trade practices, should be considered as well.

B. Factors to Be Considered in Deciding Substantial Restraint of Competition Through Coordinated Effects

300. The factors to be considered in the analysis of coordinated effects are almost the same as the determining factors for the unilateral effects.

§3. Vertical Mergers

301. The Merger Guidelines define the 'business combinations (vertical mergers)' as 'business combinations between companies which are in different trading positions, such as mergers between producers and its distributors'.

302. The guidelines indicate that vertical mergers do not reduce the number of units in a market and therefore they have less impact on competition than horizontal mergers.[72]

303. In examination of a vertical merger, the JFTC first determines whether that merger falls under one of the Safe Harbour criteria. If it does not, then, the JFTC determines both the unilateral effects and the coordinated effects of the merger.

I. Safe Harbour

304. The JFTC normally considers that a vertical or conglomerate merger will not cause substantial restraint of competition in a market when a vertical or conglomerate merger falls under the safe harbour which is indicated below:

72. *Ibid.*, Part III. 2.

i. The market share of the merging parties after the merger is not more than 10% in all of the defined market;
ii. The HHI value is not more than 2,500 and the market share of the merging parties after the merger is not more than 25% in all of the defined market.

305. According to the Merger Guidelines, the JFTC, in the light of past cases, considers that a merger will not ordinarily cause substantial restraint of competition when the HHI value is not more than 2,500 and the market share of the company group after the merger is not more than 35%.[73]

II. Unilateral Effects

306. It would be profitable for the merging parties to trade within the merging parties when a vertical merger is completed. As a result, there could be cases in which other companies would in fact lose opportunities to trade. In that case, the transactions within the merging parties may cause problems of closure or exclusivity.

307. When the market share of the merging parties is large, the company group is likely to have some ability to control the price and other factors, resulting from closure or exclusivity in trade within the merging parties through the vertical merger. In this case, the vertical merger may have effects of substantially restraining competition.

III. Coordinated Effects

308. The manufacturer can obtain information on the prices of competitors that deal with the distributor when a manufacturer and a distributor become combined vertically. As a result, manufacturers including the manufacturer of the merging parties might be able to predict each other's behaviour with higher probability. In these cases, the merging parties and their competitors are likely to have some ability to control the price and other factors; thus, the vertical merger may have effects of substantially restraining competition.

§4. Market/Product Extension Mergers

309. In the Merger Guidelines, 'conglomerate business combinations (conglomerate mergers)' are defined as "business combinations that are neither horizontal nor vertical ones. For instance, mergers between companies that engage in different types of business, or shareholdings between companies whose product ranges are in the same particular field of trade but whose geographic ranges are different."

---

73. *Ibid.*, Part V. 1(2).

310. The guidelines also indicate that conglomerate mergers do not reduce the number of units in a market and therefore, they have less impact on competition than horizontal mergers.[74]

311. In an examination of a conglomerate merger, the JFTC first determines whether that merger falls under one of the Safe Harbour criteria (the Safe Harbour criteria are the same as the ones of vertical mergers (see §3, I above)). If not, the JFTC determines both the unilateral effects and the coordinated effects of the merger.

312. Regarding the unilateral effects, the guidelines stipulate that a conglomerate merger may raise the problem of closure or exclusivity when it creates the overall business capabilities of the merging parties. In addition, the guidelines stipulate that it is also considered whether the mergers will eliminate the possibility of potential new entries if some of the parties are potential competitors of the other parties.[75]

§5. Pure Conglomerate Mergers

313. The views explained in §4 above are also applied to pure conglomerate merger cases.

§6. Joint Ventures

314. In the Merger Guidelines, 'a joint investment company' is defined as "a company jointly established or acquired by two or more companies through an agreement to pursue operations necessary to achieve mutual benefits."[76] A joint relationship between the investing companies may be formed through the joint investment company even if there is no direct shareholding relationship between the investing companies. The JFTC will examine how that fact will have an impact on competition when the business activities of the investing companies are integrated through the establishment of the joint investment company.

315. If only part of the divisions of each investing company is transferred to a joint investment company, a coordinated relationship between the investing companies may possibly be caused by the operation of the joint investment company. To determine whether a coordinated relationship between the investing companies will emerge or not, the specific details of the joint investment agreement, the actual combination and the transactions between the companies are considered. Whether the investing companies may take coordinated actions with other competitors is also considered.

74. *Ibid.*, Part III. 2.
75. *Ibid.*, Part VI. 2(1), (2).
76. *Ibid.*, Part I. 1(1) C.

Part III. Administrative Procedure

Chapter 1. Administrative Investigations Before the Antitrust Authority

§1. Initiative

I. Complaints

316. Information reported by the public to the JFTC is important for the JFTC to find a clue of a violation of the AMA and launch an investigation. Article 45 (1) stipulates that any person may report the fact to the JFTC and ask the JFTC to take appropriate measures whenever the person believes there to be a fact in violation of the AMA. Article 45 (2) stipulates that the JFTC shall make necessary investigations into the case when it receives such a report. Article 45(3) stipulates that the JFTC shall promptly notify the person who made the report of the result decision when it decides to take appropriate measures or to take no measures with respect to the case connected with the report in case where the report includes a written allegation with regard to the fact.

(Article 45)

(1) Whenever any person believes there to be a fact in violation of the provisions of this Act, the person may report the fact to the Fair Trade Commission and ask for appropriate measures to be taken.
(2) When the Fair Trade Commission receives a report as provided in the preceding paragraph, it must make the necessary investigations into the case.
(3) If a report made pursuant to the provisions of paragraph (1) includes a written allegation with regard to a specific fact pursuant to the provisions of the Rules of the Fair Trade Commission, when the Fair Trade Commission decides to take appropriate measures or to take no measures with respect to the case connected with the report, the Fair Trade Commission must promptly notify the person who made the report to that effect.

II. Ex Officio Investigations

317. Regarding an ex officio investigation, Article 45 (4) stipulates that the JFTC may take appropriate measures on its own authority whenever the JFTC believes there to be a fact in violation of the provisions of the AMA. Typically, the JFTC obtains information about simultaneous price raising in an industry by open resource such as newspapers and magazines, which leads to formal investigation of cartel case.

318. JFTC sometimes comes to believe existence of bid rigging through analysis of successful tenderers and their bidding, which support the information sent by the procurement bodies. Such analysis is an ex officio investigation.

(Article 45)

– *(4) Whenever the Fair Trade Commission believes there to be a fact in violation of the provisions of this Act or a fact falling under the purview of a monopolistic situation, the Fair Trade Commission may take appropriate measures on its own authority.*

III. Leniency Programme

A. General Remarks

319. Like many foreign competition authorities, the AMA legislation has also been equipped with the system to encourage cartel participants to voluntarily report on their violation by providing immunity or reduction of amount of surcharge. It is called as 'leniency programme' in Japan. Under this programme stipulated in paragraphs (10) to (18) of Articles 7-2, the JFTC grants immunity or reduction of amount of surcharge. Before the 2019 amendment, leniency application had been limited to up to five applicants in each case. The limitation was abolished by the 2019 amendment.

320. Concerning the relationship between leniency application and criminal accusation, the AMA provides that a crime under Articles 89 to 91 (unreasonable restraint of trade is included in these provisions) inclusive is considered only after an accusation is filed by the JFTC (Article 96 (1)). In this regard, the JFTC clearly stated in the Criminal Accusation and Investigation Policy[77] which is a policy statement of JFTC concerning criminal accusation and investigation that it would not file an accusation with the public prosecutor's office against the first successful leniency applicant who is immune from surcharge, not to make the person hesitate to apply for leniency for fear of being accused by the JFTC (*see* also Part IV, Chapter 3 below). On this point, the Ministry of Justice also supports the JFTC's policy above.

321. The leniency programme has been well functioning as a tool for cartel detection and investigation since its introduction in January 2006. The JFTC,

77. Fair Trade Commission's Policy on Criminal Accusation and Compulsory Investigation of Criminal Cases Regarding Antimonopoly Violations.

roughly speaking, has received successful leniency applications in more than 80% of the cartel cases where the JFTC took legal measures.

B. Procedure

322. The leniency programme consists of two parts, i.e., basic reduction based on the order of application for leniency and additional reduction according to the degree of cooperation to the JFTC's investigation.

(Article 7-4)

(1) Notwithstanding the provisions of Article 7-2, paragraph (1), the Fair Trade Commission may not order an enterprise that is to pay a surcharge pursuant to the provisions of Article 7-2, paragraph (1) to pay the surcharge if the enterprise falls under both of the following items:
  (i) the enterprise that is the first among the enterprises that committed the relevant violation to have individually submitted reports and materials regarding the facts of the violation to the Fair Trade Commission pursuant to the provisions of the Rules of the Fair Trade Commission (excluding when the reports and materials are submitted on or after the Investigation Start Date (the date on which the measure listed in Article 47, paragraph (1), item (iv) or the measure listed in Article 102, paragraph (1) was first taken; hereinafter the same applies in this Article) (or the date on which the enterprise received an advance notification in connection with the violation if neither the measure was taken; the same applies in the following item, in the following paragraph) for the case connected with the violation);
  (ii) the enterprise that has not committed the relevant violation since the Investigation Start Date for the case connected with the violation.
(2) In a case under Article 7-2, paragraph (1), the Fair Trade Commission is to reduce the relevant Surcharge Before Reduction (the surcharge calculated pursuant to the provisions of the preceding two Articles; hereinafter the same applies in this Article and the following Article) by twenty percent of the Surcharge Before Reduction, if the enterprise falls under item (i) and item (v) below by ten percent of the Surcharge Before Reduction, if the enterprise falls under item (ii) and (v) or item (iii) and (v) below, or by five percent of the Surcharge Before Reduction, if the enterprise falls under item (iv) and (v) below:
  (i) the enterprise that is the second among the enterprises that committed the relevant violation to have individually submitted reports and materials regarding the facts of the violation to the Fair Trade Commission pursuant to the provisions of the Rules of the Fair Trade Commission (excluding when the reports and materials are submitted on or after the Investigation Start Date for the case connected with the relevant violation);

(ii) the enterprise that is the third among the enterprises that committed the violation to have individually submitted reports and materials regarding the facts of the violation to the Fair Trade Commission pursuant to the provisions of the Rules of the Fair Trade Commission (excluding when the reports and materials are submitted on or after the Investigation Start Date for the case connected with the relevant violation);

(iii) the enterprise that is the fourth or fifth among the enterprises that committed the violation to have individually submitted reports and materials regarding the facts of the violation (excluding reports and materials related to the facts already ascertained by the Fair Trade Commission through the report provided in Article 45, paragraph (1), or the measures as provided in paragraph (4) of the same Article, or other means; the same applies in the following item) to the Fair Trade Commission pursuant to the provisions of the Rules of the Fair Trade Commission (excluding when the reports and materials are submitted on or after the Investigation Start Date for the case connected with the relevant violation;

(iv) the enterprise that is the sixth or thereafter among the enterprises that committed the relevant violation to have individually submitted reports and materials regarding the facts of the violation to the Fair Trade Commission pursuant to the provisions of the Rules of the Fair Trade Commission (excluding when the reports and materials are submitted on or after the Investigation Start Date for the case connected with the relevant violation);

(v) the enterprise that has not committed the relevant violation since the Investigation Start Date for the case connected with the relevant violation.

(3) In a case under Article 7-2, paragraph (1), the Fair Trade Commission is to reduce the relevant Surcharge Before Reduction by ten percent of the Surcharge Before Reduction, if the enterprise falls under item (i) and item (iii) below, or five percent of the Surcharge Before Reduction, if the enterprise falls under item (ii) and (iii) below:

(i) In a case where the enterprises that submitted reports and materials regarding the relevant violation pursuant to the provisions of item (i) of paragraph (1) or items (i) to (iii) inclusive of the preceding paragraph number fewer than five, the enterprise that individually submitted reports and materials regarding facts of the violation (excluding reports and materials related to the facts already ascertained by the Fair Trade Commission through the measures listed in the items under Article 47, paragraph (1) or provided in Article 102, paragraph (1), or other means; the same applies in the following item) to the Fair Trade Commission pursuant to the provisions of the Rules of the Fair Trade Commission, by the date set in the Rules of the Fair Trade Commission on or after the Investigation Start Date for the case connected with the relevant violation (limited to when the sum of the enterprise who submitted reports and materials pursuant to the provisions of item (i) of paragraph (1) or items (i) to (iii) inclusive of the preceding paragraph and the enterprise that submitted reports and materials pursuant to the provisions of this item numbers five or fewer, and when the total number of the enterprise who submitted reports and materials pursuant to the provisions of this item is three or fewer);

(ii) the enterprise that individually submitted reports and materials regarding facts of the violation to the Fair Trade Commission pursuant to the provisions of the Rules of the Fair Trade Commission, by the date set in the Rules of the Fair Trade Commission on or after the Investigation Start Date for the case connected with the relevant violation (excluding the enterprises that fall under the previous item);

(iii) the enterprise that has not committed the relevant violation since the date of submission of the reports and materials provided in the preceding two items.

(4) If two or more enterprises (limited to when the enterprises are corporations) that have violated the provisions of Article 7-2, paragraph (1) have jointly submitted reports and materials regarding the facts of the relevant violation to the Fair Trade Commission pursuant to the provisions of the Rules of the Fair Trade Commission, the relevant reports and materials are deemed to have been submitted individually and the provisions of the preceding three paragraphs apply to the two or more enterprises who have submitted the relevant reports and materials, as long as the two or more enterprises fall under item (i) below and either item (ii) or (iii) below. In such cases, the two or more enterprises are deemed to be a single enterprise for the purposes of the calculation of the number of the enterprises who have submitted the reports and materials provided in paragraph (1), item (i), paragraph (2), items (i) to (iv) inclusive and item (i) and (ii) of the preceding paragraph:

(i) that, at the time of the submission of the relevant reports and materials, the two or more enterprises are related as co-subsidiaries, etc.;

(ii) that, among the relevant two or more enterprises, the one that committed the violation in concert with another of the two or more enterprises, was related to the other enterprise as a co-subsidiary, etc. for the entire period during which it committed the relevant violation in concert with the other enterprise (limited to within ten years preceding the date on which the relevant reports or materials were submitted);

(iii) that a fact that falls under either of the following exists with regard to one of the two or more enterprises that has not committed the violation in concert with another of the relevant two or more enterprises:

(a) the enterprise has transferred all or part of the business involved in the violation to another enterprise of the relevant two or more enterprises or has alienated all or part of the business involved in the violation through a company split, and the relevant other enterprise commenced the relevant violation on the date of the relevant transfer or of the company split;

(b) the enterprise has received all or part of the business connected to the violation from another enterprise of the relevant two or more enterprises or has succeeded to all or part of the business connected to the relevant violation through a company split, and first committed the violation on the date of the relevant transfer or of the company split.

(5) Whenever the Fair Trade Commission receives the submission of reports and materials provided in item (i) of paragraph (1), items (i) to (iv) inclusive of paragraph (2), or item (i) or (ii) of paragraph (3), the Fair Trade Commission must promptly notify the enterprise that submitted the relevant reports and materials to that effect in writing.

(6) Prior to issuing an order pursuant to the provisions of Article 7-2, paragraph (1) or a notice pursuant to the provisions of the following paragraph or Article 7-7, paragraph (3) to an enterprise that submitted reports and materials regarding the fact provided in item (i) of paragraph (1), items (i) to (iv) inclusive of paragraph (2), or item (i) or (ii) of paragraph (3), the Fair Trade Commission may additionally request the relevant enterprise to submit reports or materials regarding the facts of the violation, excluding cases of agreements in paragraph (1) of the following Article (including the agreement which contains the engagement in the acts listed in each of the items of paragraph (2) of the following Article).

(7) If the Fair Trade Commission has decided not to order the payment of a surcharge pursuant to the provisions of paragraph (1), it is to notify the relevant enterprise in writing of that decision at the time it issues an order, pursuant to the provisions of Article 7-2, paragraph (1), to enterprises other than the enterprise regarding the case connected with the violation committed by the enterprises who fall under the provisions of paragraph (1) (by the time provided in the Rules of the Fair Trade Commission if the Fair Trade Commission does not issue an order pursuant to the provisions).

(Article 7-5)

(1) When the Fair Trade Commission receives the application for conference regarding the acts listed in the following items from an enterprise that submits reports and materials regarding the facts pursuant to the provisions of items (i) to (iv) inclusive of paragraph (2) or item (i) or (ii) of paragraph (3) of the previous Article (hereinafter referred to in this Article as the 'Reporting (etc.) Enterprise'), the Fair Trade Commission is to confer with the Reporting (etc.) Enterprise, and may enter into an agreement on the acts of the Reporting (etc.) Enterprise listed in item (i) below and the acts of the Fair Trade Commission listed in item (ii) below with the Reporting (etc.) Enterprise, pursuant to the provisions of the Rules of the Fair Trade Commission, taking into consideration the content of the fact pertaining to the matters provided in the Rules of the Fair Trade Commission as those contributing to revealing the truth of the case which are obtained from the facts reported or materials submitted pursuant to the provisions of items (i) to (iv) inclusive of paragraph (2) or item (i) or (ii) of paragraph (3) of the

previous Article or expected to be obtained from the facts or materials reported or submitted by the acts listed in item (i) below or other circumstances:

(i) the following acts

(a) reporting the facts or submitting the materials which the Reporting (etc.) Enterprise offered, in the conference, to report or submit to the Fair Trade Commission immediately after the agreement;

(b) reporting the facts, submitting the materials or consenting to the inspection of the materials of the Reporting (etc.) Enterprise by the Fair Trade Commission (referred to simply as 'inspection' in (c) below and (b) of item (i), in the following paragraph) or conducting other acts at the request of the Fair Trade Commission, regarding the facts or materials obtained from the submission of the reports and materials provided in items (i) to (iv) inclusive of paragraph (2) of the preceding Article or item (i) or (ii) of paragraph (3), or from the acts listed in (a);

(c) reporting the facts, submitting the materials or consenting to the inspection or conducting other acts, at the request of the Fair Trade Commission, regarding the facts revealed by the investigation of the Fair Trade Commission.

(ii) reducing the relevant Surcharge Before Reduction by the Surcharge Before Reduction multiplied by a rate specified in the relevant agreement (referred to as the 'Specified Rate' in item (ii) of the following paragraph and paragraph (3)) within the scope of rates provided in the (a) or (b) below (referred to as the 'Upper Limit Rate' in item (ii) in the following paragraph) according to the category of the enterprises listed in (a) or (b) below:

(a) the enterprise that submitted reports and materials regarding the facts provided items (i) to (iv) inclusive of paragraph (2) of the preceding Article: not more than forty percent;

(b) the enterprise that submitted reports and materials regarding the facts provided in item (i) or (ii) of paragraph (3) of the preceding Article: not more than twenty percent.

(2) In cases where the facts or materials obtained from acts listed in item (i) of the preceding paragraph, explained by the Reporting (etc.) Enterprise in the conference in the same paragraph are necessary for prompt revealing the truth of the case, and the Reporting (etc.) Enterprise are found to be likely to ascertain new facts or materials regarding the relevant case which are related to the facts with respect to the matters provided in the Rules of the Fair Trade Commission in paragraph (1) after the agreement set forth in the same paragraph, when the existence of conditions are found where a certain period is necessary for the submission of the new facts or materials, the Fair Trade Commission may request ,in the conference, the Reporting (etc.) Enterprise to make the agreement in which the Reporting (etc.) Enterprise conducts the acts listed in item (i) below in addition to the acts

listed in item (i) of the preceding paragraph, and the Fair Trade Commission conducts the acts listed in item (ii) below instead of the acts listed in item (ii) of the preceding paragraph:

(i) the following acts

(a) reporting the new facts or submitting the new materials to the Fair Trade Commission immediately when the new facts or materials are ascertained after the agreement;

(b) reporting the facts, submitting the materials or consenting to the inspection or conducting other acts, at the request of the Fair Trade Commission, regarding the facts or materials obtained from the acts listed in (a).

(ii) reducing the relevant Surcharge Before Reduction by the Surcharge Before Reduction multiplied by a rate decided by the Fair Trade Commission based on its assessment of the contents of the facts relevant to the matters provided in the Rules of the Fair Trade Commission set forth in the previous paragraph obtained from the acts listed in the preceding item, not exceeding the sum of the Specified Rate and the rate stipulated in the agreement pursuant to the provisions in the Rules of the Fair Trade Commission for the acts listed in the preceding item (limited to the rate below Upper Limit Rate) (referred to as the 'After Assessment Rate' in the following paragraph and paragraph (5)).

(3) In a case under paragraph (1), Article 7-2, when there is an agreement set forth in paragraph (1) (including the agreement which contains the engagement in the acts listed in each of the items in the preceding paragraph; the same applies in this Article and the following Article) the Fair Trade Commission is to reduce the relevant Surcharge Before Reduction by the sum of the amount to be reduced pursuant to paragraph (2) or (3) of the preceding Article and the Surcharge Before Reduction multiplied by the Specified Rate or After the Assessment Rate according to the contents of the agreement.

(4) The agreement set forth in paragraph (1) is to be concluded with its contents clarified in writing on which the Fair Trade Commission and the Reporting (etc.) Enterprise sign or register and seal.

(5) If the agreement in [sic] set forth in paragraph (1) which contains the engagement in the acts listed in item (ii) of paragraph (2) is to be concluded, The Fair Trade Commission is to state the method of the assessment and the decision of the After Assessment Rate in the writing set forth in the preceding paragraph.

(6) In the conference set forth in paragraph (1), the Fair Trade Commission may request the Reporting, (etc.) Enterprise to explain an overview of the facts or materials that it may report or submit through the acts listed in paragraph (1), item (i) (a).

(7) If the agreement set forth in paragraph (1) is not reached (excluding the cases where the Reporting, (etc.) Enterprise does not respond to the request set forth in paragraph (2) and the agreement which contains only an engagement in the acts listed in each of the items of paragraph (1) was

reached), the Fair Trade Commission may not use the documents and other materials that record the explanation by the Reporting, (etc.) Enterprise at the conference set forth in paragraph (1) as evidence.

(8) The necessary procedures regarding the conference set forth in paragraph (1) such as the deadline for application of conference shall be prescribed by the Rules of the Fair Trade Commission.

(9) The Reporting (etc.) Enterprise may appoint agents (limited to attorneys or legal profession corporations; referred to as 'Specified Agents' in the following paragraph and paragraph (11)) at the time of the conference set forth in paragraph (1).

(10) The Fair Trade Commission is to inform the Reporting (etc.) Enterprise in writing that Specified Agents may be appointed at the time of the conference set forth in paragraph (1).

(11) With respect to the application of the provisions of paragraph (1) and (4) when the Reporting (etc.) Enterprise appoints Specified Agents pursuant to the provisions of paragraph (9), the term ' confer with the Reporting (etc.) Enterprise' in paragraph (1) is deemed to be replaced with ' confer with the Reporting (etc.) Enterprise or Specified Agents (meaning the Specified Agents as provided in paragraph (9); the same applies in paragraph (4)', and the term 'and Reports, etc. enterprise' in paragraph (4) is deemed to be replaced with ' the Reporting (etc.) Enterprise and the Specified Agents'.

323. Table 3 is the chart describing how the leniency programme is applied and how much reduction the leniency applicant can receive in each case, presented by the Leniency Guidelines.[78]

Table 3 Application of Reduction Rates to the Applicants

Investigation start date	Order of the application	Reduction rates according to the order of the application	Reduction rates according to the degree of contribution to revealing the truth of the case
Before investigation	First	100% (immunity)	
	Second	20%	Up to 40%
	Third to fifth	10%	
	Sixth and after	5%	

78. Guidelines to Reduction System for Cooperation in Investigation.

Investigation start date	Order of the application	Reduction rates according to the order of the application	Reduction rates according to the degree of contribution to revealing the truth of the case
After investigation	Up to three (up to five including applicants which apply before the investigation start date)	10%	Up to 20%
	Other than above	5%	

Source: Leniency Guidelines, Table 1 (The reduction rates in the New Leniency Program) with modification by authors.

324. The leniency applicant before the commencement date of JFTC's investigation must submit a report on the outline of the violation (Form 1) via email to the address stipulated in the Leniency Rules.[79] After that, the applicant is required to submit more information (Form 2 and related materials they have) such as the name of the enterprises that jointly committed the violation. Under a certain circumstance, a part of the Form 2 report can be replaced with an oral report. The applicant must not engage in the violation since the commencement of the JFTC's investigation.

The email address for the leniency application is as follows:
genmen-2020@jftc.go.jp

325. Enterprises can submit the leniency application (Form 3 and related materials they have) even after the commencement date of the JFTC's investigation. In a certain circumstance, a part of the Form 3 report also can be replaced with an oral report. The applicant must not engage in the violation since the submission of the report to the JFTC.

326. The applicants who are fourth or after and applied before the start of the JFTC's investigation and who applied after the JFTC's investigation should submit reports and materials regarding the facts of the violation including something that the JFTC has not yet ascertained. If the reports and materials submitted by these applicants do not include any facts which are new to the JFTC, reduction is not granted.

79. Rules on Reporting the Facts and Submitting the Materials regarding Immunity from or Reduction of Surcharge.

327. In order for the subsequent leniency applicants to receive additional reduction after filing Form 1 or 3 above, they have to make a request for conference in which the JFTC and the applicants discuss what cooperation will be made in the course of investigation. In the conference, the applicant explains the content of cooperation, for example, what kind of documents or materials they have. The JFTC considers and evaluates the contents and value with regard to its investigation and presents the reduction rate.

328. The reduction rate consists of two parts. First one is the fixed rate which is granted if the applicant fulfils the conditions with regard to documents and materials which they ascertain by the time of the agreement. Second one is the range with upper and lower limits with regard to documents and materials which they will probably ascertain shortly after the agreement. After the evaluation of the value of the evidence ascertained and submitted after the agreement, the rate will be determined between the ranges.

329. When the applicant and the JFTC agree on the contents of cooperation and the reduction rate, the applicant cooperates with the JFTC abiding by the agreement and receives the additional reduction after fulfilling the conditions stipulated in the agreement. In case where the two parties have not reached an agreement, the JFTC shall not use record which the applicant has presented in the conference even if the JFTC has recorded the applicant's explanation about the information during the conference.

330. The evaluation of evidence such as information and documents that the leniency applicants voluntarily submit to the JFTC is explained in the Leniency Guidelines. They state that the JFTC evaluates applicant's cooperation from the viewpoint of how much the submitted evidence contributes to fact-finding. They also explain the information which the JFTC evaluate, e.g., rule to decide the winner of bid, participants, the period of implementation, implementation status, and the JFTC determines the reduction rates according to the content of the information.

C. Disqualification from the Leniency Programme

331. When the JFTC finds the fact falling under any of the following, the leniency applicant will be disqualified from the leniency programme. The cases in which the applicant will be disqualified are as follows:

- Reports or materials submitted to the JFTC contain false information.
- Applicant failed to submit reports or materials that the JFTC required.
- Applicants coerced other enterprises to commit the violation or blocked other enterprises from discontinuing the relevant violation.
- Applicants blocked other enterprises from cooperating with the JFTC by using the leniency programme.

– Applicants disclosed to a third party without justifiable grounds the fact that they had applied for the leniency programme.

IV. Market Surveys

332. The JFTC often conducts surveys on the status of specific markets. Most of them are not to obtain the clue of investigation case but to identify general issues in the selected area; however, some of them significantly provide the JFTC with information on a certain type of offense such as unfair trade practices.

333. The JFTC sometimes employ a provision that mandates it to execute research with penalty for negligence, at conducting market study. It emphasizes this provision as a non-investigating tool for collecting information and monitoring restricting business practices in specific sectors including IT & Digital related markets. In this regard, the JFTC established the Survey Implementation rules[80] to enhance effectiveness of this provision in 2022. The AMA sets out as follows:

> (Article 40)
>
> The Fair Trade Commission may, if necessary for the performance of its duties, order public offices, juridical persons formed by special laws and regulations, enterprises or organizations of enterprises, or their personnel to appear before the Fair Trade Commission, or require them to submit necessary reports, information or materials.
>
> (Article 94-2)
>
> A person who, in violation of the measures pursuant to the provisions of Article 40, has failed to appear or to submit a report, information or materials, or submitted a false report, information or materials is punished by a fine of not more than three million yen.

§2. Powers

334. Regarding the administrative investigation, Article 47 of the AMA sets out the power and duties of the JFTC. Article 94 of the AMA provides punishment for violation of the measures taken under Article 47:

> (Article 47)
>
> (1) In order to conduct the necessary investigation with regard to a case, the Fair Trade Commission may take the following measures:

---

80. Rules on Disposition Pursuant to Article 40 of Act on Prohibition of Private Monopolization and Maintenance of Fair Trade.

(i) order persons concerned with a case or witness to appear to be interrogated, or to collect their opinions or reports;
(ii) order expert witnesses to appear to give expert opinions;
(iii) order persons holding books and documents and other object to submit such objects, or keep such submitted objects at the Fair Trade Commission;
(iv) enter any business office of the persons concerned with a case or other necessary sites, and inspect conditions of business operation and property, books and documents, and other materials.

(2) If the Fair Trade Commission finds it to be appropriate, it may designate a staff member of the Fair Trade Commission as an investigator pursuant to Cabinet Order, and cause the staff member to take the measures set forth in the preceding paragraph.
(3) If the Fair Trade Commission causes a staff member to conduct an on-site inspection pursuant to the provisions of the preceding paragraph, the Fair Trade Commission must instruct the staff member to carry an identification card and to present it to the persons concerned.
(4) The authority to take measures pursuant to the provisions of paragraph (1) must not be construed as being granted for conducting criminal investigation.

(Article 94)

A person who falls under any of the following items is punished by imprisonment with work for not more than one year or by a fine of not more than three million yen:

(i) a person concerned with a case or any witness who, in violation of the measures taken against them, pursuant to the provisions of Article 47, paragraph (1), item (i) or paragraph (2), has failed to appear or to make a statement, or has made a false statement, or failed to submit a report, or submitted a false report;
(ii) an expert witness who, in violation of the measures taken with regard to them, pursuant to the provisions of Article 47, paragraph (1), item (ii) or paragraph (2), has failed to appear or to give an expert opinion, or submitted a false expert opinion;
(iii) a holder of the materials who, in violation of the objects taken with regard to them pursuant to the provisions of Article 47, paragraph (1), item (iii) or paragraph (2), has failed to submit the objects;
(iv) a person who has refused, obstructed or evaded the inspection pursuant to the provisions of Article 47, paragraph (1), item (iv) or paragraph (2).

I. Request for Information

335. Article 47(1)(i) stipulates that JFTC may collect opinions or reports from persons concerned with a case or witness. The JFTC usually makes an on-site inspection pursuant to Article 47(1)(v) (hereinafter referred to as the 'On-site Inspection') first and then collect reports from the enterprises if necessary.

336. The JFTC also stipulates the procedure and other matters in the Investigation Rules[81] and gives details of such request for information in the Investigation Procedure Guidelines,[82] as follows.

A. *Grounds and Legal Nature*

337. As stated in I above, the JFTC has a power to order a person concerned with an alleged violation to report information necessary for case investigation (hereinafter referred to as 'Reporting Order'). A person concerned with an alleged violation will be punished if he disobeys the order and fails to make a report or makes a false report pursuant to Article 94.

338. Nevertheless, the JFTC is used to ask the person concerned with an alleged violation to submit a report based on voluntary cooperation, rather than issuing the Reporting Order.

B. *Procedures for an Order to Report*

339. When the JFTC issues the Reporting Order to the person concerned with an alleged violation, it shall do that by serving a writ of report pursuant to Article 9 of the Investigation Rules. The person should make a report in a designated form attached to the written order. The order also contains relevant provisions of the AMA, the reporting deadline, and punishment imposed if they disobey the order (Article 94(i)).

340. The JFTC usually gives them a request for report containing the reporting deadline, attached with the form of a report in writing, when it asks the person to submit the report on a voluntary basis.

II. Investigating and Search Powers

341. The Investigation Procedure Guidelines give the details of the procedure of the JFTC's On-site Inspection as follows.

81. Rules on Japan Fair Trade Commission Investigations.
82. Guidelines on Administrative Investigation Procedures under the Antimonopoly Act.

A. Grounds and Legal Nature

342. As stated above, the JFTC has a power to enter a business office of companies involved in an alleged violation or other necessary sites to inspect conditions of their business operation, and property, books, documents, and other materials by On-site Inspection. Further, pursuant to item (iii) of the same paragraph, the JFTC is empowered to order the person who holds books, documents and other objects that are deemed necessary for case investigations to submit such materials and a right to retain them at the JFTC.

343. The On-site Inspection and other dispositions under Article 47(1)(iv) are indirectly enforceable in a sense that for administrative purposes, the parties concerned with an alleged violation are bound by the obligation to cooperate with the investigation, and the performance of the obligation is guaranteed by punishment pursuant to Article 94(iv). It means that the AMA allows the parties, on their own discretion, to decide whether to refuse the JFTC's disposition when they believe they have reasonable grounds to do so. The legitimacy of their refusal is to be judged in the court ex post facto, and the JFTC is, therefore, unable to directly or physically exercise its power to conduct the investigation on the spot.

344. In addition to the On-site Inspection, the JFTC may visit a business office of the parties concerned or other places to request them, for example, to submit materials based on their voluntary cooperation.

B. Procedures and Explanations Given for On-Site Inspection

345. At the time of an On-site Inspection, the investigator shall present its identification card to a person in charge of the place subject to On-site Inspection and then deliver a notification pursuant to Article 20 of the Investigation Rules. The notification is to notify the person that the investigation is performed under the administrative procedure and inform the title of a case, main point of the alleged fact as well as applicable provisions of the AMA, etc. It also requests cooperation to ensure smooth achievement of inspection. Further, the investigator shall explain to the person in charge that he will be punished if the party concerned refuses to cooperate with the inspection, pursuant to Article 94.

346. On the other hand, the investigator shall declare that the inspection is not conducted based on Article 47 when the investigator gives a request for submission of materials on voluntary basis with consent of the party concerned at the place where he visits.

C. Scope of On-Site Inspection

347. Investigator can perform On-site Inspection at a place that he reasonably considers necessary for case investigations, regardless of the name of the place such as the sales department, accounting department, etc. of the parties concerned with an alleged violation. Thus, even a residence of its employee can be subject to On-site Inspection when the investigator suspects that the materials related to alleged violation are present there and reasonably considers it necessary for case investigation.

D. Procedures Related to Submission and Retention of Materials

348. The investigator can give an order the party to submit materials to the extent that he reasonably considers necessary for case investigations. The materials contain those which are highly private, such as personal belongings (day planner, mobile phone, etc.) when the investigator suspects that such goods contain information useful to prove an alleged violation and reasonably considers it necessary for case investigation:

- In the case of receiving an order to submit, the party should submit originals of relevant materials on an as-is basis. As for electronic data stored on a server, client's PC, etc. (including e-mails, for example), the investigator will order to make a copy of them and store in recorded media (including client's PC itself as necessary).
- When the investigator orders the party to submit and retain the related materials to the case, he is to attach a list of the retained materials to a writ of submission and a notice on retained materials (Articles 9 to 16, Investigation Rules). Such list shall contain the titles of accounting books, documents and other materials with notes on the locations where they were present, the persons who held or managed them, etc. In the case of retention, the investigator shall show each item subject to On-site Inspection in front of a person in charge and check them with the list.
- The party concerned can ask the investigator to make copies of the materials that are subject to submission order of the JFTC, when he considers it necessary to keep them for daily use in the business, as long as it does not affect the investigation of the JFTC. The JFTC, however, admits that just for practical reasons, not as officially authorized right of the party concerned, the request for making copies of the retained materials is also accepted even after the On-spot inspection (Article 18, Investigation Rules).
- Any retained material that no longer needs to be held in custody shall promptly be returned (Article 17, Investigation Rules).

E. Presence of an Attorney During On-Site Inspection

349. The JFTC shall make a person in charge of management of the place under On-site Inspection to be present there during the inspection, as well as permit the attorney to perform witness unless it affects the inspection.

350. The JFTC, however, admits that just for practical reason, not as officially authorized right of the party concerned, does not delay the start of inspection even if the attorney does not appear in time.

III. Deposition

351. The investigators usually make deposition by interviews with the persons concerned with alleged violation in the course of collecting evidence. The Investigation Procedure Guidelines give the details of the procedures of the JFTC to interrogate the persons concerned as follows.

A. Grounds and Legal Nature

352. Interviews can be classified into two types: the interview on a voluntary basis and the interrogation executed with legal authority. The former one is conducted in cooperation with interviewees while the latter is mandatory one underpinned by Article 47(1)(i) of the AMA.

B. Procedures and Explanations Given for Interview

1. Voluntary Interview

353. As for voluntary interview, the investigator contacts the interviewee to confirm his/her schedule, directly or through the company involved in an alleged violation or his/her agent, makes clear in each case that the interview is voluntary based and then obtains its consent prior to the interview.

354. The investigator initially (at the opening of the first session when there are several sessions in the interview) presents its identification card to an interviewee. Next, the investigator explains that the interview is proceeded on voluntary basis and that the interviewee is required to state the facts based on his experience and recognition for fact-finding in the case at issue. In addition, the investigator explains as necessary that the procedure for mandatory interrogation may be initiated if the interviewee does not cooperate with a voluntary interview.

355. In the light of due process, the procedure of voluntary interview does not seem to grant little rights of interviewees, such as rights of silence or privilege of self-incrimination. It may be one of the reasons why the AMA does not provide the rights of interviewee that the JFTC relies on voluntary-based interview and depends on cooperation of the interviewee, and therefore the JFTC may not punish the interviewee even if he/she makes no reply during the interview.

2. Interrogation

356. The procedure of interrogation is usually accompanied with summons (an order to appear before the JFTC for interview). This means that the deponent who fails to appear or makes statements without justifiable reasons or makes false statements may be subject to punishment (Article 94(i)). The JFTC sends summons to natural persons respectively (Article 9 [Investigation Rules]). The summons contains the relevant provisions of the act, the date and place of appearance, and punishment imposed if the deponent disobeys the order (Article 94(i)).

357. The investigator initially presents his identification card to deponent and explains the legal nature of interrogation (the fact that interrogation is based on Article 47 of the AMA) and that the JFTC can impose punishment on the deponent if he/she refuses to make statements or makes false statements.

C. Prohibited Conducts of Investigator

358. The investigator shall not use intimidation, coercion or other means that may cause any suspicion about the voluntariness of interview in the course of interview. The investigator is also prohibited to induce a statement by, for example, implying his expectation and desires to the interviewee, or promising the interviewee to provide benefits in exchange for a certain statement.

D. Length of Interview

359. In general, an interview shall not span more than eight hours (excluding breaks) per day. The investigator shall obtain the consent of the interviewee if he foresees the interview will exceed eight hours on the day. The investigator should finish the interview by 10:00 pm unless there is an unavoidable reason.

360. The investigator shall also ensure that the interviewee can have a break time appropriately and in a timely manner, considering the party's physical condition, if the interview continues for long hours.

361. The interviewee will not generally impose any restriction on his/her activities during the break time, including contacting his/her attorney and other external persons, or taking notes based on his/her own memory.

362. When taking an interview, the investigator shall record the length of the interview and break times.

E. Procedures for Preparing Records and Affixing Signatures and Seals

363. The investigator shall prepare records of statement when he deems it necessary to do so in case where the interviewee makes a voluntary statement. On the other hand, the investigator must prepare records of interrogation when he interrogates a deponent pursuant to Articles 47(1) and 48 of the AMA (Article 10, 11 and 13 [Investigation Rules]).

364. The investigator is required to accurately record the content of statements given by interviewee that are related to the relevant case and are deemed necessary in order to make it evident to prove the fact of violation. It is not necessary, however, to record the contents of statements given by a testifying party word by word, as in the case of shorthand notes.

365. The investigator shall read out the records of voluntary statement to the interviewee or have the interviewee to peruse it and ask the interviewee if it contains any error when the investigator prepares them. It applies to records of interrogation.

366. The investigator shall have the interviewee affix his/her signature and seal on the records to complete them when he/she says that there is no error. When he/she makes a request to add, delete or change the statement he/she made, the investigator shall confirm his/her request and then modify the languages with the notes of his/her request on the record. Then, the investigator has the interviewee affix his/her signature and seal on the records.

367. In case where the interviewee refuses to affix his/her signature and seal despite he/she does not claim any error, the investigator shall write down such fact on the records (Articles 11 and 13 [Investigation Rules]).

IV. Cooperation with Other State Institutions

368. The JFTC is a sole authority of antitrust enforcement and has no relationship of cooperation with any other institution including local governments.

§3. PROCEDURE AND RIGHT OF DEFENCE

I. General Remarks

369. Before issuing a Cease and Desist Order, the JFTC shall conduct a procedure for hearing opinions of the would-be addressee of the order (hereinafter referred to as 'Procedures for Hearing') pursuant to Article 49. The same applies to the procedure regarding a Payment Order, basically (Article 62).

370. So-called Attorney Client Privileges are not accepted in the Japanese legal system. Therefore, in the process of case investigation regarding possible antimonopoly law violation, enterprises and their attorneys are not able to assert the privileges. However, taking opportunity of the 2019 amendment, a new system was introduced to protect confidential communications between an enterprise and an attorney concerning administrative investigation procedure concerning unreasonable restraint of trade cases (*see* III below) Though it is neither stipulated by the law nor applied to all the violation, it can be a milestone to pave the way for the attorney client privileges to be accepted in Japan.

II. Procedures for Hearing

A. Hearing, Access to File, Briefs

1. Hearing

371. The Procedure for Hearing is initiated by a notification to the would-be addressee of the Cease and Desist Order. Article 50 provides that the JFTC shall give a notification in a written form in advance which contains the expected contents of the Cease and Desist Order, the facts found by the Fair Trade Commission, and the application of laws and regulations. It also provides information of an oral hearing (hereinafter referred to as 'hearing') and generally called as *Jizentsuchi.*

372. Hearing is presided over by a JFTC official designated by the Fair Trade Commission (hereinafter referred to as 'Hearing Officer'). On the first date of the Hearing, the investigator in charge of the case explains the expected content of the Cease and Desist Order (Article 54(1)). At the Hearing, the person who received the notification (hereinafter referred to as the 'Party') may state their opinions, submit evidence, and, with the permission of the Hearing Officer, ask questions to the investigators (Article 54(2)).

373. After the end of the Hearing, the Hearing Officer prepares a record of the Hearing including the opinions of the party, etc., on the date (Article 58). The Hearing Officer also prepares a report describing the points at issue in the case and submits it to the Commission after the conclusion of the Hearing. The Party may request inspection of these records and reports.

374. The Commission will make a decision on a Cease and Desist Order, taking into consideration the records and reports (Article 60). The same procedure will be followed in the case of a hearing concerning a Payment Order.

> (Article 49)
>
> If the Fair Trade Commission seeks to issue an order pursuant to the provisions of Article 7, paragraphs (1) or (2) (including the cases where they are

applied mutatis mutandis pursuant to Article 8-2, paragraph (2) and Article 20, paragraph (2)); Article 8-2, paragraphs (1) or (3); Article 17-2; or Article 20, paragraph (1) ..., it must conduct a hearing of opinions with the would-be addressee of the Cease and Desist Order.

(Article 50)

(1) In a hearing set forth in the preceding Article, the Fair Trade Commission must notify the would-be addressee of the Cease and Desist Order of the following matters in writing, by a reasonable period of time prior to the date of hearing:
   (i) the expected contents of the Cease and Desist Order;
   (ii) the facts found by the Fair Trade Commission, and the application of laws and regulations thereto;
   (iii) the date and place of hearing;
   (iv) the name and location of the organization which has jurisdiction over affairs relating to hearing.
(2) The written notice set forth in the preceding paragraph must inform the following matters:
   (i) that the would-be addressee of the Cease and Desist Order may state its opinions and submit evidence on the date of hearing or submit a written statement and evidence instead of appearance on the date of hearing;
   (ii) that the would-be addressee of the Cease and Desist Order, until the conclusion of the hearing, may request inspection and a copy of evidence pursuant to the provisions of Article 52.

(Article 53)

(1) The procedures for hearing is to be presided by the staff member designated by the Fair Trade Commission for each case (hereinafter referred to as the 'Designated Staff Member').
(2) The Fair Trade Commission may not designate any staff member who performed the duties of an investigator with respect to the case pursuant to the preceding paragraph and any other staff members who conducted the administrative affairs pertaining to investigations into the relevant case as the presiding staff member for hearing.

(Article 54)

(1) The Designated Staff Member is to have the investigators designated pursuant to Article 47, paragraph (2) with respect to the case for which the procedures for hearing must be taken and any other staff members who conducted the administrative affairs pertaining to investigations into the relevant case (in the following paragraph and paragraph (3), and Article 56, paragraph (1), referred to as the 'investigators, etc.') explain to the Party appearing on the date of hearing the expected content of the Cease and

Desist Order, the facts found by the Fair Trade Commission and major evidence among those provided for Article 52, paragraph (1), and the application of laws and regulations to the facts found by the Fair Trade Commission at the outset of the first date of the hearing.

(2) The Party may appear on the date of hearing, state its opinions and submit evidence and also address questions to the investigators, etc. with the permission of the Designated Staff Member.

(3) When the Designated Staff Member finds it necessary on the date of hearing, the Designated Staff Member may address questions to parties, call upon them to state their opinions or submit evidence or request explanation from the investigators, etc.

(4) The proceedings on the date of hearing are not open to the public.

(Article 58)

(1) The Designated Staff Member is to prepare a record of the proceedings of the statement of opinions by the Party, etc. on the date of hearing and the record must clearly indicate the outline of the statements raised by parties concerned with respect to the matters listed in Article 50, paragraph (1), items (i) and (ii).

(2) The record set forth in the preceding paragraph must be prepared on each date of the hearing when the statement, etc. by the Party is conducted, and where the statement, etc. by the Party is not conducted, promptly after the hearing is concluded.

(3) The record pursuant to paragraph (1) must be accompanied by the evidence submitted (the written statements and evidence submitted, when written statements and evidence are submitted pursuant to Article 55).

(4) The Designated Staff Member must, promptly after the hearing is concluded, identify the issues of the case for a hearing, prepare a written report containing the relevant issues and submit it to the Fair Trade Commission together with the record pursuant to paragraph (1).

(5) Parties concerned may demand inspection of the record pursuant to paragraph (1) and the written report pursuant to the preceding paragraph.

(Article 60)

In making a resolution pertaining to the cease and desist order, the Fair Trade Commission must do so only after careful consideration of the contents of the record pursuant to Article 58, paragraph (1) and the report pursuant to Article 58.

(Article 62)

(1) An order issued pursuant to the provisions of Article 7-2, paragraph (1) (including the case where these are applied mutatis mutandis pursuant to Article 7-2, paragraph (2) and Article 8-3 following the deemed replacement of terms), Article 7-9, paragraphs (1) or (2) or paragraph (4) of Article 7-2, or Articles 20-2 to 20-6 inclusive ... must be rendered in writing, and the written Payment Order for a surcharge is to state the amount of the surcharge to be paid, the basis of its calculation, the violation to

which it pertains, and the time limit for payment, and the chairman and the commissioners who attended the meeting pursuant to the provisions of Article 65, paragraph (1) must affix their names and seals thereto.

(2) A Payment Order is to take effect upon service of a copy of the written Payment Order for a surcharge on the addressee thereof.

(3) The time limit for payment of the surcharge set forth in paragraph (1) is to fall on the day on which seven months have elapsed from the day on which the copy of the written Payment Order for a surcharge is issued.

(4) The provisions of Articles 49 to 60 inclusive apply mutatis mutandis to the Payment Order. In this case, in Article 50, paragraph (1), item (i), the term 'The expected contents of the Cease and Desist Order' is deemed to be replaced with 'Amount of the surcharge intended to be ordered to be paid'; the term 'The facts found by the Fair Trade Commission, and the application of laws and regulations thereto' in item (ii) of the same paragraph and the term 'the facts found by the Fair Trade Commission' in Article 52, paragraph (1) is deemed to be replaced with 'The basis of calculation of the surcharge and the violation related to the surcharge'; in Article 54, paragraph (1), the term 'the expected content of the Cease and Desist Order, the facts found by the Fair Trade Commission and major evidence among those provided for Article 52, paragraph (1), and the application of laws and regulations to the facts found by the Fair Trade Commission' is deemed to be replaced with 'Amount of the surcharge intended to be ordered to be paid, the basis of calculation of the surcharge and the violation related to the surcharge, and major evidence among those pursuant to Article 52, paragraph (1) as applied mutatis mutandis pursuant to Article 62, paragraph (4) following the deemed replacement of terms.'

2. Submission of Opinion and Access to Evidence

375. The party concerned may appear on the date of Hearing, state its opinions, submit evidence and address questions to the investigators pursuant to Article 54. It may also request to the JFTC to view and copy evidence that proves the facts recognized by the JFTC during the period from the time of notification until the conclusion of the Hearing pursuant to Article 52(1). The JFTC may not refuse the party's request unless it is likely to infringe on the interests of a third party or unless there are any other justifiable grounds.

(Article 52)

(1) The Party may, between the time when notice of a hearing is given pursuant to Article 50, paragraph (1) and the time when the hearing is concluded, submit a request to the Fair Trade Commission to inspect or copy the evidence proving the facts found by the Fair Trade Commission with respect to the case for hearing (as for copy, only limited to evidence prescribed by the Rules of the Fair Trade Commission as one that was submitted by the relevant Party or its employees or that records the statements

of the relevant Party or its employees; hereinafter the same applies in this Article). In this case, the Fair Trade Commission may not refuse the inspection or copy unless this is likely to infringe on the interests of a third party or unless there are any other justifiable grounds.

(2) The provisions of preceding paragraph do not preclude the Party from further requesting inspection or copy of the evidence, which becomes necessary in the course of the procedures for hearing.

(3) The Fair Trade Commission may designate the date, time and place for inspection or copy set forth in the preceding two paragraphs.

The detailed procedure of submission of opinions and access of the evidence is provided in the Hearing Opinions Rules.[83]

B. Statement of Objections

376. As mentioned in A above, the JFTC sends a written notification to the would-be addressee of the Cease and Desist Order before the Hearing.

377. The Hearing Opinions Rules provide the contents of the notification above in detail.

> (Article 9) [Hearing of Opinions Rules]
>
> The notice pursuant to the provisions of Article 50, paragraph (1) of the Act shall be given to the would-be addressee of the cease and desist order, by serving a document containing the matters listed in the items of the same paragraph and the items of paragraph (2) of the same Article, the title of the case, and the list of the evidence proving the facts found by the Commission with regard to the case for the hearing of opinions.

C. Final Hearing and Decision

378. The Party can request the JFTC to inspect the record and written report produced by the Hearing Officer pursuant to Article 58(5).

379. Article 60 provides that the JFTC makes a decision with regard to a Cease and Desist Order after careful consideration of the record and written report and discussion in the meeting of the Commission.

83. Rules on Hearing of Opinions by the Fair Trade Commission.

III. Attorney Client Privileges

A. Background and Overview

380. So-called Attorney Client Privileges are not accepted in the Japanese legal system. Therefore, in the process of case investigation regarding possible AMA violation, enterprises and their attorneys are not able to assert the privileges. However, regarding administrative investigation procedure concerning unreasonable restraint of trade cases, confidential communications between an enterprise and an attorney are, under certain conditions, protected. The reason why the protection is limited to unreasonable restraint of trade in the AMA is that the objectives of such treatment are not only to ensure due process but also to enhance the incentive to apply the leniency programme. Leniency applicants usually consult with their attorney. If confidential communications between them are not protected, leniency application might be hindered. Therefore, from the perspective of making the leniency programme more effective, the protection of confidential communications between enterprises and an attorney is only admitted with regard to unreasonable restraint of trade.

381. The procedures are not provided in the AMA. The treatment of objectives recording confidential communications between an enterprise and an attorney by JFTC investigator is stipulated in the Investigations Rules to clarify the procedures and the scope of the rule.

The related provisions in the Investigation Rules are as follows:

(Article 23-2) [Investigation Rules]

(1) When ordering submission of accounting books and documents or other objects pursuant to the provision of Article 47, paragraph (1), item (iii) of the Act based on the provision of Article 47, paragraph (2) of the Act (limited to the cases where such order is issued with respect to a case concerning an act alleged to be a violation under Article 7-2, paragraph (1) of the Act (including the case is applied mutatis mutandis pursuant to Article 8-3 of the Act following the deemed replacement of terms) to which the immunity from or reduction of the surcharge set forth in Article 7-4 or 7-5 of the Act may apply (such a violation referred to as a 'Violation to Which the Leniency Program may Apply' in the Article 23-3, paragraph (1), item (iii)) (such an act alleged to be a violation referred to as 'Alleged Act in Violation to Which the Leniency Program may Apply' hereinafter)), when the holder of the object (limited to the entrepreneur [sic] who committed the Alleged Act in Violation to Which the Leniency Program may Apply (when the Alleged Act in Violation to Which the Leniency Program may Apply relates to a violation stipulated in Article 7-2, paragraph (1) of the Act that is applied mutatis mutandis pursuant to Article 8-3 of the Act following the deemed replacement of terms, the constituent entrepreneur [sic] of the trade association that committed such Act; hereinafter the same) or an officer or employee thereof) notifies in writing that the objects record

contents of confidential communications between such entrepreneur [sic] and an attorney (including a law firm, and limited to the cases where the attorney engages in legal practices independently from the relevant entrepreneur [sic]) regarding legal advice on the Alleged Act in Violation to Which the Leniency Program may Apply (such communication referred to as the 'Specified Communications' hereinafter) and requests in writing application of the treatment set forth in the next Article, the investigator shall order submission of such objects after placing them in a container and sealing it, and retain them, when it is visually evident that an indication is affixed thereto to the effect that the objects record the contents of the Specified Communications and that they are stored at a specific place of storage (limited to the place managed by the division or an officer or employee of the entrepreneur [sic] that handles the affairs for consulting with the attorneys; hereinafter the same in the Article 23-3, paragraph (1), item (v)) and in a manner to ensure they are classified and separated from other objects.

(2) The entrepreneur [sic] who made the request under the preceding paragraph (hereinafter referred to as the 'Specified Party') shall submit to the Commission a document that states, for each of the Specified Communications, the title, date of preparation or obtainment, the person who conducted the Specified Communication, the person who has the knowledge of the contents of the Specified Communication, the place of storage, the outline and other necessary matters regarding the object retained pursuant to the provision of the preceding paragraph (hereinafter referred to as the 'Specified Object') (such a document is referred to as the 'Log' in the Article 23-3, paragraph (1), item (vi)) within two weeks from the day on which the submission order under the preceding paragraph was issued, unless there are extraordinary circumstances.

(Article 23-3) [Investigation Rules]

(1) When it is confirmed that all of the requirement stipulated in the following items are satisfied with respect to a Specified Object, such Object shall be returned without waiting for the closure of the case, deeming that it no longer needs to be in held custody:
   (i) It records the contents of Specified Communications;
   (ii) Nothing is included that serves as the basis of the contents of the Specified Communications or otherwise is not considered as contents of the Specified Communications or, when any statement is included that is not considered as contents of the Specified Communications, the Specified Party has submitted or reported to the Commission objects whose contents are identical to such contents;
   (iii) It does not record any contents that relate to commitment, or facilitation of commitment of a Violation to Which the Leniency Program may Apply, or obstruction of inspection or any other illegal conducts;
   (iv) The Specified Object has on its surface or on other easily visible place an indication to show that it is an object recording the contents of Specified Communications;

(v) In addition to having the indication stipulated under the foregoing item, the Specified Objects are in appropriate custody by being stored at a specific place of storage and, in a manner to visually classify and separate them from the objects that are not Specified Objects and by implementing measures with respect to the scope of persons who know the contents of the Specified Communication with the aim to maintain their confidentiality;

(vi) The Logs contain no misrepresentations.

(2) The staff members engaged in the investigation of a case concerning an Alleged Act in Violation to Which the Leniency Program may Apply under paragraph (1) of the preceding Article shall not inspect or copy the Specified Objects (excluding, however, an Object that is submitted or reported pursuant to item (ii) of the preceding paragraph) relevant to the same case while the confirmation procedures under the preceding paragraph are underway, and when the confirmation is made that all of matters stipulated in the items of the preceding paragraph are satisfied with respect thereto.

(Article 23-4) [Investigation Rules]

(1) The confirmation under paragraph (1) of the preceding Article shall be performed by a staff member designated by the Commission, for each case concerning the Alleged Act in Violation to Which the Leniency Program may Apply, from the staff of the Secretariat of the General Secretariat (hereinafter referred to in this Article and the next Article as the 'Determination Officer').

(2) The Commission shall not designate with respect to a case of an Alleged Act in Violation to Which the Leniency Program may Apply under Article 23-3, paragraph (1), any staff member who has worked for the investigation of the same case to be a Determination Officer for such case, nor shall it cause any staff member who has been appointed as a Determination Officer for a case concerning an Alleged Act in Violation to Which the Leniency Program may Apply to be involved in the investigation of the same case.

(3) The Determination Officer shall request the Specified Party to submit materials or otherwise extend cooperation as necessary when he/she finds it necessary for the purpose of performance of the confirmation under paragraph (1) of the preceding Article.

(4) When it is confirmed that all of the items stipulated in paragraph (1) of the preceding Article are satisfied with respect to the Specified Object, the Determination Officer shall notify the Specified Party to such effect.

(5) When it is confirmed that any of the items stipulated in paragraph (1) of the preceding Article is not satisfied with respect to the Specified Object, the Determination Officer shall notify the Specified Party to such effect along with the reason therefor.

(Article 23-5)

The provisions of Article 18 shall apply mutatis mutandis when the Specified Objects are inspected or copied. In this case, 'investigation of a case' as it reads in Article 18, paragraph (1) shall be replaced to read 'investigation of a case or confirmation by a Determination Officer'.

B. Determination Procedure

382. The JFTC also published the Determination Procedure Guidelines[84] to provide the detailed information on the procedures of the treatment of confidential communications between enterprises and an attorney and to ensure transparency of the treatment and predictability of the enterprises.

383. The guidelines first clarify the scope of the treatment. They include consultation document from a Specified Party to the attorney, responding document from the attorney to the Specified Party, report stating the legal advice based upon the internal investigation performed by the attorney, and memo of an internal meeting that states the discussion with the attorney on the legal advice at an internal meeting that the attorney attended.

384. The guidelines also explain the process of determination procedures. The process consists of two parts, i.e., the primary procedures and the secondary procedures. The outlines are as follows:

i. Primary Determination Procedures
   The Determination Officer shall perform the confirmation procedures under a. through c. below on the Specified Object in principle within two weeks from the day on which the submission order was issued with respect thereto:
   a. Confirmation of the descriptions on the Application: to confirm that the descriptions made on the Application are without error.
   b. Confirmation of submission of the Log: to confirm that the Specified Party submitted the Log to Determination Officer and the investigator within two weeks from the day on which the submission order was issued thereon, except to the extent that there are extraordinary circumstances, such as natural disasters.
   c. Confirmation of appropriate custody: to confirm that the requirements provided by Article 23-3, paragraph (1), items (iv) and (v) of the Investigation Rules are satisfied with respect to the Specified Object.

ii. Secondary determination procedures
   The Determination Officer shall perform the confirmation procedures under a. through e. below on the Specified Object concerning which the matters under (i) a. through c. of i. above are confirmed in principle within six weeks from the day on which the primary determination procedures are completed:
   a. Confirmation of the Specified Object Recording the Contents of the Specified Communications: to confirm that the Specified Object records the contents of the Specified Communications.

84. Guidelines on Treatment of Objects Recording Confidential Communications Between an Enterprise and an Attorney.

b. Confirmation of Non-inclusion of Ineligible Documents, etc.: to confirm that the Specified Object does not include any documents, etc. whose recorded contents do not come within the scope of the Specified Communications (hereinafter referred to as the 'Ineligible Documents, etc.) and that, if any Ineligible Documents, etc. are included, copies of such Ineligible Documents, etc. are submitted or otherwise provided to Determination Officer by the Specified Party. Examples of the Ineligible Documents, etc. include the following:
   (a) Primary materials: pocketbooks or notebooks of the Officers, etc., memos stating the details of the meetings, documents approving the business trips, etc.
   (b) Fact-finding materials; records of interview on the Officers, etc. who are considered to be involved in the Alleged Act in Violation to Which the Leniency Program may Apply, the report on internal questionnaires, etc. regarding an Alleged Act in Violation to Which the Leniency Program may Apply.
   (c) Documents, etc. stating the contents of the legal advice regarding other laws and ordinances, etc.: documents, etc. stating about the consultations that the Specified Party made to the attorneys, and the responses given from such attorneys, regarding the legal advice on the provisions of laws and ordinances other than the AMA or provisions of the AMA that are irrelevant to the Alleged Act in Violation to Which the Leniency Program may Apply.

c. Confirmation of Non-inclusion of Communications Regarding Obstruction of Inspection, etc.: to confirm that the Specified Object is not related to commitment, or facilitation of commitment, of a violation to which the leniency program may apply or commitment of obstruction of inspection or other illegal conducts.

d. Confirmation of Appropriate Custody: to confirm that the Specified Object satisfies the requirements provided by Article 23-3, paragraph (1), items (v) of the Investigation Rules.

e. Confirmation of the Contents of the Log: to confirm that the contents of the Log do not contain misrepresentations.

C. Treatment of Electronic Data

385. The Determination Procedure Guidelines, moreover, explain how electronic date is treated under the treatment procedures. The electronic data shall be treated in the same ways as objects in principals. However, considering the nature of electronic data, there are some differences. For example, with regard to custody of the objects, electronic data are considered to have been in appropriate custody if all of the requirements below are satisfied.

i. Indication

The file names of the Specified Data (subjects in the case of electronic mails) include indications to show that they are objects recording the contents of the Specified Communications: Examples of such indications include the following:

- There is an indication of '**公取審査規則特定通信**' (meaning 'Specified Communication under JFTC Investigation Rules') included in the file name of electronic data file recording the contents of the Specified Communications.
- There is an indication of '**公取審査規則第２３条の２第１項該当**' (meaning 'Document under Article 23-2, paragraph (1) of JFTC Investigation Rules') included in the subject of electronic mail recording the contents of the Specified Communications.

ii Place of storage:
The Specified Data are stored at a specific place of storage managed by the enterprise (limited to those places managed by the division or Officer, etc. that handles the affairs for consulting with the attorneys) (or managed in specific mail accounts in the case of electronic mails), and the place of storage of the Specified Data and the place of storage of data other than the Specified Data are separated by the name of the folders, etc. used as the place of storage of data. Examples of such manner of storage include the following:

- Specified Data are stored in a folder managed by the legal affairs division with an indication that electronic data recording the contents of the Specified Communication are stored therein, and no electric data other than those recording the contents of Specified Data are stored in the same folder.

iii. Scope of the Persons Who Know the Contents:
The scope of the persons who know the contents of the Specified Data is restricted to those who need to know (the persons who assume or assumed the duty to consult with the attorneys on behalf of the enterprise, etc.).

Chapter 2. Notifications and Clearance Decisions of Merger Regulations

§1. Preliminary Filing Obligations

I. Criteria and Thresholds

386. The JFTC applies an advanced notification system for some type of business combination. Notification thresholds differ in accordance with the types of business combination. The transaction within the same company group is exempted from the filing requirement.

387. Also, the JFTC request the companies submit the documents and review the planned business combination when it considers the combination may affect the competition in the domestic market and consequently may harm the interests of domestic consumers even if the business combination does not meet the criteria, for example, the sales volume of the companies concerned is less than the threshold to notify, or they are located abroad.

A. *Share Acquisition*

388. A company acquiring the shares of another company must notify to the JFTC within thirty days prior to execution of the transaction when the transaction meets the following three conditions, provided by paragraphs (1) to (3) of Article 16 of AMA Enforcement Order:

i. the total domestic sales amount of the acquiring company exceeds JPY 20 billion;
ii. the domestic sales amount of the share issuing company exceeds JPY 5 billion;
iii. the total ratio of voting rights held by the acquiring company and that of the companies which belong to the same group of the acquiring company in the share issuing company exceeds 20% or 50% after the transaction.

389. The 'total domestic sales amount of a company' referred to in i. above means the sales amount in the Japanese market, including that of the companies which belong to the same group of the company at issue, such as the ultimate parent company and its subsidiaries. This definition applies to the articles in this chapter.

390. The 'domestic sales amount of the share issuing company' referred to in ii. above includes that of its subsidiaries:

(Article 10)

(2) If a company whose domestic sales (meaning the amount stipulated by the Rules of the Fair Trade Commission as the total amount of value of goods and services supplied in Japan in the most recent business year; the same applies hereinafter) as calculated in conjunction with the domestic sales of companies, etc. other than the relevant company (meaning companies, partnerships (including equivalents of partnerships in foreign countries; the same applies hereinafter) and any other business entities that are similar to these; the same applies hereinafter in this Article) that belong to the group of combined companies to which the relevant company belongs (meaning a group consisting of the relevant company, its subsidiary companies, its parent company which is not a subsidiary company of another company, and subsidiary companies of the relevant parent company (excluding the relevant company and subsidiary companies of the relevant company); the same applies hereinafter) using a method stipulated in the Rules of the Fair Trade Commission (hereinafter referred to as the 'Total Domestic Sales Amount') exceed the amount provided by Cabinet Order, which must be no less than twenty billion yen (such a company is referred to as an 'Acquiring Company' hereinafter in this Article), intends to acquire shares of another company whose domestic sales as calculated in conjunction with the domestic sales of subsidiary companies of the relevant other company using a method stipulated in the Rules of the Fair Trade Commission exceed the amount provided by Cabinet Order, which must be no less than five billion yen (such a company is referred to as the 'Issuing Company' hereinafter in this Article) (including the cases where the Acquiring Company is a settlor or beneficiary and may exercise voting rights or give instructions to the trustee regarding the exercise of such voting rights with regard to the shares held in money or securities trust, and intends to have the trustee acquire shares issued by the Issuing Company), so that the ratio of the number of voting rights, which combines the number of voting rights for the shares of the Issuing Company to be held by the Acquiring Company after the acquisition with the number of voting rights for the shares of the Issuing Company held by companies, etc. other than the Acquiring Company that belongs to the group of combined companies to which the Acquiring Company belongs (referred to as 'companies, etc. other than the Acquiring Company' in paragraph (4) below), to the voting rights of all shareholders of the Issuing Company exceeds the numerical value provided for by Cabinet Order (when more than one numerical value is provided for, each of the numerical values pursuant to the provisions of Cabinet Order), which must be no less than twenty percent, is to give the Fair Trade Commission advance notification of the plan for the acquisition, pursuant to the provisions of the Rules of the Fair Trade Commission; provided, however, this does not apply in the case the advance submission of such a plan is stipulated as being difficult under the Rules of the Fair Trade Commission.

B. Merger

391. All the parties concerned with merger transaction must notify the JFTC of the plan within thirty days prior to its execution when the transaction meets the following two conditions (Article 18 (1) and (2) [AMA Enforcement Order]):

i. The total domestic sales amount of any one of the concerned companies exceeds JPY 20 billion;
ii. The total domestic sales amount of any one of the other concerned companies exceeds JPY 5 billion.

(Article 15)

(2) Every company that intends to become a party to a merger (hereinafter in this Article 'Merging Company') must, pursuant to the provisions of the Rules of the Fair Trade Commission, notify the Fair Trade Commission in advance of its merger plan if the total domestic sales amount of any one of the companies intending to be parties to the merger exceeds the amount provided by Cabinet Order, which must be no less than twenty billion yen, and the total domestic sales amount of any one of the other merging companies exceeds the amount provided by Cabinet Order, which must be no less than five billion yen; provided, however, that this does not apply if all of the merging companies belong to the same group of combined companies.

C. Joint Incorporation-Type Splits

392. All the companies concerned with joint incorporation-type split transaction must notify the JFTC of the plan within thirty days prior to its execution when it meets any one of the following conditions (Article 19(1)-(4) [AMA Enforcement Order]):

i. the total domestic sales amount of any one of the total succession companies exceeds JPY 20 billion, and that of the succeeding company exceeds JPY 5 billion;
ii. the total domestic sales amount of any one of the total succession companies exceeds JPY 20 billion, and that of the substantial part subject to the transaction of any one of the other substantial part succession companies exceeds JPY 3 billion;
iii. the total domestic sales amount of any one of the total succession companies exceeds JPY 5 billion, and that of the substantial part subject to the transaction of any one of the other substantial part succession companies exceeds JPY 10 billion, except for in the case (ii) above;
iv. the total domestic sales amount of the substantial part subject to the transaction of any one of the substantial part succession companies exceeds JPY 10

billion, and that of the substantial part subject to the transaction of any one of the other substantial part succession companies exceeds JPY 3 billion.

393. The 'total succession company' referred to in the conditions above means the company that intends to transfer all its business to a company established by way of joint incorporation-type split.

394. The 'substantial part succession company' referred to in the conditions above means the company that intends to transfer a substantial part of its business to a company established by way of joint incorporation-type split:

(Article 15-2)

(2) Every company that intends to become a party to a joint incorporation-type company split, pursuant to the provisions of the Rules of the Fair Trade Commission, is to notify the Fair Trade Commission in advance of its plan with regard to such a joint incorporation-type company split if any of the following items applies; provided, however, that this does not apply if all the companies intending to become parties to the joint incorporation-type company split belong to the same group of combined companies:

(i) the total domestic sales amount of any one of the companies that intend to become parties to the joint incorporation-type company split (limited to a company that intends to have the company incorporated through such a joint incorporation-type company split acquire all of its business (hereinafter in this paragraph 'Total Succession Company')) exceeds the amount specified by Cabinet Order, which must be no less than twenty billion yen, and the total domestic sales amount of any one of the other companies that intend to become parties to the same company split (limited to a Total Succession Company) exceeds the amount specified by Cabinet Order, which must be no less than five billion yen;

(ii) the total domestic sales amount of any one of the companies that intend to become parties to the joint incorporation-type company split (limited to a Total Succession Company) exceeds the amount specified by Cabinet Order, which must be no less than twenty billion yen, and the domestic sales of any one of the other companies that intend to become parties to the same company split (limited to a company that intends to have the company incorporated through such a joint incorporation-type company split acquire a substantial part of its business (hereinafter in this paragraph 'substantial part succession company')), in connection with the part of the business to be succeeded to, exceed the amount specified by Cabinet Order, which must be no less than three billion yen;

(iii) the total domestic sales amount of any one of the companies that intend to become parties to the joint incorporation-type company split (limited to a Total Succession Company) exceeds the amount specified by Cabinet Order, which must be no less than five billion yen, and the domestic sales of any one of the other companies that intend to become parties to the same company split (limited to a substantial part succession company), in connection with the part of the business to be succeeded to, exceeds the amount specified by Cabinet Order, which must be no less than ten billion yen (excluding cases that fall under the previous item);

(iv) the domestic sales of any one of the companies that intend to become parties to the joint incorporation-type company split (limited to a substantial part succession company), in connection with the part of the business to be succeeded to, exceed the amount specified by Cabinet Order, which must be no less than ten billion yen, and the domestic sales of any one of the other companies that intend to become parties to the same company split (limited to a substantial part succession company), in connection with the part of the business to be succeeded to, exceed the amount specified by Cabinet Order, which must be no less than three billion yen.

D. Absorption-Type Splits

395. All the companies concerned with absorption-type split transaction must notify the JFTC of the plan within thirty days prior to its execution when the transaction meets any one of the following conditions (Article 19(5)-(8) [AMA Enforcement Order]):

i. the total domestic sales amount of any one of the total succession companies exceeds JPY 20 billion, and that of the succeeding companies exceeds JPY 5 billion;
ii. the total domestic sales amount of any one of the total succession companies exceeds JPY 5 billion, and that of the succeeding company exceeds JPY 20 billion, except for in the case of (i) above;
iii. the total domestic sales amount of the substantial part subject to the transaction of any one of the substantial part succession companies exceeds JPY 10 billion, and that of the succeeding company exceeds JPY 5 billion;
iv. the total domestic sales amount of the substantial part subject to the transaction of any one of the substantial part succession companies exceeds JPY 3 billion, and that of the succeeding company exceeds JPY 20 billion, except for in the case of (iii) above.

396. The 'total succession company' referred to in the conditions below means the company that intends to transfer all its business to a company established by way of absorption-type split.

397. The 'substantial part succession company' referred to in the conditions below means the company that intends to transfer a substantial part of its business to a company established by way of absorption-type split:

(Article 15-2)

(3) Every company that intends to become a party to an absorption-type split must, pursuant to the provisions of the Rules of the Fair Trade Commission, notify the Fair Trade Commission in advance of its plan with regard to such an absorption-type split if any of the following items applies; provided, however, that this does not apply if all the companies intending to become parties to the absorption-type split belong to the same group of combined companies:

(i) the total domestic sales amount of any one of the companies that intend to become parties to the absorption-type split (limited to a company that intends to alienate all of its business through such absorption-type split (referred to in the following item as 'Total Succession Company')) exceeds the amount specified by Cabinet Order, which must be no less than twenty billion yen, and the total domestic sales amount of the company that intends to succeed to the business through such a split exceeds the amount specified by Cabinet Order, which must be no less than five billion yen;

(ii) the total domestic sales amount of any one of the companies that intend to become parties to the absorption-type split (limited to a Total Succession Company) exceeds the amount specified by Cabinet Order, which must be no less than five billion yen, and the total domestic sales amount of the company that intends to succeed to the business through such a split exceeds the amount specified by Cabinet Order, which must be no less than twenty billion yen (excluding cases that fall under the previous item);

(iii) the domestic sales of any one of the companies that intend to become parties to the absorption-type split (limited to a company that intends to alienate a substantial part of its business through such an absorption-type split (referred to in the following item as 'substantial part succession company')), in connection with the part of the business to be alienated, exceeds the amount specified by Cabinet Order, which must be no less than ten billion yen, and the total domestic sales amount of the company that intends to succeed to the business through such a split exceeds the amount specified by Cabinet Order, which must be no less than five billion yen;

(iv) the domestic sales of any one of the companies that intend to become parties to the absorption-type split (limited to a substantial part succession company), in connection with the part of the business to be alienated, exceeds the amount specified by Cabinet Order, which must be no less than three billion yen, and the total domestic sales amount of the company that intends to succeed to the business through such a split exceeds the amount specified by Cabinet Order, which must be no less than twenty billion yen (excluding cases that fall under the previous item).

E. Joint Share Transfer

398. All the companies concerned with joint share transfer transaction must notify the JFTC of the plan within thirty days prior to its execution when it meets the following two conditions:

i. the total domestic sales amount of any one of the concerned companies exceeds JPY 20 billion;
ii. the total domestic sales amount of any one of the other concerned companies exceeds JPY 5 billion.

(Article 15-3)

(2) Every company that intends to engage in a joint share transfer must, pursuant to the provisions of the Rules of the Fair Trade Commission, notify the Fair Trade Commission in advance of its plan with regard to the share transfer, if the total amount of the domestic sales of any one of the companies intending to be parties to the joint share transfer exceeds the amount provided by Cabinet Order, which must be no less than twenty billion yen, and the total amount of the domestic sales of any one of the other companies intending to be parties to the same joint share transfer exceeds the amount provided by Cabinet Order, which must be no less than five billion yen; provided, however, that this does not apply if all the companies intending to be parties to the joint share transfer belong to the same group of combined companies.

F. Acquisition of Business

399. All the companies concerned with acquisition of business transaction whose total domestic sales amount exceeds JPY 20 billion must notify the JFTC of the plan within thirty days prior to execution of the transaction when it meets any one of the following conditions (Article 21 [AMA Enforcement Order]).

i. the total domestic sales amount of the company transferring its all business exceeds JPY 3 billion;
ii. the total domestic sales amount of the substantial part of business subject to the transaction of the company transferring its business exceeds JPY 3 billion.

(Article 16)

(2) Any company whose total domestic sales amount exceeds the amount provided by Cabinet Order, which must be no less than twenty billion yen (hereinafter referred to as 'assignee company' in paragraph (4)) must, pursuant to the provisions of the Rules of the Fair Trade Commission, notify

the Fair Trade Commission in advance of its plan with regard to the acceptance of assignment of the business or the fixed assets used for the business (hereinafter referred to as 'Business, etc.' in this Article) if either of the following items applies; provided, however, that this does not apply if the company intending to accept assignment of the Business, etc. and the company intending to assign the relevant Business, etc. belong to the same group of combined companies:

(i) the company intends to accept assignment of the whole business of another company whose domestic sales exceeds the amount provided by Cabinet Order, which must be no less than three billion yen;

(ii) the company intends to accept assignment of a substantial part of the business or the whole or a substantial part of the fixed assets used for the business of another company, and the domestic sales in connection with the subject of such acceptance of assignment exceeds the amount provided by Cabinet Order, which must be no less than three billion yen.

II. Notification Form

400. The notifying party should submit several documents to the JFTC in accordance with the Business Combination Rules. A filing fee is unnecessary.

401. A person who has failed to notify or submitted a written notification with a false description in violation of the AMA provisions is punished by a fine of not more than JPY 2 million.

(Article 91-2)

A person who falls under any of the following items is punished by a fine of not more than two million yen:

(i) a person who, in violation of the provisions of Article 9, paragraph (4), has failed to submit a written report or submitted a written report with a false description;

(ii) a person who, in violation of the provisions of Article 9, paragraph (7), has failed to notify or submitted a written notification with a false description;

(iii) a person who, in violation of the provisions of Article 10, paragraph (2), has failed to notify or submitted a written notification with a false description;

(iv) a person who has acquired shares in violation of the provisions of Article 10, paragraph (8);

(v) a person who, in violation of the provisions of Article 15, paragraph (2) has failed to notify or submitted a written notification with a false description;

(vi) a person who, in violation of the provisions of Article 10, paragraph (8) as applied mutatis mutandis pursuant to Article 15, paragraph (3) following the deemed replacement of terms, has effected a register of an incorporation or a change as a result of a merger;
(vii) a person who, in violation of the provisions of Article 15-2, paragraphs (2) and (3) has failed to notify or submitted a written notification with a false description.
(viii) a person who, in violation of the provisions of Article 10, paragraph (8) as applied mutatis mutandis pursuant to Article 15-2, paragraph (4) following the deemed replacement of terms, has effected a register of incorporation as a result of a joint incorporation-type company split or a register of change as a result of an absorption-type split;
(ix) a person who, in violation of the provisions of Article 15-3, paragraph (2), has failed to give notification or submitted a written notification with a false description;
(x) a person who has effected a register of incorporation as a result of a joint share transfer in violation of the provisions of Article 10, paragraph (8) as applied mutatis mutandis pursuant to Article 15-3, paragraph (3) following the deemed replacement of terms;
(xi) a person who, in violation of the provisions of Article 16, paragraph (2), has failed to give notification or submitted a written notification with a false description;
(xii) any person who, in violation of the provisions of Article 10, paragraph (8) as applied mutatis mutandis pursuant to Article 16, paragraph (3) following the deemed replacement of terms, has carried out an act falling under Article 16, paragraph (1), item (i) or (ii);
(xiii) a person who, in violation of the provisions of Article 23, paragraph (6), has failed to notify or has submitted a written notification with a false description.

§2. Structure of Proceedings

I. Time Framework

402. The structure of merger review comprises two aspects in its timeframe. The first one is 'primary review' and the latter is 'secondary review.' The purpose of the primary review is to discern whether the transaction needs to go to secondary review. On the other hand, the goal of the secondary review is to determine whether the JFTC should issue a Cease and Desist Order to stop the transaction.

403. In this regard, the JFTC, to clarify the comprehensive framework of the review, made public its policy statement in the Merger Review Policy[85] (Figure 1).

85. Policies Concerning Procedures of Review of Business Combination.

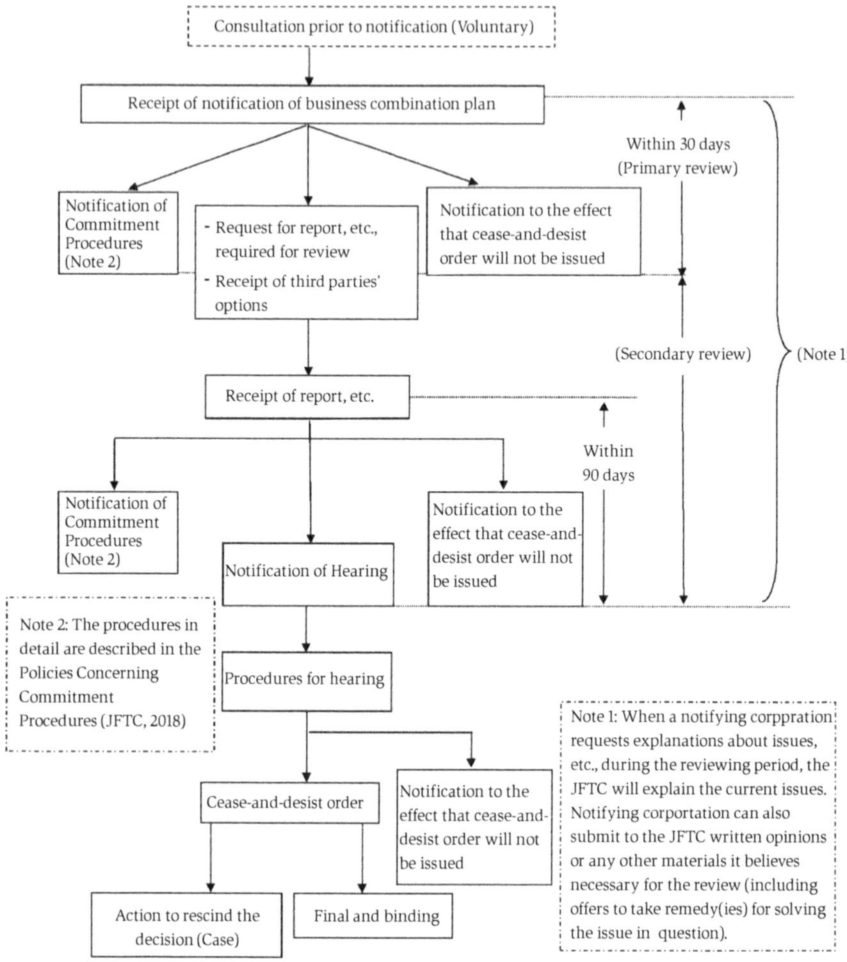

Figure 1 Flowchart of Business Combination Review

Source: https://www.jftc.go.jp/en/legislation_gls/imonopoly_guidelines_files/191217policy.pdf.

A. Consultation Prior to Notification (Voluntary)

404. The company that intends to notify the JFTC of its business combination plan can apply to the JFTC for consultation on a voluntary basis. It may apply at the JFTC's Merger and Acquisition Division or any of eight local offices.

405. In the consultation, the JFTC will give the applicant any explanation on the specific case based on the materials that the applicant provides, in accordance with the Merger Review Policy. The company, however, is not bound by this explanation and whether it applies for consultation absolutely depends on its own decision. It will not be given, therefore, disadvantageous treatment even if it does not ask for consultation. The JFTC may also correct its *ex ante* explanation as a result of reviewing the case after it is officially notified.

B. Primary Review

406. The primary review starts when the company notifies its plan of transaction of the JFTC and the notification is officially filed. The notifying company is prohibited from proceeding the transaction until the expiration of the thirty-day waiting period from the day when the notification is filed (the thirty-day waiting period can be shortened following the procedure stipulated by the JFTC).

407. During the primary review, the JFTC decides whether it is necessary to bring the transaction to the secondary review so as to examine in detail its competitive effect on competition. When the JFTC considers unnecessary, it terminates the review and provides the notifying company a notification to the effect that Cease and Desist Order will not be issued concerning the transaction pursuant to Article 9 of the Business Combination Rules. This notice is generally called as the 'Article 9 Notice'. In case where the notifying company requests to shorten the waiting period in writing, the JFTC may shorten the waiting period and issue Article 9 Notice before thirty days elapse.

> (Article 9) [Business Combination Rules]
>
> When the Fair Trade Commission decides not to issue a notice pursuant to the provisions of Article 50, paragraph (1) of the Act regarding an acquisition of shares, merger, company split, share transfer or Business Acquisition, etc. under a Business Combination Notification ..., it shall provide the notifying company with notice using Form No. 43, 44, 45, 46, 47 or 48.

408. Among the cases cleared in the primary review, the JFTC makes public the cases which are informative to the other parties. Such cases include those which the JFTC gives clearance on condition that the notifying company should take a remedy to execute the transaction.

C. Secondary Review

409. As noted above in B., the JFTC should determine whether it issues a Cease and Desist Order to stop the transaction. The JFTC, therefore, sends the notifying company a written request to submit reports, documents, etc. that contain necessary information to conduct detailed analysis of the impact of the transaction on competition. In the request, the JFTC briefly explains the reason why the submission is required for the secondary review.

410. The JFTC makes announcement on its website that the case is brought to the secondary review procedure to invite opinions of the third parties. The parties with any opinion about the case can submit written opinion to the JFTC within thirty days after the said publication.

411. The JFTC should send a notification of Hearing to the notifying company when it believes that the notified transaction may substantially restrain competition and therefore it should initiate the Procedure for Hearing for issuing a Cease and Desist Order. The notification should be issued within ninety days after the date of the receipt of all reports from the notifying company. The procedures after the prior notice are basically the same as those of investigation of cartels, etc. (*see* Part III, Chapter 1, §3, II above).

412. On the contrary, the JFTC issues Article 9 Notice to the notifying company when it will give clearance to the case after the secondary review. In this case, the JFTC explains to the notifying company in writing the result of the review. All the results of the secondary review are published by the JFTC.

II. Explanation of Issues and Submission of Written Opinions by the Notifying Company

413. Through the primary and secondary review, the notifying company can request the JFTC to explain what the competitive issues of the transaction are.

414. The notifying company can submit to the JFTC written opinions or any other documents it believes necessary for the review. Such opinions may include offers to take remedies regarding the notified transaction. The JFTC gives examples of materials, for the reference of the companies, in the review of the notified transactions in the Merger Review Policy.

415. There is no deadline for the submission of such opinions, so the notifying company can submit any time in the course of the primary and secondary review. It should also be noted that such opinions may not be reflected in the JFTC's judgment depending on the time of its submission.

III. Commitment Procedure in the Business Combination Review

416. Throughout the procedure of the review, the JFTC may give a Notice of Commitment Procedures to resolve suspected violations. The same procedures stated in Part I, Chapter 5, §1, I, C, 2 above are applied after the issuance of Notice of Commitment Procedures also in the business combination review process.

§3. Clearance and Conditional Clearance

I. Conditions and Undertakings

417. Among the business combinations, which the JFTC considers substantially restrain competition in the market, some are remedied by certain appropriate measures taken by the companies concerned (such measures are referred to as 'Remedial Measures' hereinafter).

418. What kind of Remedial Measures is appropriate depends on conditions of each case. The basic idea stipulated in the Merger Guidelines is that the Remedial Measures should, in principle, be formed of structural measures, transfer of business, for example. A behavioural measure can be admitted as appropriate one in the case where the market structure is changing rapidly because of technological innovations.

419. The guidelines illustrate typical measures of the Remedial Measures as follows.[86]

A. *Transfer of Businesses*

420. The most effective measures to solve issues of substantial restraint of competition by the business combination are to establish new independent competitors, or to strengthen existing competitors so that they serve as an effective competitive constraint. Such measures include transferring all or part of the business of the company group or dissolving the business combination (the disposition of voting rights, reduction in the percentage of voting rights held or termination of interlocking directorates in another company, etc.) and the business alliances with a third party.

B. *Supply of Products under Special Conditions*

421. There may be, however, some exceptional cases to adopt the structural measures. The cases are, for example, where it is difficult for the companies at issue to find an adequate transferee to take over all or part of their business due to declining demand, and it is less important for maintaining competition to promote research and development activities or improvement of goods and services because the market has been enough matured. In such cases, it may be more effective to take alternative measures that include setting up the conditions under which the companies concerned provide their competitors with privilege to purchase their products at a low-price equivalent to the production cost.

86. Merger Guideline, Part VII.

C. Promotion of Imports and Market Entry

422. Some companies employ the measures of promoting import or market entry as another option to remedy the anticompetitive effect of business combination when the market is in the exceptional circumstances as stated in B above.

423. Indeed, The JFTC has approved the Remedial Measures of the company concerned that the company group to which the concerned company belonged made the storage and other importing facilities, which a company in the group owned available to the third party importers. The JFTC considered that such measures would make importers as an effective competitor by promoting import, and that the concerns that the transaction would substantially restrain the competition.

424. In another case, the JFTC admitted the Remedial Measures that the company group would grant licences of patents the group had to its competitors or new entrants. Such measures would encourage newcomers to enter the market and resolve the concerns of the JFTC that the transaction would substantially restrain competition in the market.

D. Measures Concerning Behaviour of the Company Group

425. The behavioural measures of the company concerned would be better to resolve the competitive concerns though the Remedial Measures should be primarily structural measures as stated in I above.

426. For example, the JFTC may accept the remedial measures to insulate communication on sales among the concerned companies and to ensure independence of new company in a case in which the investing companies will establish a manufacturing company to jointly produce goods, but they will maintain selling products separately. In another case of business combination of service providers, the Remedial Measures to prohibit discriminatory treatment of non-affiliated companies with respect to use of essential facilities for the business may resolve the concerns of emerging foreclosure or exclusivity in the markets.

II. Timing

427. In principle, the concerned companies should have completed the Remedial Measures before execution of the business combination. In such cases where the companies are to take actions for Remedial Measures, the companies should make appropriate and definite period to implement the measures. In the case of business transfer, it is desirable to have determined the transferee of the business in advance of execution of transaction. Otherwise, the parties may need to reach an agreement with the JFTC concerning the possible transferee, at least.

Chapter 3. Challenging Administrative Decision

§1. General Remarks

428. The recipient of a Cease and Desist Order or Payment Order may challenge the order in Tokyo District Court. Before the 2013 amendment, the recipient of such an order could not file a lawsuit with the court without challenging the order under the JFTC's administrative hearing procedures. After the hearing procedures, the enterprise may bring a lawsuit in Tokyo High Court.

429. The administrative hearing procedure above was abolished by the 2013 amendment, and Procedures for Hearing related to Cease and Desist Order and Payment Order have replaced it. This procedural revolution changed the way of enforcement as well as brought enactment or revision of other relevant laws and regulations, including the establishment of the Hearing Opinions Rules, Investigation Rules, etc. Such rules specify the procedures related to the JFTC's administrative orders and other dispositions as well as provide the procedures for inspection and copying of evidence relied on by the JFTC in its findings as stated above (*see* Chapter 1, §3, II above).

430. The lawsuit challenging the JFTC's administrative order is implemented under the Administrative Case Litigation Act (Act No. 139 of 1962) and the rules concerning general civil litigation.

§2. Administrative Appeals Procedure

431. An enterprise can file an action for revocation of an administrative order to a court before six months has elapsed from the day on which it became aware of the fact that the orders were made. These cases are subject to the exclusive jurisdiction of the Tokyo District Court. It is because antitrust cases, different from usual administrative litigation cases, handle complex economic affairs and require high expertise. This exclusive jurisdiction is supposed to ensure the unity of judgments and accumulate high expertise in the court. In practice, the Commercial Division (Division Eight of the Civil Department) of the court handles all cases filed for revocation of JFTC's administrative orders. The division, with the Insolvency Division and the Intellectual Property Division, consists of a brunch, commonly called as the Business Court.

432. As stated in §1 above, before the 2013 amendment, these cases were subject to the exclusive jurisdiction of the Tokyo High Court and the Tokyo High Court reviewed the cases under the substantial evidence rule and the rule restricting submission of new evidence. However, the amendment has abolished these two rules. The Tokyo District Court conducts a proceeding and makes a judicial decision by a panel consisting of three judges or, when necessary, the panel of five judges because these orders are made by the JFTC with high expertise, so more careful review is required.

433. When the case is appealed to the Tokyo High Court after a final judgment made by the Tokyo District Court, the Tokyo High Court conducts a proceeding by the panel of three judges or, when necessary, the panel of five judges. According to the Administrative Litigation Case Act, the filing of an action for the revocation of the orders does not preclude the execution of the orders, but the court may, upon petition, stay the whole or part of the execution of the orders by an order in case where it is needed to urgently respond to serious damage that would be caused by the execution of the orders. An enterprise who has complaint against Tokyo High Court decision may appeal to the Supreme Court.

(Article 77)

The Fair Trade Commission is the defendant in the action for the judicial review of an administrative disposition provided for in Article 3, paragraph (1) of the Administrative Case Litigation Act (Act No. 139 of 1962) in connection with a Cease and Desist Order, etc.

(Article 85)
Any following action and case is subject to the exclusive jurisdiction of the Tokyo District Court: (i) action for the judicial review of an administrative disposition under Article 3, paragraph (1) of the Administrative Case Litigation Act in connection with the Cease and Desist Order, etc.

(Article 86)
(1) The Tokyo District Court is to conduct a proceeding and make a judicial decision by a panel consisting of three judges for action and case provided for in Article 85, as well as actions provided for in the preceding Article.
(2) Notwithstanding the provisions of the preceding paragraph, the Tokyo District Court, with regard to the action and case preceding paragraph, may make a ruling by the panel of five judges who are to conduct a proceeding and make a judicial decision.
(3) In the case of the preceding paragraph, the panel may not contain three or more assistant judges simultaneously, and no assistant judge may serve as the presiding judge.

(Article 87)
With regard to the case subject to appeal to the Tokyo High Court against a final judgment made by the Tokyo District Court for the action or suit set forth in Article 85, item (i) or the action or suit pursuant to Article 85-2 or the case subject to appeal to the Tokyo High Court against a ruling made by the Tokyo District Court for the case as set forth in Article 85, item (ii), in the Tokyo High Court, a panel may make a ruling that the panel of five judges is to conduct a proceeding and make a judicial decision on that case.

Part IV. Criminal Procedure

Chapter 1. General Remarks

§1. Background

434. The Chapter XII of the AMA sets out the details of criminal investigation procedure. This procedure has been inserted into the AMA in 2005. The provisions are similar to those of tax fraud investigation, which the national tax agency enforces. Before the 2005 amendment, although the AMA provided that the JFTC, where it considers that a crime violating the provisions of this Act exists, shall file a criminal accusation with the Prosecutor General, there were no criminal investigation provisions in the act. All investigations, even some of which led to criminal accusation, were conducted through administrative procedures.

435. On this point, there was criticism in the business community that the practice was incompatible with due process, because the investigation under criminal procedure should be accompanied with a more rigid system to protect the rights of the parties concerned. There was another argument that the lack of criminal investigation power made it difficult for the JFTC to detect and charge serious and vicious cartels and bid riggings. For example, JFTC's investigators were not given the authority to conduct compulsory inspection. Another reason is that the prosecutors could not divert the evidence seized by JFTC staff under administrative procedure due to the protection of due process. That is why the criminal investigation power was introduced. Along with the introduction of criminal procedure, the department of criminal investigation which engages in criminal investigation was established in the JFTC.

436. Under such circumstances, the JFTC had made public the policy statement on criminal accusation. In the policy statement '*Fair Trade Commission's Policy on Criminal Accusation of Criminal Cases Regarding Antimonopoly Violations*' (1990, hereinafter referred to as 'Old Policy Statement'). In the Old Policy Statement, the JFTC declared that it would accuse the case where the infringement might seriously damage the consumer welfare like price-fixing, market allocation, etc. and the alleged enterprises had been involved in the violation repeatedly so that the market would not be remedied by administrative measures even though they involve monetary sanction.

437. The JFTC reviewed the Old Policy Statement and newly published the Criminal Accusation and Investigation Policy[87] in accordance with the 2005 amendment which provided the JFTC for the criminal procedure and incorporated the leniency application into the AMA. It has been revised in 2009 and 2020 according to amendment of AMA.

438. Maintaining its policy of vigorously filing criminal accusation against serious and vicious infringements, the Criminal Accusation and Investigation Policy makes it clear that the JFTC will assign the staff members of the JFTC who are specially designated to engage in criminal investigation (hereinafter referred to in this part as 'Staff Members') to investigate the suspicious case of the violation of the AMA in case where there is a considerable reason for suspicion of being fallen under the policy statement mentioned above. It also provides that the JFTC files a criminal accusation as the result of the criminal investigation in case where it is convinced that a criminal offense takes place.

§2. Overview of Criminal Investigation Procedure in AMA

439. The difference between administrative and criminal investigation is roughly described as following; the former one is oriented to issue administrative measures in order to eliminate the anticompetitive conduct in question and prevent similar violation in future, and the latter is aimed at punishing the related persons and companies to make them learned that the anticompetitive business practice is deserved felony. Consequently, the violation which can be targeted as the criminal procedure is limited to the conduct which is deemed to substantially restrain competition in the market, in particular, unreasonable restraint of trade; however, there has been no criminal accusation so far in private monopoly cases.

440. The criminal investigation procedure of the AMA is, however, slightly different from investigation conducted by a police officer and public prosecutor. According to the Supreme Court decision on a tax evasion case, criminal investigation under the Act on General Rules for National Taxes (Act No. 66 of 1962), which is almost identical to the criminal investigation procedure of the AMA, is a kind of administrative proceedings. The nature of the AMA procedure is, therefore, construed to be a kind of 'administrative' proceeding. Consequently, the AMA has special rules, unlike those under the criminal one, which are provided in the light of due process. It is not required, for example, to notify a suspect that they have the right to remain silent, although they have it. It is also a difference that the AMA does not grant JFTC investigators the authority to arrest a suspect.

87. Fair Trade Commission's Policy on Criminal Accusation and Compulsory Investigation of Criminal Cases Regarding Antimonopoly Violations.

Chapter 2. Investigating and Search Power

441.

(Article 101)

(1) Whenever necessary in the investigation of a criminal case (cases related to crimes in Articles 89 to 91 inclusive; hereinafter the same applies in this Chapter), a staff member of the Fair Trade Commission (limited to the staff members designated by the Fair Trade Commission; hereinafter referred to in this Chapter as 'FTC Staff Member(s)') may request a criminal suspect or witness (hereinafter referred to in this paragraph as 'Criminal Suspect(s), etc.') to appear before the Fair Trade Commission, may question a Criminal Suspect, etc., inspect an object possessed or abandoned by a Criminal Suspect, etc., and may retain an object voluntarily submitted or abandoned by a Criminal Suspect, etc.
(2) In the course of an investigation in a criminal case, an FTC Staff Member may inquire with a public agency or public or private organization and request that the agency or organization report the necessary matters.

(Article 102)

(1) Whenever necessary in the investigation of a criminal case, an FTC Staff Member may conduct an on-site inspection, search, or seizure, by virtue of a Warrant issued in advance by a judge of the district court or summary court having jurisdiction over the location of the Fair Trade Commission (Note: Tokyo District Court and Tokyo Summary Court).
(2) In a case under the preceding paragraph requiring urgency, an FTC Staff Member may take the measures under the preceding paragraph by virtue of a warrant issued in advance by a judge of the district court or the summary court having jurisdiction over the location of the site to be inspected, the site, body or an object to be searched, or the object to be seized.
(3) When an FTC Staff Member requests a warrant provided for in paragraph (1) or the preceding paragraph (hereinafter referred to in this Chapter as a 'Warrant'), the FTC Staff Member must submit materials that confirm the existence of a criminal case.
(4) When a request provided in the preceding paragraph is made, the judge of the district court or the summary court must issue a Warrant to the FTC Staff Member with the judge's name and seal affixed thereto, and the following information entered thereon: the site to be inspected; the site, body or object to be searched; or the object to be seized; the government position and name of the person making the request; the Warrant's valid period; the fact that the inspection, search or seizure may not be initiated and the Warrant must be returned after the expiration of the valid period; the date of issuance of the Warrant; and the name of the court to which the judge belongs. In this case, the name of the criminal suspect and the fact of a criminal offense, if known, must also be written.

(5) An FTC Staff Member may deliver a Warrant to another FTC Staff Member and have that FTC Staff Member conduct the on-site inspection, search or seizure.

(Article 103)

(1) Whenever necessary in the investigation of a criminal case, after receipt of a Warrant, an FTC Staff Member may seize postal items, correspondence or documents related to telegrams that are sent by or to a criminal suspect and stored or possessed by persons handling communication affairs pursuant to the provisions of laws and regulations.
(2) After receipt of a Warrant, an FTC Staff Member may seize postal items, correspondence or documents related to telegrams that are stored or possessed by persons handling communication affairs pursuant to the provisions of laws and regulations and do not fall under the provisions of the preceding paragraph, to the extent that there are sufficient grounds to suspect each of the items are related to a criminal case.
(3) When the measures under the preceding two paragraphs have been taken, FTC Staff Members must notify the sender or recipient of the items to that effect; provided, however, that this does not apply when notifying the sender or recipient is likely to hinder the investigation of the criminal case.

(Article 104)

(1) No on-site inspection, search or seizure may be conducted during the period from sunset to sunrise unless it is specified on the Warrant that the Warrant may be executed at night.
(2) When it is considered to be necessary, an on-site inspection, search or seizure that was initiated before sunset may be continued beyond sunset.

(Article 105)

Warrants for on-site inspection, search or seizure must be shown to the person that is subject to such measures.

(Article 106)

When conducting questioning, inspection, retention, on-site inspection, search or seizure pursuant to the provisions of this Chapter, an FTC Staff Member must carry an identification card that indicates their official status and produce it at the request of persons concerned.

(Article 107)

(1) Whenever necessary for conducting an on-site inspection, search, or seizure, an FTC Staff Member may open locks, open seals and take other necessary measures.
(2) The measures set forth in the preceding paragraph may be taken in relation to objects retained or seized.

(Article 108)

FTC Staff Members may prohibit any person from entering or leaving the site without permission while the questioning, inspection, retention, on-site inspection, search or seizure pursuant to the provisions of this Chapter are being conducted.

(Article 109)

(1) When conducting an on-site inspection, search or seizure of a person's residence, or a residence, building or other site guarded by a person, an FTC Staff Member must have the owner or superintendent (including their representative or agent or other person who can act on their behalf), or their employee or cohabitating relative who has attained the age of majority witness it.
(2) If it is not possible, in a case under the preceding paragraph, to have a person provided in that paragraph witness the on-site inspection, search, or seizure, an FTC Staff Member must have a neighbor who has attained the age of majority or a local police official or local government official witness it.
(3) Any body-search of a female must be conducted in the presence of a female witness over the age of majority; provided, however, that this does not apply to urgent cases.

(Article 110)

– If necessary in the course of an on-site inspection, search or seizure, an FTC Staff Member may request the assistance of police officials.

(Article 111)

After carrying out questioning, inspection, retention, on-site inspection, search or seizure pursuant to the provisions of this Chapter, an FTC Staff Member must prepare a written report that states the date when the measures were taken and the findings, and show it to the person who was questioned or the witness, and, along with the person who was questioned or the witness, affix the person's name and seal thereto; provided, however, that if the person who was questioned or the witness does not affix the person's name and seal thereto or is unable to do so, it is sufficient to make supplementary note to that effect.

(Article 112)

After carrying out retention or seizure, an FTC Staff Member must prepare an inventory of the objects retained or seized and deliver a copy of the inventory to the owner or holder of the objects retained or seized or a person who can act in lieu of the owner or holder.

(Article 113)

Regarding a retained or seized object that is difficult to transport or store, an FTC Staff Member may, with the consent of the owner or holder of the object or other person that the FTC Staff Member finds to be appropriate, have such a person store the object after receiving a safekeeping receipt.

(Article 114)

(1) After a retained or seized object no longer needs to be held in custody, the Fair Trade Commission must return the object to the person to whom it should be returned.
(2) If the Fair Trade Commission cannot return a retained or seized object set forth in the preceding paragraph because it does not know the domicile or residence of the person to whom the object should be returned or because of another reason, the Fair Trade Commission must issue a public notice to that effect.
(3) If no request is made for the return of a retained or seized object regarding which a public notice has been issued pursuant to the preceding paragraph after six months have elapsed since the day of the public notice, the object belongs to the national treasury.

(Article 115)

After completing the investigation of a criminal case, a FTC Staff Member must report the results of the investigation to the Fair Trade Commission.

(Article 116)

(1) In the case where an accusation is filed pursuant to the provisions of Article 74, paragraph (1) as a result of the investigation of a criminal case, when there are any retained or seized objects, the Fair Trade Commission must hand over the objects together with the inventory thereof.
(2) If a retained or seized object set forth in the preceding paragraph is being stored pursuant to the provisions of Article 113, the Fair Trade Commission must hand over the safekeeping receipt set forth in that Article and notify the person storing the object pursuant to that Article to that effect.
(3) When a retained or seized object is handed over pursuant to the provisions of the preceding two paragraphs, the object is deemed to have been seized pursuant to the provisions of the Code of Criminal Procedure.

(Article 117)

The provisions of Chapters II to IV inclusive of the Administrative Procedure Act do not apply to measures taken or administrative guidance implemented by the Fair Trade Commission or an FTC Staff Member in accordance with the provisions of this Chapter.

(Article 118)

Measures taken by the Fair Trade Commission or an FTC Staff Member pursuant to the provisions of this Chapter cannot be appealed under the Administrative Appeal Act.

442. Article 101 provides that the Staff Member may exercise their authority to request criminal suspects or witnesses to come to the JFTC's office and to submit objects and materials that they possess.

443. Also, the Staff Members may conduct on-the-spot investigation and search, seizure or seizure with ordering records, with the permission of the court, at the facilities of the suspects and the residence of the related persons pursuant to Article 102, if necessary. Moreover, the Staff Members, when necessary to investigate a criminal case, may seize postal items, correspondence mails and telegrams that are sent by or to criminal suspects and stored or possessed by persons, with the permission of the court, pursuant to Article 103.

444. As provided in Article 102(4), the research warrant is issued by the judge of the district court or the summary court in the form of a document with the judge's name and such information in writing as the site to be inspected; the site, person or objects to be searched; or the objects to be seized; the government position and name of the person making the request; the permission's valid period.

445. As Article 101(2) sets out, the search is conducted by the staff members alone in some cases and in cooperation with public prosecutors in other cases. It depends on the cases.

446. The staff members usually initiate the search in the morning, and it may last in the evening, pursuant to Article 104. At the beginning of the search, the Staff Members shall indicate the search warrant issued by the court to permit to execute disposition, i.e., on-site inspection, search or seizure, to those whom such measures are to be made. The staff members shall also, when conducting questioning, inspection, retention, on-site inspection, search or seizure pursuant to the provisions of this chapter, carry an identification card so that they can indicate their identity to the criminal suspects upon their request (Article 106). With respect to the seizure, the Staff Members seize original materials and documents, not the copies of them.

447. The Staff Members may request, if necessary, in the course of on-the-spot investigation and search or seizure, the assistance of police officials (Article 110). Pursuant to Article 111, the Staff Members, after conducting questioning, inspection, retention, on-the-spot investigation, search or seizure, shall prepare a written report that states the date of the measures were made and the findings, show it to the person who was questioned or has witnessed it and, along with the person who was questioned or has witnessed it, affix their names and seals thereto. Also, the Staff Members shall, after conducting retention or seizure, prepare an inventory of the objects retained or seized and deliver a transcript of the inventory to the owner or holder of the objects retained or seized or a person who can act in lieu of the owners or holders (Article 112).

448. When the JFTC, after conducting criminal investigation, files a criminal accusation with the Prosecutor General, the JFTC has to transfer the objects, which

Staff Members retained or seized to the public prosecutor's office with the inventory of such objects. The objects possessed by the public prosecutor's office through the transfer procedure shall be deemed as seized pursuant to the provisions of the Code of Criminal Procedure (Article 116).

449. Even if a company has a complaint against any measures made by the JFTC or the Staff Members pursuant to the provisions of criminal investigation power, the company is not allowed to appeal under the Administrative Appeal Act (Article 118). This is because the criminal investigation is conducted aiming at criminal charge and therefore it is not appropriate that an administrative organ judges the right or wrong of such measures. Such measures are also exempted from the application of relevant provisions of the Administrative Procedure Act (Article 117). Thus, those who have a complaint against such a measure will file an administrative lawsuit against the measure pursuant to the Administrative Case Litigation Act.

450. The related provisions are as follows:

(Article 101)

(1) Whenever necessary in the investigation of a criminal case (cases related to crimes in Articles 89 to 91 inclusive; hereinafter the same applies in this Chapter), a staff member of the Fair Trade Commission (limited to the staff members designated by the Fair Trade Commission; hereinafter referred to in this Chapter as 'FTC Staff Member(s)') may request a criminal suspect or witness (hereinafter referred to in this paragraph as 'Criminal Suspect(s), etc.') to appear before the Fair Trade Commission, may question a Criminal Suspect, etc., inspect an object possessed or abandoned by a Criminal Suspect, etc., and may retain an object voluntarily submitted or abandoned by a Criminal Suspect, etc.

(2) In the course of an investigation in a criminal case, an FTC Staff Member may inquire with a public agency or public or private organization and request that the agency or organization report the necessary matters.

(Article 102)

(1) Whenever necessary in the investigation of a criminal case, an FTC Staff Member may conduct an on-site inspection, search, seizure, or seizure with ordering records ('seizure with ordering records' as used in this Act shall mean having a custodian of the electromagnetic records ('electromagnetic records' as used in this Act shall mean any records which are produced by electronic, magnetic or any other means unrecognizable by natural perception and are used for data-processing with a computer; the same applies hereinafter) or other persons with the authority to use electromagnetic records copy the necessary electromagnetic records onto the recording medium or print them out, and seizing such recording medium; the same applies hereinafter) by virtue of a Warrant issued in advance by a

judge of the district court or summary court having jurisdiction over the location of the Fair Trade Commission (Note: Tokyo District Court and Tokyo Summary Court).

(2) *Where the object to be seized is a computer, and with regard to a recording medium connected via telecommunication lines to the computer, it may be reasonably supposed that the recording medium is used to retain electromagnetic records, which have been made or altered using the computer or which may be altered or erased using the computer, the Fair Trade Commission may seize the computer or other recording medium after the electromagnetic records have been copied onto such computer or other recording medium.*

(3) *In a case under the preceding paragraphs requiring urgency, an FTC Staff Member may take the measures under the preceding paragraphs by virtue of a warrant issued in advance by a judge of the district court or the summary court having jurisdiction over the location of the site to be inspected, the site, body or an object to be searched, or the object to be seized, or the person to whom it may cause to record or print the electromagnetic record.*

(4) *When an FTC Staff Member requests a warrant provided for in paragraphs (1) or the preceding paragraph (excluding Article 114-3, paragraph (4) and (5), hereinafter referred to in this Chapter as a 'Warrant'), the FTC Staff Member must submit materials that confirm the existence of a criminal case.*

(5) *If a request provided in the preceding paragraph is made, the judge of the district court or the summary court must issue a Warrant to the FTC Staff Member with the judge's name and seal affixed thereto, and the following information entered thereon: the site to be inspected; the site, body or object to be searched; or the object to be seized; the electromagnetic records to be recorded or printed; the government position and name of the person to be made to record or print the electromagnetic records, and the government position and name of the person making the request; the Warrant's valid period; the fact that the inspection, search or seizure may not be initiated and the Warrant must be returned after the expiration of the valid period; the date of issuance of the Warrant; and the name of the court to which the judge belongs. In this case, the name of the criminal suspect (for a corporation, this means its name) and the fact of a criminal offense, if known, must also be written.*

(6) *In a case under paragraph (2), other than the matters provided by the preceding paragraph, the scope of the recording medium requiring duplication of the relevant electromagnetic records connected to the computer to seize via telecommunication lines must be written on the Warrant.*

(7) *An FTC Staff Member may deliver a Warrant to another FTC Staff Member and have that FTC Staff Member conduct the on-site inspection, search or seizure or seizure with ordering records.*

(Article 103)

(1) Whenever necessary in the investigation of a criminal case, after receipt of a Warrant, an FTC Staff Member may seize postal items, correspondence or documents related to telegrams that are sent by or to a criminal suspect and stored or possessed by persons handling communication affairs pursuant to the provisions of laws and regulations.

(2) After receipt of a Warrant, an FTC Staff Member may seize postal items, correspondence or documents related to telegrams that are stored or possessed by persons handling communication affairs pursuant to the provisions of laws and regulations and do not fall under the provisions of the preceding paragraph, to the extent that there are sufficient grounds to suspect each of the items are related to a criminal case.

(3) If the measures under the preceding two paragraphs have been taken, FTC Staff Members must notify the sender or recipient of the items to that effect; provided, however, that this does not apply if notifying the sender or recipient is likely to hinder the investigation of the criminal case.

(Article 103-2)

(1) Whenever necessary for seizure or seizure with ordering records, an FTC Staff Member may request in writing to a person who conducts business with one's own facilities for telecommunication of other persons, or a person who has facilities to mediate communication of an unspecified number of persons for the business not to erase the electromagnetic records' communication history as specified for the senders, destinations, date and time, etc. for a period not exceeding thirty days. In this case, if found it unnecessary to seize or seize by ordering records the relevant electromagnetic records, an FTC Staff Member must render a decision to rescind the request.

(2) The time period set forth in the preceding paragraph asking for non-erasing may be extended not exceeding thirty days if necessary; provided, however, the total time period asking for non-erasing shall not exceed sixty days.

(3) If a request is made pursuant to the provisions of paragraph (1), and if it considers it particularly necessary, an FTC Staff Member may ask not to divulge the matters concerning the request without good reason.

(Article 103-3)

If an object to seize is a recording medium pertaining to electromagnetic records, an FTC Staff Member may take any of the following measures instead of seizure.

(i) to copy the electromagnetic records recorded on the recording medium which is to be seized onto some other recording medium, print them out or transfer them, and seize such other recording medium.

(ii) to have the person undergoing the seizure copy the electromagnetic records recorded on the recording medium which is to be seized onto some other recording medium, print them out or transfer them, and seize such other recording medium.

(Article 104)

(1) No on-site inspection, search, seizure or seizure with ordering records or seizure may be conducted during the period from sunset to sunrise unless it is specified on the Warrant that the Warrant may be executed at night.
(2) If it is considered to be necessary, an on-site inspection, search, seizure or seizure with ordering records that was initiated before sunset may be continued beyond sunset.

(Article 105)

Warrants for on-site inspection, search, seizure or seizure with ordering records must be shown to the person that is subject to such measures.

(Article 106)

When conducting questioning, inspection, retention, on-site inspection, search, seizure or seizure with ordering records pursuant to the provisions of this Chapter, an FTC Staff Member must carry an identification card that indicates their official status and produce it at the request of persons concerned.

(Article 107)

(1) Whenever necessary for conducting an on-site inspection, search, seizure or seizure with ordering records, an FTC Staff Member may open locks, open seals and take other necessary measures.
(2) The measures set forth in the preceding paragraph may be taken in relation to objects retained, seized or seized with ordering records.

(Article 107-2)

If an object to inspect or object to seize is a recording medium pertaining to electromagnetic records, an FTC Staff Member may ask for cooperation in the operation of a computer and others from a person to be inspected, searched or seized.

(Article 108)

FTC Staff Members may prohibit any person from entering or leaving the site without permission while the questioning, inspection, retention, on-site inspection, search, seizure or seizure with ordering records pursuant to the provisions of this Chapter are being conducted.

(Article 109)

(1) When conducting an on-site inspection, search, seizure or seizure with ordering records of a person's residence, or a residence, building or other

site guarded by a person, an FTC Staff Member must have the owner or superintendent (including their representative or agent or other person who can act on their behalf), or their employee or cohabitating relative who has attained the age of majority witness it.

(2) If it is not possible, in a case under the preceding paragraph, to have a person provided in that paragraph witness the on-site inspection, search, or seizure, an FTC Staff Member must have a neighbour who has attained the age of majority or a local police official or local government official witness it.

(3) Any body-search of a female must be conducted in the presence of a female witness over the age of majority; provided, however, that this does not apply to urgent cases.

(Article 110)

If necessary in the course of an on-site inspection, search, seizure or seizure with ordering records, an FTC Staff Member may request the assistance of police officials.

(Article 111)

After carrying out questioning, inspection, retention, on-site inspection, search, seizure or seizure with ordering records or seizure pursuant to the provisions of this Chapter, an FTC Staff Member must prepare a written report that states the date when the measures were taken and the findings, and show it to the person who was questioned or the witness, and, along with the person who was questioned or the witness, affix the person's name and seal thereto; provided, however, that if the person who was questioned or the witness does not affix the person's name and seal thereto or is unable to do so, it is sufficient to make supplementary note to that effect.

(Article 112)

After carrying out retention, seizure or seizure with ordering records, an FTC Staff Member must prepare an inventory of the objects retained or seized and deliver a copy of the inventory to the owner or holder of the objects retained, seized or seized with ordering records (including a person subjected to the measure under the provisions of Article 103-3) or a person who can act in lieu of the owner or holder.

(Article 113)

Regarding an object retained, seized or seized with ordering records that is difficult to transport or store, an FTC Staff Member may, with the consent of the owner or holder of the object or other person that the FTC Staff Member finds to be appropriate, have such a person store the object after receiving a safe-keeping receipt.

(Article 114)

(1) After an object retained, seized or seized with ordering records no longer needs to be held in custody, the Fair Trade Commission must return the object to the person to whom it should be returned.
(2) If the Fair Trade Commission cannot return an object that is retained, seized, or seized with ordering records set forth in the preceding paragraph because it does not know the domicile or residence of the person to whom the object should be returned or because of another reason, the Fair Trade Commission must issue a public notice to that effect.
(3) If no request is made for the return of an object retained, seized, or seized with ordering records regarding which a public notice has been issued pursuant to the preceding paragraph after six months have elapsed since the day of the public notice, the object belongs to the national treasury.

(Article 114-2)

(1) If the seized object is a recording medium which was seized after transferring the electromagnetic records or having the electromagnetic records transferred pursuant to the provisions of Article 103-3 and does not need to be placed in custody, where the person who underwent the seizure and the owner, possessor or custodian of such recording medium differ, the Fair Trade Commission must deliver the recording medium to the person who underwent the seizure or shall allow the copying of the electromagnetic records.
(2) The provisions of paragraph (2) of the preceding Article apply mutatis mutandis to the delivery or duplication pursuant to the provisions of the paragraph of the preceding Article.
(3) If neither delivery nor duplication is requested under the preceding paragraph after six months from the date of public notice as provided for under paragraph (2) of the preceding Article, which provision is applied mutatis mutandis under the preceding paragraph, neither delivery nor duplication shall be required to be made. The provisions of paragraph (2) of the preceding Article apply mutatis mutandis to the delivery or duplication pursuant to the provisions of the paragraph of the preceding Article.

(Article 114-3)

(1) Whenever necessary in the investigation of a criminal case, an FTC Staff Member may commission persons who have knowledge and experience to give expert opinions on objects retained, seized or seized with ordering records, or commission interpreters or translators.
(2) The persons commissioned to give expert opinions pursuant to the provisions of the preceding paragraph (referred to in the paragraphs (4) and (5) as "expert witness") may destruct the objects involved with the permission by a judge of the district court or summary court having jurisdiction over the location of the Fair Trade Commission.
(3) A request for permission under the preceding paragraph must be made by an FTC Staff Member.

(4) If a request provided in the preceding paragraph is made, the judge must issue a Warrant to the FTC Staff Member with the judge's name and seal affixed thereto, and the following information entered thereon: the name of the suspect(for a corporation, this means its name), the charge, the object to destruct, the names of the expert witnesses; the government position and name of the person making the request; the Warrant's valid period; the fact that the inspection, search or seizure may not be initiated and the Warrant must be returned after the expiration of the valid period; the date of issuance of the Warrant; and the name of the court to which the judge belongs.
(5) The expert witnesses must show the Warrant under the provisions of paragraph (2) to the person that is subject to such measures.

(Article 115)

After completing the investigation of a criminal case, an FTC Staff Member must report the results of the investigation to the Fair Trade Commission.

(Article 116)

(1) If an accusation is filed pursuant to the provisions of Article 74, paragraph (1) as a result of the investigation of a criminal case, if there are any objects retained, seized or seized with ordering records, the Fair Trade Commission must hand over the objects together with the inventory thereof.
(2) If any objects retained, seized or seized with ordering records set forth in the preceding paragraph is being stored pursuant to the provisions of Article 113, the Fair Trade Commission must hand over the safekeeping receipt set forth in that Article and notify the person storing the object pursuant to that Article to that effect.
(3) When any objects retained, seized or seized with ordering records is handed over pursuant to the provisions of the preceding two paragraphs, the object is deemed to have been seized pursuant to the provisions of the Code of Criminal Procedure.

(Article 117)

The provisions of Chapters II to IV inclusive of the Administrative Procedure Act do not apply to measures taken or administrative guidance implemented by the Fair Trade Commission or an FTC Staff Member in accordance with the provisions of this Chapter.

(Article 118)

Measures taken by the Fair Trade Commission or an FTC Staff Member pursuant to the provisions of this Chapter cannot be appealed under the Administrative Appeal Act.

Chapter 3. Coordination with Administrative Procedures

451. There is a firewall between the criminal investigation section and the administrative investigation section from the viewpoint of the protection of due process. It is prohibited by the AMA that the JFTC utilizes the evidence or information obtained under administrative investigation in the criminal case (Article 47(4)). If not, the protection of due process would be significantly impaired since criminal penalty is applied to refusal to allow administrative investigation that is conducted without search warrant. In other words, such transfer creates a loophole of protection of the privilege against self-incrimination and undermines search warrant requirement in criminal proceedings. The firewall is established pursuant to provisions of the Criminal Investigation Rules.[88]

452. For example, section 4 of the Criminal Investigation Rules provide that the investigator shall, when the contacted facts in the case where he took the measures of administrative investigation power are considered to be the incipiency of a criminal case, immediately report to the director general of the investigation bureau of the general secretariat and follow his instructions, and shall not report on the facts directly to the staff members for criminal investigation. The rules also provide that the director general of the investigation bureau shall, upon coming into contact with the incipient facts of a criminal case, report to the commission. The commission, when it finds appropriate, assigns the Staff Members to initiate a criminal investigation.

453. On the other hand, the JFTC is allowed to use information or evidence obtained in the criminal investigation when it takes an administrative measure because any due process problems are not raised in such circumstances. In Japan, as already described in Part I, Chapter 5, §3 above, cartels and bid riggings are subject to both administrative measures and criminal penalty. Thus, the JFTC usually issues administrative orders after it files criminal accusation, and in the course of proceedings to issue these administrative orders, it uses the evidence and information obtained under criminal investigation.

88. Rules on Investigation of Criminal Cases by the Fair Trade Commission.

Chapter 4. Implementation of the Criminal Investigation

454. Just after the 2005 amendment was enacted, the newly introduced criminal investigation power was exercised in the bid rigging investigation concerning night-soil treatment plant construction in 2006, which led to criminal accusation by the JFTC against eleven companies and eleven individuals.[89] The companies and individuals were convicted in the following criminal trial. Including the nightsoil bid rigging case, in ten cartel or bid rigging cases criminal investigation power has been implemented by 2023. In some of these cases, the JFTC and the public prosecutor's office allegedly conducted a joint investigation. A joint investigation between them had been impossible before the introduction of the criminal investigation power in 2005.

89. Nightsoil Treatment Plant Construction Case (JFTC Criminal Accusation on 23 May and 12 Jun. 2006, followed by JFTC Cease and Desist Order on 16 Jan. 2007).

Chapter 5. Role of Prosecutors

455. Article 96 provides that the Prosecutors' Office can consider the act as a crime only after an accusation is filed by the JFTC (Article 96, AMA). This is called the JFTC's 'Exclusive Accusation System'. When the JFTC considers that a criminal offense has taken place, it shall file an accusation with the Prosecutor General pursuant to Article 74. If the Prosecutor General decides not to prosecute, the Prosecutor General should promptly notify, in writing, the reason to the Prime Minister through the Minister of Justice. The decision by the Prosecutor General not to prosecute regardless of criminal accusation by the JFTC has never been made in the last half century.

456. Practically, however, the JFTC and the Public Prosecutors Office have close contact with each other before accusation by holding the Conference of Criminal Accusation for ensuring smooth and appropriate accusation. In this regard, Criminal Accusation and Investigation Policy states as follows:

> *'At the time of consideration of criminal accusations, in order to ensure smooth and appropriate criminal accusation, the FTC with the prosecutorial authorities will hold "the Conference of Criminal Accusation" consisting of prosecutors under the Prosecutor in Finance and Economic Article of Supreme Public Prosecutors Office ... and the Director General and officers of the Compulsory Investigation Department ..., and exchange opinions and information on concrete problems of each of the said case.'* [90]

90. Criminal Accusation and Investigation Policy, para. 3.

Part V. International Aspects

Chapter 1. Cooperation under Administrative Agreement

§1. General Remarks

457. International cooperation with foreign competition authorities has been one of the priorities of the JFTC. The first visible event in the international cooperation was the bilateral meeting with US antitrust agencies in 1977 in Washington D.C. Since then, the JFTC has been holding various bilateral meetings with foreign competition authorities such as US, EU, UK Germany, France, South Korea, Canada, Australia and China. The JFTC has also actively participated in the Organization for Economic Co-operation and Development (OECD) competition committee since its foundation as well as the United Nations Conference on Trade and Development (UNCTAD) Competition Law and Expert Group, the Asia Pacific Economic Cooperation (APEC) Competition Policy and Law Group (CPLG) and the International Competition Network (ICN). In addition to these activities, the JFTC has also engaged in technical assistance to young competition agencies in mainly East Asia region since 1990s.

458. Such international cooperation and other daily-basis communications with foreign competition authorities have increased in the quantitative as well as the qualitative sense with the globalization of the world economy. Under the circumstances the momentum towards conclusion of administrative cooperation agreement with foreign government had become larger in the late 1990s.

459. The Japanese government in 1999 concluded the first bilateral administrative cooperation agreement, 'Agreement between the Government of Japan and the Government of the United States of America concerning Cooperation on Anticompetitive Activities' with US. After the conclusion of the first bilateral cooperation agreement, the Japanese government concluded a similar agreement with EU in 2003, and Canada in 2005.

460. In parallel with this movement, the Japanese government actively pursued bilateral free trade agreements in the 2000s. The first bilateral EPA, which is a kind of free trade agreement, was with Singapore concluded in 2002. The EPA includes competition chapter, which contains similar provisions of the above-mentioned bilateral administrative cooperation arrangements.

461. Since the mid-2000s, the Japanese government has taken the position that it chooses to include provisions of cooperation in competition policy into EPA, rather than pursuing administrative cooperation agreement specialized in competition policy. In line with this policy, after concluding cooperative agreement with Canada, there has been no other administrative cooperation agreement on competition policy, while the Japanese government has concluded several bilateral EPAs containing competition chapter. The jurisdictions with which Japan has concluded EPAs with competition chapter cover various areas, Asia, Europe, and Latin America.

462. In terms of the form of law, EPA is a treaty that the governments conclude between other jurisdictions and requires the approval of the Diet to take into effect, while a cooperation agreement is deemed as an administrative arrangement that the governments can conclude on a diplomatic basis. Also, the JFTC has come to more employ a way of exchanging notes with foreign competition authorities in order to establish the matters concerning cooperation with them. This is called as 'MOC' and the JFTC has concluded MOCs with more than ten jurisdictions. Some of them are those which comprise provisions that substantially take the form of cooperation agreements, and others are those which set out details just to complement fundamental agreements including EPAs. When it comes to practical matters for competition authority, however, there is no conceivable difference no matter how they are formulated.

463. To deepen such cooperative relationships, the JFTC recently concluded with Australia and Canada so-called second-generation agreements aiming at facilitating communication of information obtained through enforcement activities including investigations. The JFTC expects that those cooperation agreements (including EPAs, administrative arrangements, MOCs and any other type of cooperative agreements, the same apply hereinafter) with other jurisdictions will be upgraded to the second-generation agreements.

§2. Cooperation Agreement on Competition Policy

464. The three agreements (with US, EU and Canada) on competition policy consists of five basic provisions, i.e., notification, cooperation and coordination on enforcement activities between competition authorities, request for enforcement activities (positive comity), and paying consideration to the important interests of the other party (negative comity).

465. Some agreements also have a provision of periodical bilateral consultations between competition authorities of the parties under which the JFTC and its counterparties have held bilateral meetings where top officials discuss various policy and enforcement issues once a year or two years. This structure was established when the first bilateral cooperation agreement was concluded between JFTC and US authorities (Antitrust Division of Department of Justice and Federal Trade

Commission). The provisions in other agreements are identical to those of this cooperation agreement. The followings are typical provisions of those cooperation agreements.

I. Notification of Enforcement Activities

466. Some cooperation agreements provide that each party shall notify the other party of its enforcement activities that, the notifying competition authority considers, may affect the important interests of the other party. The notification system plays a key role in the cooperation agreements since it provides an opportunity for cooperation and coordination on enforcement activities. It also enables that negative comity clause works well by letting each party know the enforcement activities of the other party.

467. The basic framework of the notification system was modelled after the notification scheme under the recommendation of the OECD in 1995 (Revised Recommendation of The Council concerning Co-operation between Member Countries on Anticompetitive Practices Affecting International Trade). The typical case where the notification is required is that the competition authority investigates an enterprise that is incorporated or organized under the applicable laws and regulations within the territory of the other country.

468. Notification shall be given as promptly as possible when the competition authority becomes aware that its enforcement activities may affect the important interests of the other party. That means each competition authority does not necessarily notify its enforcement activities in advance. The objective of the prior notification requirement is possible when the notified party would like to ask the notifying party to hold consultation before the latter takes formal action.

469. The cooperation agreements stipulate that notification shall be sufficiently detailed to enable the notified competition authority to make an initial evaluation of the effect on its party's important interests. It depends on the case and circumstances how detailed the notified information should be, but at least the notified competition authority needs information necessary to evaluate the overall impact on its party's important interests. In that sense, the provision requires 'sufficiently detailed' notification.

470. There is no agreement that has provision with regard to the way of notification. Telephone and email are, however, acceptable for implementation of notification. The notification can be made directly between the competition authorities. In some cooperation agreements, the notification shall be confirmed in writing through the diplomatic channel and the confirmation shall be made as promptly as practically possible after the communication concerned between them.[91]

91. For example, Art. 11 of the administrative cooperation agreement between Japan and US sets out as follows: *In the event that information communicated by a Party to the other Party pursuant to this*

II. Cooperation on Enforcement Activities Between Competition Authorities

471. Not a few agreements have specific scheme for cooperation between the authorities. The authorities cooperate under each domestic laws and regulations. The relevant provisions of the cooperation agreements stipulate some examples of forms of cooperation, but cooperation is not limited to those forms. The cooperation forms are as follows:

i. Inform the competition authority of the other Party with respect to its enforcement activities involving anticompetitive activities that the informing competition authority considers may also have an adverse effect on competition within the territory of the other country. In some agreements, the authorities are required to notify the other party of its enforcement activities, for example, taking formal actions, in advance. Those include administrative orders, such as Cease and Desist Order and Payment Order.
ii. Provide the competition authority of the other Party with any significant information, within its possession and that comes to its attention, about anticompetitive activities that the providing competition authority considers may be relevant to, or may warrant, enforcement activities by the competition authority of the other Party.
iii. Provide the competition authority of the other Party, upon request and in accordance with the provisions of agreements, with information within its possession that is relevant to the enforcement activities of the competition authority of the other Party.

472. With respect to ii and iii above, providing the information that the JFTC possesses, whether voluntarily or upon request of the other party, is limited to public information in many cases, since the cooperation shall be subject to Japanese domestic laws and regulations. However, as globalization of economy is rapidly developing and cross-border violation is becoming an everyday affair, closer cooperation between competition authorities including those they obtained in the course of investigation, has come to be essential for effective enforcement. That is the reason that it becomes necessary for competition authorities to conclude the 'second-generation agreements'.

473. On the other hand, it is needed to give a basis for competition authorities to provide confidential information to the third parties, i.e., foreign competition authorities. In general, the competition authorities are under strict prohibition to release the information that they obtained in their activities because such information contains secret intelligence of enterprises, and it should be strictly protected. To remove this restriction, therefore, the laws should authorize the staff of the

---

Agreement, except publicly available information, is needed for presentation to a grand jury or to a court or a judge in criminal proceedings, that Party shall submit a request for such information to the other Party through the diplomatic channel or other channel established in accordance with the law of the requested Party (https://www.jftc.go.jp/en/int_relations/agreements_files/usagree.pdf).

authorities to pass on the information to other competition authorities. In this regard, 2009 amendment incorporated a new article as follows:

(Article 43-2)

(1) The Fair Trade Commission may provide any foreign authority responsible for enforcement of any foreign laws and regulations equivalent to those of this Act (hereinafter referred to in this Article as a 'Foreign Competition Authority') with information that is deemed helpful and necessary for the execution performance of the Foreign Competition Authority's duties (limited to duties equivalent to those of the Fair Trade Commission as provided in this Act; the same applies in the following paragraph); provided, however, that this does not apply if the provision of the relevant information is found likely to interfere with the proper execution of this Act or to infringe on the interests of Japan in any other way.

(2) Whenever the Fair Trade Commission provides information to a Foreign Competition Authority pursuant to the provisions of the preceding paragraph, the Fair Trade Commission must confirm the matters listed in the following items:

(i) that the relevant Foreign Competition Authority is capable of providing information equivalent to the information provided pursuant to the provisions of the preceding paragraph;

(ii) that the secrecy of information provided as secret pursuant to the provisions of the preceding paragraph will be protected under the laws and regulations of the relevant foreign country to a degree that is equivalent to the degree to which the secrecy of such information is protected in Japan;

(iii) that the information provided pursuant to the provisions of the preceding paragraph will not be used by the relevant Foreign Competition Authority for purposes other than those contributing to the performance of its duties.

(3) Appropriate measures must be taken so that the information provided pursuant to the provisions of paragraph (1) is not used for criminal proceedings undertaken by a court or a judge in a foreign country.

474. This article is just to authorize the JFTC staff to provide foreign authorities with information necessary for enforcement and the details of exchange of information are generally set out in the cooperation agreements. The administrative agreements between JFTC and Australian competition authority (Australian Competition and Consumer Commission) were concluded for this reason.

III. Coordination on Enforcement Activities Between Competition Authorities

475. Where the competition authorities of both parties are pursuing enforcement activities with regard to related matters, it would be beneficial to both sides that the competition authorities coordinate their enforcement activities. The coordination provisions require each competition agency to consider coordination of their enforcement activities in that case.

476. A typical example in which coordination between competition authorities is required is a merger review where the proposed transaction may have an adverse effect on competition in the relevant markets in both countries. If the competition authority of one party imposes remedy including divestiture of facility located in the other party, the remedy may affect competition condition in the relevant market in the county. In such a case, coordination between competition authorities would be necessary and beneficial to the business and both authorities.

477. The agreements list the following factors which competition authorities should consider when they coordinate their enforcement activities:[92]

i. the effect of such coordination on their ability to achieve the objectives of their enforcement activities;
ii. the relative abilities of the competition authorities of the parties to obtain information necessary to conduct the enforcement activities;
iii. the extent to which the competition authority of either party can secure effective relief against the anticompetitive activities involved;
iv. the possible reduction of cost to the parties and to the persons subject to the enforcement activities;
v. the potential advantages of coordinated relief to the parties and to the persons subject to the enforcement activities.

IV. Negative Comity

478. Negative comity is the very traditional principle of international law. Any country must consider the important interests of other countries when it enforces its domestic laws and regulations in the international context. That includes refraining from enforcement. The cooperation agreement explicitly confirms this concept, i.e., it provides that each party shall give careful consideration to the important interests of the other party throughout all phases of its enforcement activities, including decisions regarding the initiation/termination of enforcement activities, the scope of enforcement activities and the nature of penalties or relief sought in each case. Whether or not to take actions, and what measures they would choose, is left to the discretion of each competition agency.

479. The agreement also lists some factors, which should be considered by the competition authorities under the negative comity clause. They are as follows:[93]

92. *See* Art. 4(2) of the Agreement Between the Government of Japan and the European Community Concerning Cooperation on Anticompetitive Activities (https://www.jftc.go.jp/en/int_relations/agreements_files/J-ECagreement.pdf).
93. *Ibid.*, Art. 6(3).

i. relative significance to the anticompetitive activities of conduct or transactions occurring within the territory of the country of the enforcing party as compared to those occurring within the territory of the other country;
ii. relative impact of the anticompetitive activities on the important interests of the respective parties;
iii. presence or absence of evidence of an intention on the part of those engaged in the anticompetitive activities to affect consumers, suppliers, or competitors within the territory of the country of the party conducting the enforcement activities;
iv. extent to which the anticompetitive activities substantially lessen competition in the market of each country;
v. degree of conflict or consistency between the enforcement activities by a party and the laws of the other country, or the policies or important interests of the other party;
vi. whether private persons, either natural or legal, will be placed under conflicting requirements by both parties;
vii. location of relevant assets and parties to the transaction;
viii. degree to which effective penalties or relief can be secured by the enforcement activities of the party against the anticompetitive activities;
ix. extent to which enforcement activities by the other party with respect to the same persons, either natural or legal, would be affected.

V. Positive Comity

480. The cooperation agreement does not use the phrase 'positive comity', but provides 'request of enforcement activity'. In other words, if the competition authority of a party believes that anticompetitive activities carried out in the territory of the other country may adversely affect the important interests of the former party, the former requests that the latter initiates appropriate enforcement activities with expectation that the requested authority will more effectively address the activities. This scheme is based on the concept of positive comity.

481. This notion is incorporated in the Revised Recommendation of the Council concerning Co-operation between Member Countries on Anticompetitive Practices Affecting International Trade, issued by the OECD in 1995. In case where anticompetitive activity has an adverse effect on the market of the country, which is carried out in the territory of the other country, and if the competition authority of the former country immediately takes an action against the anticompetitive activity, conflicts regarding jurisdiction might arise. The main purpose of the positive comity clause is to avoid such conflicts and to achieve effective enforcement activity.

482. Under this scheme, the requested competition authority shall carefully consider whether to initiate enforcement activities, or whether to expand ongoing enforcement activities if it has already engaged in any enforcement actions, with respect to the anticompetitive activities identified in the request. The requested agency does not have to accept the request. It has to inform, however, the requesting competition authority of its decision as soon as practically possible. In case where the requested competition authority has already initiated enforcement activities, it shall inform the requesting competition authority of their outcome and, to the extent possible, of significant interim developments.

§3. Competition Chapter of EPA

483. Cooperation agreement on competition policy is only related to competition issues between the two authorities in each country. EPA deals with wide range of economic issues including competition policy and therefore the contents of each EPA differ depending on economic circumstances of the countries.

484. The competition chapters of EPAs, which Japan has so far concluded, generally contain the above-mentioned five basic clauses. However, in some EPAs their competition chapters have only broad agreement to cooperate without any forms or methods of cooperation since the competition authorities in some countries are very young and have not yet established a system to enforce their competition laws. Considering such circumstances, some EPAs and the related agreements emphasize the importance of technical cooperation and the JFTC has provided technical assistance to its counterparts based on them.

Chapter 2. Other Types of Cooperation and Coordination

§1. Cooperation and Coordination Through Multilateral Forum

485. The JFTC has been actively participating in multilateral competition cooperation frameworks such as the ICN and the OECD. The ICN has been getting the most important cooperation scheme in the competition community with increase in the number of member agencies. The JFTC was one of the original members and has been a member of the steering group, which manages all ICN activities, since its establishment. With respect to ICN activities, the JFTC hosted the seventh ICN annual conference in Kyoto in 2008, the 2010 Cartel Workshop in Yokohama, 2018 Merger Workshop and 2023 Unilateral Conduct Workshop in Tokyo.

486. There is also a regional multilateral forum for competition cooperation. In Asia-Pacific area, the CPLG of the APEC plays that role. The CPLG was established to enhance understanding of the importance of competition policy so that trade and investment would be facilitated and privatized. The JFTC has been the Chair of the CPLG since 2005 and contributed to facilitate cooperation among member competition authorities in this region.

487. There is also a regional multilateral forum for competition cooperation. In Asia-Pacific area, the CPLG of the APEC plays that role. The CPLG was established to enhance understanding of the importance of competition policy so that trade and investment would be facilitated and privatized. The JFTC has been the Chair of the CPLG since 2005 and contributed to facilitate cooperation among member competition authorities in this region.

§2. Cooperation and Coordination in East Asia Region

I. Top Level Meeting and Conference

488. Japan has a strong economic relationship with countries in East Asia region because of geographical and cultural factors. On the other hand, in that area there were a few countries which had vigorous competition policy since the late 1990s. The JFTC, against that background, has positively engaged in technical assistance activities. In the 2000s many East Asian jurisdictions has established comprehensive competition laws and competition authorities were created. That means the importance of cooperation and coordination among competition agencies in that region would be increasing.

489. In this context, the JFTC, which is the oldest competition authority in the region, proposed to establish the framework in which competition agencies share experience and discuss important topics in competition policy and top officials meet and make face-to-face dialogue. That proposal, in 2005, led to the 'Top Level Officials' Meeting on Competition Policy in East Asia' (hereinafter referred to as 'Top

Level Meeting'), and the first meeting was held in Bogor, Indonesia, in May 2005. The Top Level Meeting has been annually held since then.

490. In the nineteenth Top Level Meeting, held in Kuala Lumpur, Malaysia in 2024, sixteen competition agencies in each jurisdiction got together and they discussed recent issues in competition policy in East Asia. Along with the Top Level Meeting, international conference on competition policy in East Asia is usually held. In addition to competition agencies' officials, private practitioners, scholars and businesses take part in the conference and share their views and experiences.

II. Technical Assistance

491. The JFTC has been actively engaging in technical assistance activity in East Asia. The JFTC has more than seventy years' experience in competition law enforcement and other competition policy-related activities, and Japan has, in some aspects, common or similar business regulations and practices with East Asian countries. Therefore, technical assistance by the JFTC may have good advantages for younger competition agencies in this region.

492. The JFTC, in collaboration with the Japan International Cooperation Agency (JICA), invites officials of younger agencies and holds training course, dispatches its officials to seminars held in the region, and occasionally a JFTC official is stationed in a country as advisory staff to its competition authority. In recent years, the JFTC has been providing technical assistance in collaboration with the KFTC (South Korean competition authority) and the TFTC (Taiwanese competition authority). These two agencies are well-experienced competition authorities in the region, and the collaboration has enriched the technical assistance activities by sharing experience among the three agencies.

Selected Bibliography

Koki Arai, 'Law and Economics in Japanese Competition Policy' (Springer, 2019).
Akira Inoue, 'Japanese Antitrust Law Manual: Law, Cases and Interpretation of Japanese Antimonopoly Act (International Competition Law)' (Kluwer Law International, 2007).
Japan Fair Trade Commission's website, https://www.jftc.go.jp/en/index.html.
Mitsuo Matsushita, 'Introduction to Japanese Antimonopoly Law' (Yuhikaku, 1990).
Anderson Mori & Tomotsune, 'Introduction to Japanese Business Law & Practice (Fifth Edition)' (LexisNexis, 2021).
Masako Wakui, 'Antimonopoly Law: Competition Law and Policy in Japan (Second Edition)' (Independently published, 2018).

Selected Bibliography

Index

The numbers here refers to paragraph numbers.

2005 amendment, 9, 434, 437, 454
2009 amendment, 9, 197, 213, 235, 473
2013 amendment, 428, 429, 432
2019 amendment, 319, 370

Abuse of superior bargaining position (ASBP), 15, 30, 176, 213, 232–239
Accepting (Acceptance of) assignment, 66, 67, 77, 237
Administrative Guidance, 30, 53, 132, 441, 450
Administrative hearing, 10, 109, 133, 275, 428, 429
Administrative investigation, 30, 186, 316–385, 451, 452
Antimonopoly Act (AMA), 35–45, 439–440
AMA Enforcement Order, 25, 83, 170, 388, 391, 392, 395, 399
Attorney Client Privileges, 370, 380–385
Article 9 Notice, 407, 412

Behavioural measures, 418, 425
Bid rigging, 13, 85, 86, 105, 121, 122, 125, 156, 189, 190, 195, 318, 435, 453, 454
Business combination, 26, 30, 31, 66, 68, 69, 89, 98, 99, 119, 146, 148, 276–279, 301, 309, 386, 387, 400, 403, 404, 407, 416, 417, 420, 422, 426, 427
Business Combination Rules, 26, 69, 400, 407

Cabinet Order, 23–25, 83, 173, 175, 176, 334, 390, 391, 394, 397–399
Cartel, 9, 34, 46, 48–50, 55, 85, 86, 105, 109, 125, 137, 146, 147, 155, 156, 173, 188, 192–198, 202–204, 208, 317, 319, 321, 411, 435, 453, 454, 485
Cease and Desist Order, 58, 65, 68, 75, 82, 115, 154, 168, 188, 220, 230, 234, 235, 257, 267, 272, 273, 277, 369, 371, 372, 374, 376, 377, 379, 402, 407, 409, 411, 428, 429, 433, 454, 471
Clearance, 252, 386–427
Comity, 464, 466, 478–482
Commission rule, 55
Commitment Procedure, 11, 26, 31, 155–162, 416
Communication of intent, 108–110
Concerted refusal to trade, 77, 78, 80, 176
Conglomerate merger, 304, 309–313
Consultation, 49, 206, 207, 383, 384, 404, 405, 465, 468
Cooperation agreement, 21, 201–208, 458, 459, 461–483
Cooperative, 22, 35, 38–41, 48, 173, 220, 230, 461, 463
Coordinated effect, 281, 299, 300, 303, 308, 311
Criminal accusation, 31, 320, 434, 436–439, 448, 453–456
Criminal investigation, 26, 152, 334, 434, 435, 438–440, 448, 449, 451–454

Damage (suit), 58, 75, 82, 93, 115, 180–184, 231, 433, 436
Determination procedure, 30, 382–385
Discriminatory pricing, 78, 176
Distribution Guidelines, 30, 85, 87, 209, 263, 266

Economic Partnership Agreement (EPA), 22, 460–462, 483
Efficiency, 2, 5, 47, 124, 131, 206, 214, 231, 295
Enterprise, 51–54, 250–251

Index

Excessive concentration of economic power, 30, 63–65, 144
Exemption, 8, 18, 35–51, 94
Exclusionary conduct, 240, 241, 253, 255, 258, 265, 269, 272
Exclusionary Private Monopolization Guidelines, 30, 123, 141, 241, 253, 258, 269

Franchise, 30, 213
Freelancers Act, 15, 23, 25

General concentration, 63, 143–145
General Designation, 27, 28, 73, 77, 78, 80, 210, 228, 240, 266, 267, 271
General Secretariat, 150, 381, 452

Hardcore cartel, 105, 193, 198, 202–204, 208
Hearing, 10, 26, 109, 133, 156, 275, 369, 371–379, 411, 428, 429
Hearing officer, 372, 373, 378
Herfindahl Hirschman Index (HHI), 282–284, 304, 305
Horizontal merger, 279–300, 302, 310

ICN, 457, 485
Import, 48, 210, 271, 290, 422–424
Injunction, 178, 180, 184
Intellectual property (IP), 17, 30, 36, 37, 84, 216, 217, 431
Investigation Rules, 26, 336, 339, 345, 348, 356, 363, 367, 381, 384, 385, 429, 451, 452
Involvement Prevention Act, 13, 23, 190

Japan Fair Trade Commission (JFTC), 7–11, 14, 15, 19–22, 26–32, 34, 36, 41–45, 49, 51–55, 58, 59, 69, 71, 73, 79, 80, 84–86, 88, 89, 96–102, 109, 111, 112, 123, 132–135, 137, 149–157, 159, 161–169, 172, 174, 177–179, 187, 188, 191, 194, 196, 202, 206–209, 212, 216, 220–223, 225, 226, 230, 234, 235, 251, 252, 255, 259, 263, 267, 269, 271–273, 275, 278, 281, 282, 287–291, 295, 303–305, 311, 314, 316–322, 324–327, 329–344, 348–351, 355–357, 368, 369, 371, 372, 375, 376, 378, 379, 381, 382, 385–388, 391, 392, 395, 398–400, 402–417, 423, 424, 426–432, 434–438, 440, 442, 448, 449, 451, 453–457, 462, 463, 465, 472, 474, 484–489, 491, 492
Joint Venture, 147, 148, 314, 315

Leniency programme, 9, 11, 319–331, 380

Market concentration, 63, 66, 143, 146
Merger, 25, 30, 31, 48, 66, 67, 71, 89, 97, 98, 119, 122, 146, 148, 150, 154, 155, 174, 276, 278–314, 386–427, 476, 485
Monopolistic situation, 72, 83, 84, 318

Notification form, 31, 400, 401
Notification threshold, 386
NTT-East Case, 53, 121, 223, 267

OECD, 457, 467, 481, 485
On-site inspection, 334, 335, 341–350, 441, 446, 450

Particular field of trade, 38, 41, 56, 57, 60, 66–68, 97, 118, 146, 171, 173, 175, 177, 185, 194, 279, 309
Payment Order, 58, 82, 168–170, 174, 177, 235, 257, 272, 369, 374, 428, 429, 471
Predatory Sales Guidelines, 30, 247, 248, 250, 252, 263
Premerger (Prior) notification, 14, 322, 468
Premiums and Representation Act, 14, 23
Primary review, 402, 406–408
Private monopolization, 7, 25, 26, 30, 48, 53, 60–62, 69, 74, 77, 83, 86, 88, 104, 111, 119, 121–123, 133, 138, 141, 142, 169, 175, 185, 188, 202, 217–220, 223, 240, 241, 253, 257, 258, 262, 264, 265, 267, 269, 270, 272, 275, 333
Procedures for Hearing, 369, 371–379, 429

Rebate, 230, 239, 258–263
Remedial measures, 417–419, 423–427
Resale price maintenance, 35
Research & Development (R&D), 30, 105, 129, 202–204, 214, 215

Safe Harbour, 281–284, 303–305, 311
Search warrant, 446, 451
Secondary review, 402, 407, 409–413, 415
Seizure, 152, 441, 443, 446, 447, 450
Share holding, 63
Specific designation, 28
Structural Impediments Initiative (SII), 9
Structural measures, 418, 421, 425
Subcontract Act, 12, 23, 25

Substantial restraint of competition, 56, 57, 60, 119–126, 185, 193, 229, 257, 262, 273, 282, 288–298, 300, 304, 305, 420
Surcharge, 9, 11, 25, 26, 58, 59, 75, 115, 137, 169–177, 187, 192, 193, 195, 197, 198, 213, 272, 273, 319, 320, 322, 324, 374, 381
Survey (Market survey), 26, 332–333

Trade association, 30, 72, 77, 90, 95, 96, 115–118, 147, 177, 183, 184, 199, 200, 381
Trading on exclusive terms, 266
Trading on restrictive terms, 77, 78, 210
Tying, 77, 253–257

Unfair trade practice, 14, 19, 27, 28, 30, 38, 41, 42, 49, 67, 72–81, 87, 105, 111, 118, 133, 134, 137, 142, 169, 176, 183, 184, 191, 197, 202, 209, 211, 213, 217, 218, 224, 229, 240, 244, 257, 262–264, 266, 277, 332
Unilateral Effect, 281, 285–298, 300, 303, 306, 307, 311, 312
Unjust low-price sales, 78, 212, 248, 263
Unreasonable restraint of trade, 19, 56–59, 61, 62, 74, 81, 105–111, 113–115, 119, 169, 171–175, 177, 183, 185, 191, 192, 195, 199, 201, 202, 205, 208, 209, 217, 320, 370, 380, 439

Vertical merger, 301–308, 311

Zaibatsu, 4, 7

Index

www.ingramcontent.com/pod-product-compliance
Ingram Content Group UK Ltd.
Pitfield, Milton Keynes, MK11 3LW, UK
UKHW020142290926
15471UKWH00004B/656

9 789403 526096